Water in a Thirsty Land

Ruth R. Ealy

David G. Thomas, Editor

Mesilla Valley History Series, Vol 10

Copyright © 2022 by Doc45 Publishing

All Rights Reserved

This book, or parts thereof, may not be reproduced in any form, including information storage and retrieval systems, without explicit permission from Doc45 Publishing, except for brief quotations included in articles and reviews.

Doc45 Publishing, P. O. Box 5044, Las Cruces, N. M. 88003
books@doc45.com

To obtain books, visit:
doc45.com

YouTube Channel
youtube.com/c/Doc45Publications

Cover artwork by Dusan Arsenic.

ISBN 978-1-952580-11-6

DOC45 PUBLISHING

Mesilla Valley History Series

La Posta – From the Founding of Mesilla, to Corn Exchange Hotel, to Billy the Kid Museum, to Famous Landmark – by David G. Thomas

Giovanni Maria de Agostini, Wonder of The Century – The Astonishing World Traveler Who Was A Hermit – by David G. Thomas

Screen with a Voice – A History of Moving Pictures in Las Cruces, New Mexico – by David G. Thomas

Billy the Kid's Grave – A History of the Wild West's Most Famous Death Marker – by David G. Thomas

Killing Garrett, The Wild West's Most Famous Lawman – Murder or Self-Defense? – by David G. Thomas

The Stolen Pinkerton Reports of Colonel Albert J. Fountain Investigation – David G. Thomas, Editor

The Trial of Billy the Kid – by David G. Thomas

The Frank W. Angel Report on the Death of John H. Tunstall by David G. Thomas

Water in a Thirsty Land – by Ruth R. Ealy, David G. Thomas, Editor

Mesilla Valley Reprints

When New Mexico Was Young – by Harry H. Bailey

Acknowledgments

I thank Dan Aranda, Lanty Wylie, and Josh Slatten for proofing the manuscript and making corrections and suggestions.

Special thanks to the many who sought out source materials and provided invaluable help in my research efforts: Dennis Daily, Elizabeth Villa, and Teddie Moreno, Library Archives & Special Collections, NMSU; Heather Hultman, Montana Historical Society; Rick Hendricks, New Mexico State Records Administrator; Josh Slatten, Billy the Kid's Historical Coalition; Tomas Jaehn, Special Collections, UNM; Joseph R. Diaz and Patricia Ballesteros, Special Collections, UA; Connie Hurtt, Old Log Church Historical Society; Lynda Sanchez; Kenneth Walter; and Brian Otto.

Unattributed photos are from the author's collection.

Contents

Acknowledgments iv
List of Images vii
Editor's Introduction 1
Preface 21
Introduction 23
1. Fort Arbuckle 27
2. Lincoln 37
3. Zuni 85
4. Second Year 103
5. The Silent Year – 1880 139
6. The End of Life in Zuni 147
7. Conclusion 165
Appendix A – Taylor F. Ealy's Testimony at Dudley Court of Inquiry 167
Appendix B – Rynerson Letter to "Friends Riley and Dolan" 175
Appendix C – Timeline 177
Notes 181
Index 189

Doc 45

Buenas noches boys,
A social call no doubt –
Do we talk it over,
Or do we shoot it out?

I'm Doc 45,
Toughest man alive.
Hand over those golden bills
Or I'll dose you up with dirty leaden pills.

List of Images

1. Mary and Taylor Ealy, marriage photo, 1874 xiii
2. John Henry Tunstall, 1875 photo 2
3. Alexander Anderson McSween 4
4. Susan Ellen (Hummer) McSween 4
5. David Pugh Shield 4
6. Elizabeth (Hummer) Shield 4
7. Drawing McSween/Shield building, Lincoln, NM 6
8. Nathan Augustus Monroe Dudley, 1863 photo 8
9. Zuni Pueblo, 1863 photo 12
10. Ealy family home in Schellsburg 24
11. Taylor Filmore Ealy 25
12. Mary Elizabeth (Ramsey) Ealy 25
13. Taylor Filmore Ealy 26
14. Mary Elizabeth (Ramsey) Ealy, 1914 photo 26
15. Plan of Mission House at Fort Arbuckle 30
16. Mission House at Fort Arbuckle 34
17. Aerial view of Las Vegas, NM, photo circa 1880 38
18. Andres Nelson & Co. General Store/Hotel, Anton Chico 38
19. Fort Stanton, 1898 photo 44
20. Aerial view of Lincoln, NM 44
21. Robert Adolph Widenmann 51
22. William Brady 51
23. George W. Coe showing missing "trigger" finger 54
24. Trader store at Fort Stanton, 1870s photo 71
25. Zuni Pueblo in 1878 88
26. Zuni Pueblo showing Dowa Yalanne ("Corn Mountain") in distance, 1879 88
27. Bill of sale, October 23, 1878 90
28. House Dr. Ealy built at Zuni 94
29. Drawing of plans for house at Zuni 94
30. Sheldon Clinton Jackson 98
31. Pedro Pino, Governor of Zuni, 1878 photo 100
32. José Ynes Perea, 1909 photo 101
33. Fort Wingate, New Mexico, 1873 photo 102
34. Two Views of Zuni Pueblo, 1879 photos 104
35. Grinding grain at Zuni 109
36. Zuni cornfield with its scarecrows 116
37. Detail showing shelter in corn field 116
38. Frank Hamilton Cushing in Zuni dress 126
39. Zuni Children with Teachers, 1879 photo 132
40. Four students from Zuni, before Carlisle trip 144
41. Four students from Zuni, after Carlisle trip 145
42. We'wha (we-wa), 1886 photo 148
43. Patricio Pino, Zuni Governor after Pablo Pino 150
44. The Dance of the Great Knife, Zuni 152

Mary and Taylor Ealy, marriage photo, 1874. Courtesy Center for Southwest Research and Special Collections, UNM.

Introduction by Editor

"*Water in a Thirsty Land*" is a chronicle by Ruth Rea Ealy of her father's sojourns as a Presbyterian missionary in Indian Territory (Oklahoma) and New Mexico Territory. Her father was Dr. Taylor Filmore Ealy, her mother was Mary Elizabeth Ramsey. The sources of her account are her father's extensive, contemporaneous diaries; correspondence by both Taylor and Mary with family members, government authorities, and Presbyterian officials; memories by the author of conversations with her parents; and historical sources cited by the author.

Taylor Filmore Ealy was born September 12, 1848, in Schellsburg, PA, the oldest of seven siblings. In 1869, he graduated from Washington and Jefferson College and entered Western Theological Seminary. In 1872, he entered the medical department of the University of Pennsylvania and earned a medical degree.

Mary Elizabeth Ramsey was born December 23, 1850, in East Waterford, PA. She was educated as a teacher.

From an early age, Taylor sought to be a Presbyterian missionary. The Presbyterian Church mandated that its missionaries be married; so, on October 1, 1874, to satisfy that requirement as well as his personal wishes, he married Mary Ramsey. Five days later, on October 6, he was licensed as an evangelist by the Presbytery of Pittsburgh.

Taylor was offered two positions, one as a teacher at Western Theological Seminary and one as a missionary at Fort Arbuckle, Indian Territory. The Presbytery had a special relationship with the U.S. Government at Fort Arbuckle. Any missionary sent to the Fort, which was located within the Chickasaw Reservation, was also an employee of the Department of Indian Affairs and received a Federal salary as a teacher in addition to what the Presbytery paid.

Taylor accepted the Fort Arbuckle assignment. Fort Arbuckle, around which the town developed, was founded in 1851 and named after U.S. General Matthew Arbuckle. The site was located a few miles northwest of present-day Davis, Oklahoma. The fort was decommissioned as a military fort in 1870, but remained Federal property.

Fort Arbuckle

By early November, 1874, Taylor and Mary were in Fort Arbuckle. They traveled by train from Schellsburg to Caddo, Indian Territory, and from Caddo, by horse-drawn, concord stage.

On September 3, 1875, Taylor and Mary had their first child, Anna Margarette, known as "Pearl," at Fort Arbuckle (Taylor delivered the baby).

After 18 months of service, on June 5, 1876, Taylor and family returned to Schellsburg for what was intended to be a brief vacation. Instead, Taylor decided not return to Fort Arbuckle, even though he was offered an annual salary of $900.00 to return. Mary was offered $600.00.

On October 15, 1877, they had their second child, Ruth Rea (author of this book), at East Waterford, PA.

John Henry Tunstall. 1875 photo. Courtesy Palace of the Governors Photo Archives (NMHM/DCA), 066009.

Lincoln

In November, 1877, the Presbytery offered Taylor a position in Lincoln, New Mexico. Lincoln at the time had a population of about 600 people, and, based on the census of 1880, about 150 dwellings. A prominent resident of the city, Alexander A. McSween, a Presbyterian, had asked his church to send a missionary to Lincoln to start a church and a primary school.

Taylor, Mary, their two infant children, and Susan Gates arrived in Lincoln on February 19, 1878. That was the day after John Henry Tunstall was sadistically murdered. The murder of Tunstall, while being chased by a posse of 30 men, kicked off the event known to historians as the Lincoln County War. The Lincoln County War lasted roughly two years and involved an estimated 200 men. A description of the events and consequences of the War is beyond the scope of this introduction. Of the many books written about the War – and they are certainly multitudinous – this editor recommends two of his: *"The Trial of Billy the Kid"* and *"The Frank W. Angel Report on the Death of John H. Tunstall."*

Miss Susan Gates was with the Ealys because she had agreed to accompany Taylor as an assistant schoolteacher. The five were lodged with the Shield family, which consisted of attorney David P. Shield, wife Elizabeth, and their five children.[1] The Shields occupied the Western wing of a U-shaped house located on Lincoln's only street. The Eastern wing of the house belonged to Alexander McSween and his wife Susan. The two wings of the structure enclosed a courtyard and were connected on the south by an enclosed passageway (see drawing page 6).

Elizabeth (Hummer) Shield was the sister of Susan (Hummer) McSween. Alexander McSween and David Shield were law partners.

In the evening of the day they arrived, Tunstall's body was brought into Lincoln. He had been shot in the back of the head and in the chest. The following day, Tunstall's funeral was held in the McSween home. Taylor gave the funeral oration (which was translated into Spanish for the Spanish speakers present) and his wife played "two or three hymns."

Albert Howe, who was with the posse that chased after and killed Tunstall, gave the following sworn account of his murder:

> *"That he did not see the shooting but was informed how Tunstall was killed by the boys."*
>
> *"That Tunstall was some distance off from the road, and when he found that he had been deserted by his party. He turned and rode towards Hill & Morton. That when he came in sight of them, he seemed very much surprised and hesitated. That Hill called to him to come up and that he would not be hurt at the same time both Hill & Morton threw up their guns, resting the stocks on their knees. That after Tunstall came nearer, Morton fired and shot Tunstall through the breast and then Hill fired & shot Tunstall through the head. Someone else fired and wounded or killed Tunstall's horse at the time Tunstall was shot through the head by Hill. That two barrels of Tunstall's revolver were emptied after he was killed. That Tunstall fired no shots and that Tunstall was killed in cold blood."* [2]

Alexander Anderson McSween. Undated photo. Courtesy Maurice G. Fulton Papers, Special Collections, UA.

Susan Ellen (Hummer) McSween. Undated photo. Courtesy Courtesy Maurice G. Fulton Papers, Special Collections, UA.

David Pugh Shield. Undated photo. Courtesy Center Courtesy Maurice G. Fulton Papers, Special Collections, UA.

Elizabeth (Hummer) Shield. Undated photo. Courtesy Maurice G. Fulton Papers, Special Collections, UA.

Forty-one days after Tunstall's funeral, the Ealys witnessed the next explosive event of the Lincoln County War, the killing of Lincoln County Sheriff William Brady and Deputy George Hindman.

On March 30, McSween met with a group of supporters at John Chisum's South Springs Ranch, where he was sheltering, because he was afraid to stay in Lincoln due to numerous death threats, including an explicit threat by Sheriff Brady. He told those present that he intended to come into Lincoln and appear before the District Court on its opening day. His intention was to demand protection of the Court.[3] (page 61)

Six men responded to McSween's urgent request: Billy the Kid, Fred Waite, John Middleton, Frank MacNab, Henry Brown, and Jim French. On March 31, just after dark, they sneaked into Lincoln and positioned themselves in Tunstall's horse corral. During the night, they were joined by Robert Widenmann and Sam Corbet. They were expecting McSween to come into town the following morning, April 1, and walk down Main Street to the courthouse.

About 9:00 a.m., Sheriff Brady and deputies Jacob Mathews, George Hindman, Jack Long, and George Peppin left the Murphy/Dolan store and began walking toward McSween's residence. They were confident McSween was there – and they intended to arrest him. What they did not know was that McSween was delayed by a rainstorm. He was still a few miles outside of Lincoln.

As the five officers neared Tunstall's corral, a sudden flurry of gunshots broke the crisp, morning air, issuing from behind the structure.

Sheriff Brady, who was closest to the corral, was hit by three shots: head, back, left side. He died instantly.

George Hindman was hit by one shot. He stumbled a few steps and fell, mortally wounded. As he was dying, he screamed out, begging for a glass of water (suggesting heavy bleeding).

Jack Long was wounded slightly. He, Mathews, and Peppin raced for and gained shelter.

Two men sprinted from behind the corral wall – Billy and French – and leant over Sheriff Brady's body. Some sources say they were trying to grab the papers Brady carried for McSween's arrest. Others, that Billy was trying to recover his Winchester rifle that Brady had confiscated several weeks earlier. A shot by Mathews wounded French – Taylor describes treating French's wound in his diary (page 61).

Juan Peppin, son of George Peppin, who was 12 at the time of the shooting, later gave the following description of the shooting:

> *"On the morning of April 1st... about 9 o'clock I heard shooting, but did not give it much thought until someone came by the house with the news that Sheriff Brady had been killed.... I left my work and went into town.... I saw Major Brady lying on his back in the street dead, all covered with blood, and one of his deputies, George Hindman, lying mortally wounded a few yards further along the street. My father was alive but had had a narrow escape."*

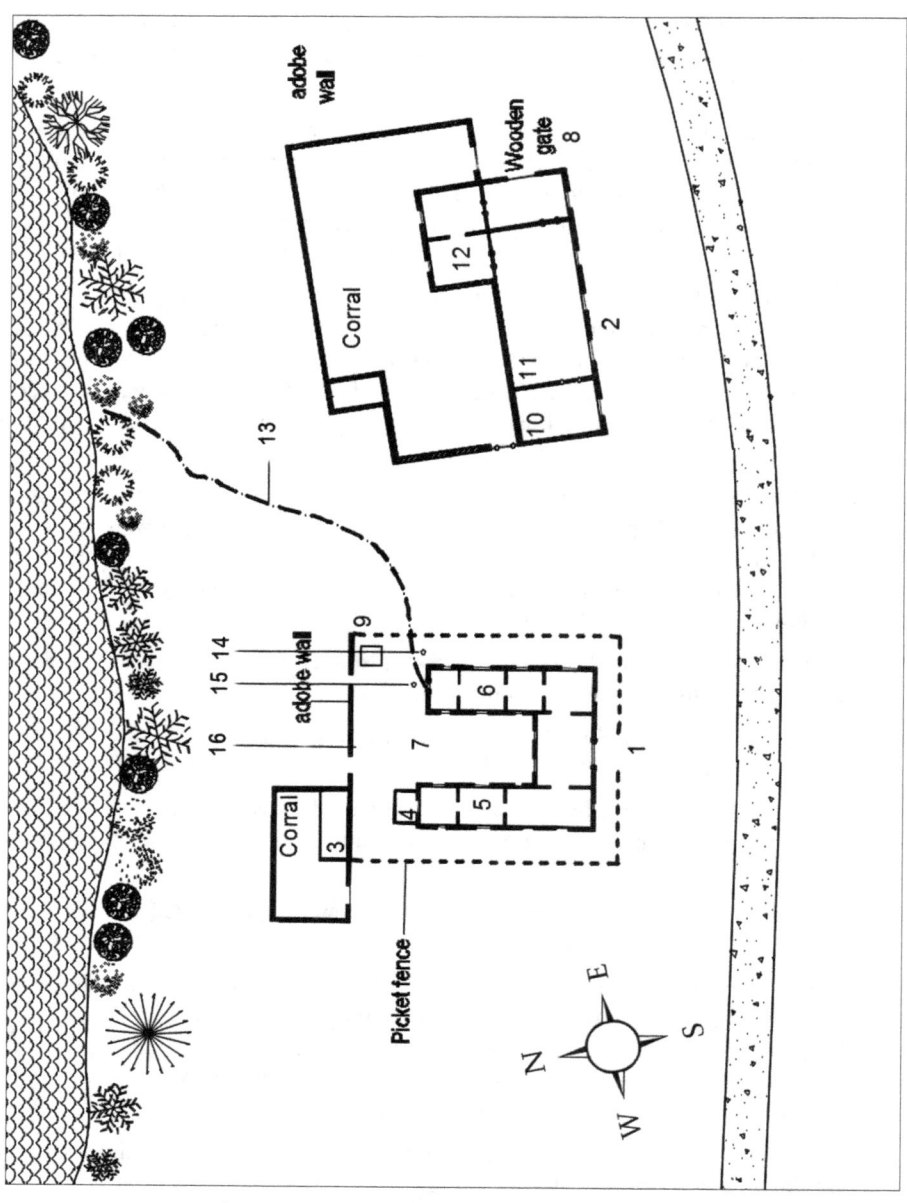

Lincoln, New Mexico, July 19, 1878, detail. (1) McSween/Shield building, (2) Tunstall store/residence, (3) Stable, (4) Kitchen shed, (5) McSween's wing, (6) Shield's wing, (7) Courtyard, (8) Corral gate (9) Outdoor toilet, (10) McSween law office, (11) Tunstall's store, (12) Tunstall's residence, (13) Route Billy, Thomas O'Folliard, Jim French, and José Chavez y Chavez took to escape burning building, (14) Harvey Morris killed here, (15) McSween killed here, (16) Francisco Zamora and Vincente Romero killed here.

> "From hearing him tell about it, I am able to give what happened....They were walking down the street... and had just past the gateway to the corral when five or six McSween men fired at them from behind the adobe wall of the corral.... They had drilled port holes in the east wall of the corral, so that they could level their rifles through them." [4]

The result of the killing of Brady and Hindman was all-out war between the two parties.

The final explosive event of the War witnessed by the Ealys was the 5-day shootout in Lincoln.

On July 14, in the evening, a sleepy Sunday, McSween, Billy, and as many as 60 supporters, in small groups, slipped silently into Lincoln, undetected by the residents. They had been riding as a band for several weeks, avoiding when they could – and fighting otherwise – a party of gunmen controlled by James Dolan.

The men took positions on the north side of the street, in McSween's house and several stores owned by allies. McSween had decided to occupy Lincoln with sufficient firepower to protect him from Dolan while he sought sanctions and redress in the District Court for Dolan and his allies' extralegal behavior.

Dolan, who was living at the Wortley Hotel in Lincoln, was caught by surprise. He had few of his men with him. He frantically ordered his ally Sheriff George Peppin to round up armed supporters. Peppin had replaced the deceased Brady as Lincoln Sheriff.

By late afternoon, Sheriff Peppin was back in Lincoln with a party almost as large as McSween's. Dolan's men took positions in buildings opposite the McSween men. Firing between the two sides commenced – described as "promiscuous" by one participant – and continued with fleeting pauses for the next four days.[5]

Taylor and Mary's accounts of the next four days are given in the book.

On the fifth day of the fighting, at 10 a.m., Colonel Nathan Dudley, the Commander of Fort Stanton, marched into Lincoln with his entire command: officers, cavalry, infantry:

> "On the morning of the 19th inst. I took every officer of the post including the post surgeon... [and] proceeded to Lincoln taking with me the Gatling Gun and 2,000 rounds of ammunition, also the Howitzer with ample supply of ammunition for any emergency that might arise, with three days rations."
>
> "I personally headed the column..." [6]

Colonel Dudley pitched camp in the center of town, between the two sides. Dudley informed the McSween side that if a shot was fired into his camp *"wounding or killing any of my officers or men,"* he would open fire on the source with his Howitzer canon.[7] With this action, Dudley was using his military force to support the Murphy-Dolan faction.

Dudley did nothing, however, to stop the Murphy-Dolan side from firing into the McSween home. Dudley later reported:

> "The estimate made by my officers was that over two thousand shots were exchanged during the evening." [8]

Nathan Augustus Monroe Dudley. 1863 photo. Courtesy Library of Congress.

About one o'clock in the afternoon, Jack Long sneaked up on the northeast corner of the Shield house and poured coal oil on it. Inside the home were Elizabeth Shield and her children. Long lit the oil, but the fire, after flaring, failed to take.[9]

After that firing failure, Andrew Boyle, at Sheriff Peppin's direct order, crept up on McSween's home and using coal oil, succeeded in starting the house on fire.[10] Inside the house were Alexander and Susan McSween and twelve men who had vowed to protect McSween. After the fire had burned awhile, Susan was permitted by Dudley to leave the house. Elizabeth and her children were permitted to leave the Shield house.

The fire burned all afternoon, consuming one room after another, forcing the men inside to crowd into a smaller and smaller space. By evening, the entire structure was burning, except for one room. The men in the house faced a stark choice, stay and burn to death or run for it.

In an attempt to save McSween's life, Billy, Thomas O'Folliard, Jim French, José Chavez y Chavez, and Harvey Morris volunteered to make a break for Tunstall's store, exiting the house to the east. That was the most exposed route and would draw the most fire. Simultaneously, McSween, Yginio Salazar, Thomas Cullins, George Bowers, Ignacio Gonzales, Francisco Zamora, Vincente Romero, and Florencio Chaves would dash straight back, aiming for the cover of the river.

Billy and his group dashed into a wall of fire. Morris, who was in the lead, was killed before he got six feet, *"inside the gate inside the McSween yard."* [11]

McSween, Romero, and Zamora were killed at the back of the house. Robert Beckwith, one of Dolan's men, was killed in the fiery exchange during the escape, possibly by his side. The other McSween men, including Billy, escaped.[12]

The next morning, when the Ealys dared to look out from their shelter in the Tunstall store, they saw:

> *"...five corpses lying in the McSween yard [four corpses – Beckwith's body had been removed to Fort Stanton during the night]. None of us went to see the terrible scene except Miss Gates. She described it as being so horrible I stayed away. I gave her a [bed] sheet and [Bates and Washington] before mentioned made a rude coffin and buried McSween in the same place Tunstall was buried. One other of the bodies was buried there at the same time [Harvey Morris], and one had been buried there before, so the plot contained six graves." (page 69)*

Dudley reported to his superiors that:

> *"McSween's body, unwashed was wrapped up in a blanket, placed in a box and buried without ceremony."* [13]

About 4 p.m. that day, the Ealys, Susan Gates, and Elizabeth and her children were escorted by troops to Fort Stanton. They never returned to Lincoln.

On May 12, 1879, 296 days later, Taylor and Mary were subpoenaed to testify in the Dudley Court of Inquiry. The Inquiry was a formal hearing by the Army at Fort Stanton to determine whether Dudley should be court martialed for his behavior in Lincoln. By that time the Ealys were living in Zuni, New Mexico.

The Court of Inquiry had begun May 7. Taylor refused to subject his wife to the hardship of a trip to Fort Stanton, so only he showed up on May 26, after a difficult trip. He was called to testify June 2 as a prosecution witness, in the afternoon. The prosecutor, representing the Army, was Captain Henry H. Humphreys. Assisting Captain Humphreys, in a rather bizarre arrangement, was Susan McSween's personal attorney, Ira Leonard. Defending Colonel Dudley was Santa Fe lawyer Henry L. Waldo.[14]

Taylor gives his description of his testimony on page 115. His testimony, as recorded in the trial transcript, is given in Appendix A.

After his testimony, Taylor clandestinely left for Zuni by way of Roswell, the opposite direction in which he needed to travel. He did so because he believed Dudley and his allies had vowed to kill him before he got home. (page 117)

The Court of Inquiry ended July 6, 1879, having lasted over 60 days. The costs to the army exceeded $25,000. Dudley had been charged with six counts of misbehavior. He was acquitted of all counts.[15]

There are many details about the conflict in Taylor and Mary's accounts that are not recorded in other sources. Here are examples:

- The Ealys had their wagon searched by Lawrence Murphy, James Dolan, and John Riley the day they arrived in Lincoln. (page 65)
- McSween owned about 70 chickens. (page 46).
- Tunstall's funeral was held at 3 pm. His bullet-holed, bloody clothes were lying on the dirty ground in McSween's back yard during the service. (page 50)
- The Lincoln county jail when Sheriff Brady was shot was *"a hole in the ground with a watch-tower over it."* (page 61).
- Sheriff Brady had handcuffs in his pocket when he was shot. (page 61)
- The wound that Jim French suffered after the shooting of Sheriff Brady was in the thigh, not in the "bowels," as other sources report. (page 61).
- The book provides many details about Tunstall's store: *"The floors were good ones and the windows were large."* (page 55) One room was *"12 feet high, 18 feet long, and 18 feet wide, with a huge window and a door with a large glass in it."* (page 56) That room was *"large enough to hold three hundred people."* (page 57) The store lot was five acres in size and fully fenced. (page 57)
- The Lincoln Post Office was in the Murphy-Dolan store. Mail to members of the McSween side was opened by Dolan before it was delivered. (page 56). To prevent his mail from being read, McSween had his mail delivered *"in a brass-locked private mail sack from Roswell."* (page 62)
- Two of McSween's front windows were shot out on the second day of the 5-day shootout in Lincoln. (page 59)
- When the McSween house was fired during that 5-day shootout, one of Elizabeth Shield's children stepped in the coal oil used to ignite the fire. (page 77)
- Among the items in McSween's house destroyed by the fire were an elegant piano, a Brussels carpet, costly furniture, rich curtains, and fine paintings. (page 76)

- McSween was buried wrapped in a sheet supplied by Mary Ealy. (page 64)
- After the Ealys fled Lincoln for Fort Stanton, they were ordered by the Fort Commander, Colonel Dudley, to not talk about the events they witnessed in Lincoln. (page 64)
- After Taylor testified at the Dudley Court of Inquiry, he was warned by anonymous note that he would be killed before he got back to his home in Zuni (a "coffin note"). (page 115).

Zuni

After leaving Lincoln, Taylor accepted a position as a missionary teacher at Zuni Pueblo, New Mexico. Chapters 3-6 detail his nearly three years of service, from October 12, 1878, to June 21, 1881. As she had at Lincoln, Susan Gates accompanied Taylor as an assistant teacher.

The day they arrived in Zuni, the Zunis were holding a dance. That was a providential introduction to the cultural shock they would experience at Zuni. They were entering a physical and cultural environment which could hardly be more different from their existing life.

Frank Hamilton Cushing, an anthropologist and ethnologist, who would visit Zuni in September, 1879, and end up staying for years, described Zuni Pueblo this way:

"Imagine numberless long, box-shaped, adobe ranches, connected with one another in extended rows and squares, with other, less and less numerous, piled up on them lengthwise and crosswise, in two, three, even six stories, each receding from the one below it like the steps of a broken stair-flight – as it were, a gigantic pyramidal and mud honey comb with far outstretching base...."

"Everywhere this structure bristled with ladder-poles, chimneys, and rafters. The ladders were heavy and long, with carved slab crosspieces at the tops, and leaned at all angles against the roofs. The chimneys looked more like huge bamboo joints than anything else I can compare them with, for they were made of bottomless earthen pots, set one upon the other and cemented together with mud, so that they stood up, like many-lobed, oriental spires, from every roof-top. Wonderfully like the holes in an ant-hill seemed the little windows and doorways which everywhere pierced the walls of this gigantic habitation; and like ant-hills themselves seemed the curious little round-topped ovens which stood here and there along these walls or on the terrace edges."

"All round the town could be seen irregular, large and small adobe or dried-mud fences, inclosing gardens in which melon, pumpkin, and squash vines, pepper plants and onions were most conspicuous." [16]

The only shelter available to the new arrivals was a room in one of the Pueblo homes. Two days later, Taylor, with the help of Zunis, began digging a well. He also began planning a residence/school:

"I have decided to build it well as I go; first dig out all the foundations so as to make a good cellar under the whole house – four rooms and hall on first floor, and four rooms and hall on second floor." (page 89)

Zuni Pueblo. 1863 photo. Courtesy Library of Congress.

By November 17, Taylor had enough of the house completed to move in his family and Susan Gates.

Three men play a huge role in Taylor's life at Zuni: José Ynes Perea, Pedro Pino, and Dr. Sheldon Jackson. Perea was at Zuni when Taylor arrived. Pino [Zuni name Lai-iu-ahtsai-lu] was the Governor (the secular/administrative leader) for Zuni. Dr. Sheldon Jackson was the superintendent of the Presbyterian mission work of the Rocky Mountains, Taylor's boss.

On December 24, Susan Gates married Pedro Perea. Susan was 28 and Perea was 41. The couple remained at Zuni until February 3, 1879, when they moved to St. James, Arizona. With Susan gone, Taylor needed a new assistant teacher. He recommended 23-year old Miss Jennie M. Hammaker, a cousin of his wife, from his home town of Schellsburg. She agreed to accept the position and was hired by the Presbytery. When Taylor was returning from testifying at the Dudley Court of Inquiry, he met her by prior arrangement in Las Vegas and escorted her to Zuni. (page 117)

In July, 1880, Taylor decided to resign his missionary work and return to his hometown of Schellsburg. That was shortly after his five-month-old baby son Albert "Bertie" Ealy, born at Zuni and delivered by him, had died. He agreed to defer leaving until a replacement was found. He was finally relieved by the Presbytery and permitted to depart Zuni on June 21, 1881. He was back in Schellsburg by July 4, 1881.

Jennie stayed behind at Zuni as a teacher. She died there suddenly of typhoid fever in September, 1881. (page 163)

Cast of Characters

Here are brief biographies of the most important persons appearing in this book. Many of the individuals mentioned are too obscure today to find identifying information.

Angel, Frank Warner. Born May 28, 1845, in Watertown, NY. Angel was appointed special investigator for the U.S. Department of Justice April 15, 1878, charged with investigating John Henry Tunstall's murder in Lincoln. After a 102-day stay in New Mexico, he submitted his report on the murder to the Justice Department October 3, 1878. His interviews with the participants in the Lincoln County War are of immense value to historians. Angel died March 15, 1906, in Jersey City, NJ.[17]

Appel, Daniel Mitchell. Born October 28, 1854, in PA. Appel graduated Jefferson Medical College in 1875 and entered the army a year later. Appel was the serving medical officer at Fort Stanton when Tunstall was murdered and did the post mortem examination of Tunstall's body. He died April 21, 1914, in Hawaii.

Axtell, Samuel B. Born October 14, 1819, in Franklin County, OH. Axtell was appointed governor of New Mexico July 30, 1875. He was fired as governor September 3, 1878, by President Rutherford B. Hayes as a direct result of the report on his behavior in the aftermath of Tunstall's murder submitted by Angel. He was appointed chief justice of the New Mexico Territorial Supreme Court in 1882 and served until he resigned in 1885. Axtell died August 6, 1891, in Morristown, NJ.[18]

Brady, William. Born August 16, 1829, in Ireland. Brady immigrated to the U.S. and joined the U.S. Army in 1851, serving two five-year terms. He joined the 2nd N.M. Volunteer Infantry August 19, 1861, to fight for the Union. He was promoted to Brevet Major and appointed commander of Fort Stanton April 29, 1864. He was discharged from the army October 8, 1866. In 1868, he purchased a large ranch east of Lincoln. He was elected sheriff of Lincoln County September 6, 1869. After serving two years, Brady was elected to the Territorial House for one term. In November, 1876, Brady was re-elected sheriff of Lincoln County. Brady was killed April 1, 1878, by shots fired from Tunstall's horse corral. Billy the Kid was tried for and convicted of murdering Brady.[19]

Crane, William W. Born 1832 in NY. During the Civil War, Crane served as a scout and teamster for Kit Carson. After the War ended, he built a house and store at Bacon Springs, which became a stage stop on the route between Santa Fe and Prescott, Arizona. His house was described in 1883 as:

> "...a model eastern home, with every appliance of the most advanced civilization – every adornment that beautifies, every comfort that makes home delightful." [20]

Ralph E. Twitchell, in *"Leading Facts of New Mexico History,"* wrote:

> "Crane... supplied the post at Wingate with beef, hay, and other commodities and accumulated quite a fortune, all of which he lost in gambling with the officers at the post. Crane was known far and wide and among the Navajos, who were very friendly with him; he was known as "Hostin Kloee," the man who makes hay." [21]

After the railroad arrived at Bacon Springs, the name of the settlement was changed to Coolidge. Crane died December 11, 1904, at his home.

Cushing, Frank Hamilton (adopted Zuni name Teai-e-se-u-lu-ti-was). Born July 22, 1857, in North East Township, PA. Cushing became interested in Native Americans at the age of nine when a plow on his father's farm turned up a flint arrowhead. Fascinated by the object, he started collecting arrowheads. He created a private museum in his parents' house to display his finds. In an attempt to learn how they were made, he began chipping his own arrowheads. At 18 he went to Cornell University, already a self-taught expert in Native American artifacts. He was hired as a curator at the Department of Ethnology Museum in Washington, DC, and appointed to staff of the newly created U.S. Bureau of Ethnology.[22]

Cushing was invited to join the 1879 James Stevenson anthropological expedition to New Mexico, and arrived in Zuni September 19, 1879. He stayed 4½ years. He learned the language, adopted Zuni dress and customs, and in 1880, was accepted as a member of the tribe. He was invited to join the Bow priesthood and after several months became its head. While at Zuni, Cushing was pressured to marry a Zuni wife to validate that he truly wanted to be a member of the tribe. He said he refused because:

"...he feared the Zuni would become convinced that he had duped them in order to learn their secrets." [23]

Cushing really was interested in discovering their religious secrets, and in 1884 he published an extensive article called "Zuni Breadstuff" in which revealed the legends and ceremonial practices of the Corn Clan, "the Guardians of the Seed," a violation of their trust.[24]

In later years he suffered serious health problems possibly related to the hardship of his Zuni life. While a patient at a Washington, D.C. hospital April 10, 1900, he choked to death on a fish bone.[25]

Dolan, James J. Born May 2, 1848, in Ireland. Dolan served in 17th Regiment, NY Zouaves, during the Civil War. He reenlisted after the war and was discharged at Fort Stanton. He was hired by Murphy as a bookkeeper and clerk. He became a Murphy partner in April, 1874. When Murphy retired in 1877, the company became Dolan & Co. A few years after Tunstall's killing, Dolan purchased Tunstall's Lincoln store and his Rio Feliz ranch. Dolan died February 26, 1898, of cerebral hemorrhage.[26]

Dudley, Nathan Augustus Monroe. Born August 20, 1825, in Lexington, MA. Dudley joined the army in 1855. In 1857, he participated in the "Mormon War" in Utah. In 1861, he was court-marshaled on the charge of lying to a fellow officer, but acquitted. During the Civil War he was promoted to both colonel and brigadier general. Following the Civil War, he served in Arizona, then in New Mexico. In 1877, at Fort Union, he was court-marshaled and convicted of being too drunk to perform his duties. He was given command of Fort Stanton on April 5, 1878. Dudley's intervention in the 5-day shootout in Lincoln led to a court of inquiry to determine whether Dudley should be court-martialed. He was acquitted of all charges after two months of testimony. Dudley retired from the army on August 20, 1889. He died April 29, 1910, in Boston, MA, and was buried in the Arlington National Cemetery, Washington, D.C.[27]

Ealy, Albert Elijah. Born January 4, 1846, in Schellsburg, PA. Older brother of Taylor Ealy. Albert obtained a medical degree in 1870 from the University of Pennsylvania. In 1878, he moved to Albuquerque, New Mexico, "for reasons of health," according to one source. In 1882, he was listed as one of the six licensed physicians in the town. That same year he was elected county coroner. In 1888, he moved to Arizona. Albert died October 22, 1919, in Schellsburg.[28]

Ealy, Mary Elizabeth (Ramsey) (Tsai au-tit-sa). Born December 23, 1850, in East Waterford, PA. Mary trained as a teacher. She married Taylor Ealy October 1, 1874. She died May 31, 1935, in Schellsburg.

Ealy, Ruth Rea. Born October 15, 1878, in Schellsburg, PA. Ruth is the author of "Water in a Thirsty Land." She spent her professional life as a public school teacher. Ruth died October 5, 1959, in St. Petersburg, PA.[29]

Ealy, Taylor Filmore (Tra-wa-ea-tsa-lun-kia). Born September 12, 1848, in Schellsburg, PA. Ealy attended a theological seminary and received a medical degree from the University of Pennsylvania in 1874. He served as a Presbyterian medical missionary and school teacher at Fort Arbuckle, Indian Territory, from 1874 to 1876, and at Lincoln and Zuni, New Mexico Territory, from 1878 to 1881. He gave up missionary work June 21, 1881, and returned to Schellsburg where he joined his father's medical practice. Ealy died February 20, 1915, in Schellsburg.

Gates, Susan. Born September 6, 1850, in Schellsburg, PA. Gates served as an assistant teacher to Taylor during his service in Lincoln. When he was assigned to Zuni, she agreed to serve there too. Shortly after arriving in Zuni, she accepted a marriage proposal from José Ynes Perea. They were married Christmas Day, December 25, 1878. They had seven children together. She died November 26, 1924, in Falmouth, KY.

Douglas D. Graham, born June, 1849, in New York. Graham opened the first trader store at Zuni in 1879. He spoke Zuni well. In 1902, he was appointed the Superintendent and Disburing Agent for Zuni. In 1904, frustrated by the repeated failure by authorities to build a telephone line to Zuni, he built it himself. He died Aug 18, 1914, in Summertown, Tennessee.

Hammaker, Jennie M. (Jan-i-uh-tit sa). Born in 1856 in Schellsburg, PA. A relative of Mary Ealy's. When Gates resigned as Taylor's assistant teacher at Zuni, Hammaker agreed to come from Schellsburg and replace her. She arrived in Zuni June 11, 1879. When Taylor left Zuni to return to Schellsburg, Hammaker elected to stay in Zuni and continue teaching. She died there suddenly of typhoid fever in September, 1881.

Hillers, Johann "John" Karl. Born in 1843 in Hanover, Germany. Hillers migrated with his parents to the U.S. at age nine. During the Civil War, he served in both the N.Y. Naval Brigade and the U.S. Army. He re-enlisted when the War ended and served until 1870 in various Western garrisons. In 1871, he joined John Wesley Powell's second expedition down the Colorado River. It was then that he learned photography. He was appointed the first staff photographer of the U.S. Bureau of Ethnology, and in capacity was invited to join the 1879 James Stevenson anthropological expedition to New Mexico. He arrived in Zuni September 19, 1879, with Cushing and the other members of the expedition. He died November 14, 1925.[30]

Hindman, George W. Birth date unknown. Arrived in Lincoln in 1875. Hindman was crippled, having been mauled in both the arms and legs by a bear. Hindman was in the posse that chased after and killed Tunstall. He and Sheriff Brady were killed April 1, 1878, by firing from behind Tunstall's corral wall. No one was ever tried for his killing.

Jackson, Sheldon Clinton. Born May 18, 1834, in Minaville, NY. Jackson graduated from Princeton Seminary in 1857 with a doctorate in theology. In December that year, he was licensed by the Albany Presbytery as a missionary. He spent 13 years teaching and evangelizing in Indian Territory, Minnesota, Wisconsin, and Iowa. In February, 1870, he was placed in charge of the Rocky Mountains Presbyterian Mission. The Mission was charged with overseeing missionary work in Colorado, Wyoming, Montana, Utah, New Mexico, and Arizona. It was based in Denver, Colorado. In 1872, he founded the "Rocky Mountain Presbyterian" newspaper. He visited Zuni for the first time in March, 1877. He died September 6, 1930, in Nassau, NY.[31]

Long, Jack "John." Known variously as Frank Rivers, Barney Longmont, John Mont, and Frank Ridden. Long arrived in Lincoln in 1876 and went to work for John Chisum as a cowhand. He bragged to the Ealys that he had helped hang a priest in Arizona. He was in the posse that chased after and killed Tunstall. He was indicted for killing Tunstall, but his murder charge was dropped when he pled Governor Lew Wallace's amnesty. He was walking down the street in Lincoln with Sheriff Brady when Brady and Hindman were killed and he was wounded slightly. Long left New Mexico for locations unknown in 1879.[32]

McCarty, William Henry, known variously as William Henry Antrim, William Henry Bonney, and famously as Billy the Kid. Most historians believe Billy was born in New York City in 1859, although no records documenting his birth or his paternal parentage have been found. Some authors have suggested he was born December 20, 1859.

Billy's birth name was William Henry McCarty. His mother may not have been married. Billy, his younger brother Joseph, and his mother Catherine McCarty left New York in 1872 for Wichita, Kansas. There they lived with William H. Antrim, a farmer, who later would become Billy's stepfather. Catherine and her sons were probably taken on by Antrim as a charity case, and as free labor. Within a few months, Antrim and his three wards left Kansas for New Mexico, where Antrim married Catherine in Santa Fe on March 1, 1873.[33]

Shortly after the marriage, the family moved to Silver City, N.M. There, on September 16, 1874, Catherine died of tuberculosis. One year after his mother's death, Billy was arrested and jailed for concealing stolen property. Billy was manipulated into hiding the purloined items by George Schafer, a much older tough known around Silver City as "Sombrero Jack." Billy escaped from the jail by shinnying up a fireplace chimney in the corner of his cell. Following his escape, Billy fled Silver City, beginning his now famous life as an adult.

During his life, in court records, Billy was referred to as William Bonney, alias "Kid,' alias William Antrim. It is unknown why Billy began calling himself Bonney. It is possible that his birth father's surname was Bonney. Billy went by Henry Antrim while growing up in Silver City. In letters, Billy signed his name as W. H. Bonney, or occasionally, W. Bonney.

Billy was killed about midnight, July 14, 1881, by Sheriff Pat Garrett in Pete Maxwell's bedroom at Fort Sumner.[34]

McSween, Alexander Anderson. Born in 1843 on Prince Edward Island in Canada. Little is known about McSween's early years. He may have practiced as a Presbyterian minister. He did not finish his law training. Nevertheless, in 1873, he began practicing law in Eureka, Kansas, where he met his future wife Susan Ellen Hummer. The same year he was elected Justice of the Peace. McSween and Susan were married August 13, 1873. They moved to Lincoln on March 3, 1875. On October 29, 1876, McSween met Tunstall in Santa Fe, which began their close friendship and later business association. McSween was killed attempting to flee his burning house on July 19, 1878, during the last day of the 5-day shootout in Lincoln.[35]

McSween, Susannah Ellen "Susan." She always gave her maiden name as Homer, but it actually was Hummer. Born December 30, 1845, in Adams County, PA. She was raised as a Dunkard, a sect of the German Baptist Brethren. The denomination mandated conservative dress and banned the use of alcohol and tobacco. In 1863, a party of Confederate forces on their way to what would become the Battle of Gettysburg raided the Hummer farm, demanding food supplies and stealing two horses. When the battle began, the family took what shelter they could. They were close enough to the battle to experience house-rattling cannon fire. Following the battle, Susan ran away from home. The next ten years of her life are a mystery. She appears in April, 1873, in Eureka, Kansas. On August 13, 1873, she married McSween using the name Sue E. Homer. Two years after McSween's murder, she married George L. Barber. In 1885, they acquired the Three Rivers Ranch. The couple divorced on October 16, 1892. Following the divorce, Susan retained ownership of the Three Rivers Ranch. She sold most of the ranch in 1902, and in 1906 moved to White Oaks, *"because in my old age I wanted peace,"* where she died January 3, 1931.[36]

Morton, William Scott "Buck." Born in 1856 in Charlotte County, VA. By early 1877, Morton was in Lincoln working for Murphy and Dolan as their ranch foreman. He was the leader of the posse that chased after Tunstall. Morton and Tom Hill reached Tunstall ahead of the other posse members. Morton shot Tunstall in the breast; Hill shot him in the head. Then Morton shot Tunstall's horse. Morton was arrested for Tunstall's murder by a posse led by Richard Brewer using warrants issued by Justice of the Peace Wilson. While being taken to Lincoln on March 9, 1878, Morton tried to escape and was shot and killed.[37]

Peppin, George W. Born in 1838 in Chittenden County, VT. Peppin was a California Column veteran, having joined the Fifth Regiment of the California Infantry at he start of the Civil War. He was mustered out at Mesilla in November, 1864. Trained as a stone mason, he moved to Lincoln and built several of the town's buildings, including McSween's house and the two-story Murphy-Dolan store that later became the Lincoln Courthouse. He was appointed deputy sheriff by Brady and was with Brady when Brady and Hindman were killed. He was appointed Lincoln County sheriff on June 14, 1878, by Governor Axtell. He was removed as sheriff in February, 1879. In later years, he worked as a mason, Fort Stanton butcher, deputy, and, for a while, Lincoln jailor. Peppin died January 14, 1909.[38]

Perea, José Ynes. Born April 23, 1837, on a large sheep ranch near Bernalillo, NM. His parents were wealthy landowners. At an early age he was sent to the Pingry School in Elizabeth, New Jersey, a college preparatory school. Although the school was non-denominational, the founder was a Presbyterian minister. While at the school Perea lost his Catholic faith and became a Protestant. When he returned home, he was banished by his family for his Catholic apostasy. He *"became an exile and wanderer for sixteen years. During this time he visited the principal seaports of Europe and Asia, and resided for a time in California."* When Taylor arrived in Zuni, he found Perea already there, working for the Rocky Mountains Presbyterian Mission. On December 25, 1878, Perea and Susan Gates were married. On September, 5, 1880, Perea was ordained as an Evangelist in the Presbyterian Church. Perea died July 17, 1910, in Albuquerque.[39]

Pino, Patricio (Pah-lo-wah-ti-was). Son of Pedro Pino. Succeeded Pedro as Governor of Zuni in 1878. Birth and death dates unknown to author.

Pino, Pedro (Lai-iu-ahtsai-lu). Born in 1788 in Zuni. On his mother's side, he was born into the Eagle Clan; on his father's side, the Deer Clan. In his early teens, while on a war party raid with his father, Pino was captured and enslaved by Navajos. After two years of servitude, he was ransomed by Don Pedro Bautista Pino, a wealthy Spaniard living in Santa Fe (Mexico did not receive Independence from Mexico until 1821), who gave him his Spanish name. He remained a servant for Don Pedro until about 1812, when it was decided that he should become a priest. He was sent back to Zuni under the authority of the Catholic mission at Zuni. After several years under the rigorous discipline of the Church, he rebelled and escaped to the Zuni village of Heshota. The Catholic mission was abandoned in 1830, and that same year, Pino became Governor of Zuni. His education and ability to speak Zuni, Navajo, and Spanish well qualified him for the position.

Pino served as Governor of Zuni from 1830 to 1878. During those years, he saw Zuni move from Mexican to U.S. jurisdiction. In February, 1882, Pino, over ninety years old, accompanied Cushing and five other Zunis to Washington, D.C. They took the train from Fort Wingate, and arrived at D.C. by way of Santa Fe, Denver, and Chicago. In Washington, they met President Chester A. Arthur.[40]

Pino's death date, some time after he returned to Zuni, is unknown. He was buried by the Eagle Clan.

Purington, George A. Born July 21, 1837, in Athens, OH. Purington was appointed commander of Fort Stanton in 1877. He was replaced as fort commander by Colonel Dudley on April 5, 1878. After leaving New Mexico, he served as commander of Fort Thomas in Arizona, then as commander of Forts Stockton, Ringgold, and McIntosh in Texas. He retired from the Army July 17, 1895. Purington died May 31, 1896, in Metropolis, Illinois.[41]

Rynerson, William L. Born February 22, 1828, in Mercer County, KY. In 1852, he travelled to California as one of the thousands attracted there by the gold discoveries. When the Civil War started, he enlisted in the First California Infantry, attaining the rank of Lieutenant Colonel. During the events in Lincoln covered in this book, Rynerson was District Attorney of the Third Judicial District. He was an unprincipled supporter of the Murphy-Dolan faction during the Lincoln County War. He died September 26, 1893, in Las Cruces.[42] See Appendix B for a copy of his letter inciting physical violence against the Tunstall-McSween side.

Shield, David Pugh. Born December 5, 1835, in Reynoldsburg, OH. Shield married Elizabeth Hummer, Susan McSween's sister, November 11, 1859. In 1877, he, Elizabeth, and their children moved to Lincoln. Shield formed a law partnership with McSween and bought one wing of his Lincoln home. Shield was in Santa Fe on business when McSween was killed and never returned to Lincoln. He set up a law practice in Las Vegas. In 1884, he was appointed San Miguel County Judge. Shield died March 6, 1888, in Las Vegas.[43]

Shield, Elizabeth (Hummer). Born January 18, 1840, in Gettysburg, PA. Older sister of Susan McSween. Elizabeth married David P. Shield November 11, 1859. According to one account, Elizabeth and Susan quarreled a few months after the 5-day shootout in Lincoln and never spoke to one another afterward. Elizabeth died of pneumonia December 13, 1916, in Los Angeles, CA.[44]

Stevenson, James. Born December 24, 1840, in Maysville, KY. Stevenson was one of the founders of the U.S. Geological Survey. He led the expedition named after him that arrived in Zuni September 19, 1879. The goal of the expedition was to study the language, mythology, philosophy, and sociology of the Pueblo Peoples of New Mexico and Arizona. He died July 25, 1888, in New York City of heart disease.[45]

Tunstall, John Henry. Born March 6, 1853, in London, England. Tunstall left England on August 18, 1872, for Victoria, Canada. After four years there, he left Victoria for California. His goal was to make a fortune by establishing a sheep business. After investigating opportunities in California, he decided land was cheaper in New Mexico and business prospects were better. Tunstall arrived in Lincoln November 6, 1876, and, with his father's money, began building his empire. Tunstall was murdered by Buck Morton and Tom Hill February 18, 1878.[46]

Widenmann, Robert A. Born January 24, 1852, in Ann Arbor, MI. Widenmann's early life is obscure. He was in Santa Fe by August, 1876, when he met Tunstall. He was riding with Billy, Richard Brewer, and John Middleton when Tunstall fled to Lincoln with his horses and was murdered. He was behind Tunstall's corral wall with Billy when Sheriff Brady was shot. Afterwards, he claimed he was there only to feed Tunstall's dog and he saw and knew nothing of the shooting. He left New Mexico in October, 1878. In early 1879, Tunstall's father paid his expenses to travel to London, where he lived with the Tunstall family for six months. On Widenmann's return to the U.S., he settled in Nanuet, NY. Sometime after 1920, he moved to Haverstraw, now Stoney Point, NY, where he died April 15, 1930.[47]

About this Book

The full text of *"Water in a Thirsty Land"* by Ruth Rea Ealy begins on page 21. The supplementary information inclosed in brackets in the text are my editorial additions. I am also responsible for adding the images not identified as being from the original book, the appendices and footnotes, and the index.

– David G. Thomas, editor

Preface

For a number of years I have toyed with the idea of doing something with the diaries, notes, and letters which Father had left concerning his experiences in the mission field in Indian Territory, MDR Oklahoma, and in New Mexico, but the constant demands of a school room kept me from carrying out my plan. I thought for awhile that my brother Charles would work up the papers and notes into a consecutive account, but when he died suddenly a few years ago, I realized that he had not been able to do what I hoped.

When Father died in 1915, the home in Schellsburg soon was broken up and many of the papers were scattered among the various branches of the family. It is true that Mother brought some of them with her when she came to live with me in Pittsburgh, but not all by any means. By the time I was ready to get to work I had to try to find the missing diaries and papers. Most of those have been collected and have formed the basis for this book.

Last summer was the first time that I felt able to begin my project. First I took the diaries and put them into my own hand writing, since often the original writing was blurred or dim, for it had been many years since Father had written them. Furthermore, he had no idea they would ever be used and so took no particular pains. At times I found it necessary to use a magnifying glass to find out what he wrote. Then, when I had something written, new material would be sent to me. I found it rather exacting work. The project, though, has been exceedingly fascinating and one that will prove valuable for the first hand report of the West at a crucial period of its history. Father gave frankly his opinion about persons who were responsible for the Lincoln County War; he also brought out the poor travel conditions at that time and other unique customs and beliefs found among the Zuni Indians.

In this book I have tried to retain as far as possible Father's own words. He had a gift of saying things in a concise and spritely way. It seems to me marvelous that he was able to keep up his diary in the midst of the hazards and frustration of his busy life and make it so much alive.

The Smithsonian Institution gave me some books on the Zuni Indians, books that have proved most helpful. I wish to thank them. A number of people too have proved especially kind in the words of encouragement they have given me. The novelist, Conrad Richter, helped me by his inspiring books about the Indians and by his suggesting my name to the editor of the New Mexico Magazine.

Mr. Robert N. Mullin from Toledo, Ohio gave me a reconstructed map of Lincoln on which he had worked long and arduously; Mr. Aubrey H. Williams from Erdenheim, Philadelphia shared with me some copies of Father's letters which he had secured from the Presbyterian Board; the Board itself has been most kind in sending me all Father's letters posted with the Board; Father Finnigan, formerly stationed at Zuni, at my request sent me information about modern Zuni; Mr. George Fitzpatrick, the editor of the "New

Mexico Magazine," published three articles of mine in his magazine and has shown me many courtesies; my nieces and nephews have applauded me in my efforts. All these people have my hearty thanks. I am also grateful to many other people who have encouraged me in my writing.

Introduction

In nature frequently there is at work some quiet force which brings about great changes. The sun does not announce that his beams are busy day by day changing the garb of nature, but we see the effect in the bursting bud, the ripening fruit, and the waving fields of golden grain. Among people the same force is shown. The person who has the most influence in a family or community usually goes about his daily life so unobtrusively that few realize his power until he has obeyed the call of the great Master and slipped quietly away. Such a person was my father, Dr. T. F. Ealy.

Those characteristics which he showed as a medical missionary in New Mexico during the early part of his life were in evidence through his entire life. His manner always was quiet and unassuming so that he did not in a crowd attract special attention. All around him, though, instinctively refrained from using improper language in his presence, and no one, having once told a questionable story to him, ever repeated the offense. He had a way of looking straight at the narrator that made him ashamed of his words. Having high ideals himself he naturally expected others to have them. Thus, unconsciously he gained the respect of those about him.

His love and loyalty to his town and to his fellow-townsman made him somewhat intolerant of those who did not try to make the most of themselves. In fact, when he talked with one who was not leading the right sort of life, he was likely to speak too plainly about this person's faults to win his friendship. So sometimes he made enemies of those who were vicious and evil, but his forgiving disposition was such that many, at first his enemies, became his staunch friends.

The joy of living permeated his whole being. Even though sixty-six years of age when he died, he never lost his quick step and abounding vitality. This result was largely due to his interest in everything and everybody. One of his last acts of life was to give up his office, the office in which he had passed almost his entire professional life, to a man who wished to establish a town bank, for he said, "I can use any office, but the bank must be in a good location."

When I was a child, I used to marvel at his physical courage, his seeming disregard of disagreeable weather, his lonely night rides, his fearlessness of his fractious pony; but I wondered still more in later years at his moral courage. While he never forced people to listen to his arguments upon a subject, yet, having made up his mind upon a point he kept to his decision with a pertinacity found only in a quiet person. He first decided what was right and then went on his course unflinchingly.

From what I have said you would be led to think Father was grave and serious at all times. On the contrary, there was no one who could enjoy a joke more than he. I recall the zest with which he would repeat the words of a friend, "My wife, she is the readingest woman I ever saw." Father seldom laughed, it is true, but when he did, one felt that his enjoyment, as shown by his laugh, came from his very soul.

When I think of his life, of his ever-youthful interest in living, of his loyalty to his family, his town, his profession, of his unswerving devotion to the cause of Christ, I am

Ealy family home in Schellsburg where Taylor Ealy grew up and to where he returned after leaving Zuni. He later turned the building over to the First National Bank. The people in front may be Taylor and his family. Courtesy Connie Hurtt.

proud that he was my father. As Hamlet said of his father, "He was a man, take him for all in all. I shall not look upon his like again."

Taylor Filmore Ealy, my father, was born September 12, 1848 and died February 19, 1915. It is of his life I wish to write, particularly of that part revealed in the diaries kept of his three pastorates during the years 1874-1881, when he was a medical missionary in the West during the early days of its settlement. It has been my good fortune to examine carefully those diaries during this past summer.

All three charges were in lands which had not yet become states; the first in Indian Territory, now Oklahoma; and the other two in New Mexico, before it became a state in 1912.

The black people in Fort Arbuckle to whom Father was first sent heard him gladly. They were delighted indeed to find some one interested in their educational advancement and in their soul's salvation. They seized every chance to improve their condition. Having recovered just recently from slavery, their studies were hard especially for the older people, but they applied themselves diligently and did remarkably well; while in their Christian development they drank deeply from the "wells of salvation." All their work was a great joy.

New Mexico, the second place, has always been a dry country. Water flows from the snow clad hills in the spring time and creates a flood in the valleys below. With no adequate means of storing that water, it either disappears rapidly into the dry soil or runs off into the streams, which for a short time overflow their banks and then have no moisture except a small amount in the river bed.

Much has been done in later years to improve this condition, but this state is still dependent upon the infrequent rains for its water supply. More needs to be done.

Not only was New Mexico arid physically when Father went there as a home missionary, but the spiritual side was even worse; most people were either openly hostile to the Christian religion as in Lincoln or indifferent as in Zuni, perfectly satisfied as they were. All these people needed to be given a satisfying drink of the "living water."

Left: Taylor Filmore Ealy as a student at Washington and Jefferson College, Washington, Pa. Right: Mary Elizabeth (Ramsey) Ealy as a young woman. Images from book.

Taylor Filmore Ealy. Undated photo. Courtesy Taylor F. Ealy papers, Special Collections, UA.

Mary Elizabeth (Ramsey) Ealy. 1914 photo. Courtesy Taylor F. Ealy papers, Special Collections, UA.

Chapter 1 | Fort Arbuckle

The travel to the West in those days was far from comfortable and frequently hazardous. Father did not reach any of these places in the modern fashion – by plane, in a luxurious train, by a motor car. He went as far as he could by the trains of those days, frequently in poor coaches, and then finished the trip in springless wagons, drawn by mules or oxen for the most part. Often he could not find a place to stop over night, but he did not hesitate to sleep on the ground, even though it was covered by snow. He had with him for his first trip only his wife, but later, his two girls as well. Sometimes it was a difficult matter to keep his family and himself from freezing. Besides, it was not unusual to hear wolves not far away from the place he had selected to camp. Lawless characters too roamed around and once stopped the buckboard in which the family was riding. It truly took courage in those days to be a minister.

Father's first charge was at Fort Arbuckle in Indian Territory. At this place he was under both the United States Government and the Freedmen's Board of the Presbyterian Church. He was under the Department of the Interior of the Government because his assignment was in the reservation of the Chickasaw Nation and Indians were then wards of the United States Government, and under the Presbyterian Church because this body had been allowed to place a minister on that reservation to minister to the people located there. (The Indians since 1924 are citizens of the United States.)

To secure the place at Fort Arbuckle, Father had to accept a difficult field in which to work, and to agree to marry. He said he was eager and willing to accept the difficult field and as for the latter condition he was on his way to fulfilling it.

His preparation had been adequate. As a boy he had had a great desire for military service and hoped when he was old enough to enlist in the regular army. For several years he acted as captain of a group of boys in his home town of Schellsburg. This was during the stirring days of the Civil War. When his older brother enlisted in Company H, 55th Regular Pennsylvania Volunteers, Father, himself, decided to go too, and went as far as Harrisburg, Pennsylvania. There his brother saw him and promptly sent him home. Grandfather, realizing Taylor, or Tay, as he was called, would enlist at the first opportunity, packed him off to a preparatory school at Elder's Ridge Academy. So his formal education began. At this school in Pennsylvania he spent two and a half years.

At the end of this time Father was ready for college. He entered the junior class of Washington and Jefferson College; he was graduated with the class of 1869. Dr. Moffett [James D. Moffat], later president of the college, was one of his classmates. After his graduation Father was enrolled in the Western Theological Seminary, Allegheny, Pennsylvania, from which school he was graduated with the class of 1872. His vacations meanwhile were spent in Schellsburg, Pennsylvania, reading medicine in the office of his father and brother Albert. After his graduation from the Seminary, he went to Philadelphia, Pennsylvania to the medical department of the University of Pennsylvania. Here he finished his formal education when he was graduated with the class of 1874.

He was ready now for his first call. From the first he had desired to be a foreign missionary and had chosen Japan for his field of work, but Mr. Hepburn, a missionary who had just returned from Japan, discouraged him from this choice. Meanwhile, he was busy practically every Sabbath supplying some vacant pulpit in and around Pittsburgh. I recall that one place at which he preached was East Liberty Presbyterian Church. Those of you who are familiar with the marvelous cathedral which now stands at the corner of Highland and Penn will be surprised to learn that to reach his appointed place from Old Allegheny, Father had to drive a long distance through the woods. One Monday morning, after he had preached at a place 20 miles north of Old Allegheny, he was approached by an elder of the church where he had preached day before, who said, "The church is divided about calling you and we will not make out a call unless it is unanimous." Father was greatly surprised that he was being considered as a candidate, such an idea had not entered his head, since it was understood that he was to become a missionary.

Just after this encounter he went to his room and dropped upon his knees to ask the Lord to show him his work. Later, that same day when he returned to his room he found there a note requesting him to go to the Freedmen's Board. There, Mr. McClelland, the secretary, told him there were two fields for which they were hunting a suitable man, one a teaching position in the seminary, the other, a much harder one, a position in the government school at Fort Arbuckle. He chose the latter place.

He had asked the Lord to give him a wife suitable for his work and to give him a field in which to work for Him. The latter had now been fulfilled. Mother, with her good preparation and her great teaching ability, was surely the proper wife for him. When the call came, though, it took rapid moving around for him to be ordained and married and to have all the preparations made for his journey to Fort Arbuckle in the time designated. He was married on October 1, [1874], to Mary E. Ramsey at East Waterford, Juniata County, Pennsylvania. He was ordained as an evangelist by the Presbytery of Pittsburgh on October 7 [October 6 according to Presbytery records].

Soon after his ordination he and his bride started for Indian Territory to begin their work. It must have been a most trying experience for both. They went by way of the Vandalia Line through Indianapolis; then over the M. K. & T. R. R. to Caddo, Indian Territory, sixty miles from Fort Arbuckle.

Leaving the railroad at Caddo late at night, they went to a hotel which had been pointed out to them. Since it was an exceedingly late hour, the hotel was dark and no answer came to repeated knocks and calls. Always resourceful, Father simply went to a room and took it for the night. He failed to say what happened in the morning. He does say that the latter part of their trip from Caddo to Fort Arbuckle was carried out in a stage, drawn by four horses. So he and Mother took the stage at about three o'clock in the afternoon.

At the edge of town two armed men rode up and stopped the stage. Father thought that these men wanted to see just who were in the stage and later kill them. Evidently, they were looking for someone else and so did not bother the occupants. On they went and by daybreak the driver's bugles announced their approach to the Exchange [Hotel] where travelers on the stage were able to get an early breakfast of coffee and what Father designated as "truck." An old woman made many apologies for the meal; said that when nice folks came she was not prepared with any good things to eat.

Next day at noon the stage pulled into Paul's Valley. Because it was Saturday, Father was determined to push on to Fort Arbuckle in order not to travel on the Sabbath. People advised them to wait until the next day, but nothing would detain him, so he hired a driver and a team of horses, bought such eatables as he thought they might need to begin housekeeping, and started for the fort.

Pushing along at as rapid a rate as the roads allowed, they came to Fort Arbuckle by sundown. On the way flocks of pigeons flew over the wagon and filled the sky as far as the eye could see. This sight was too much for Father and so he stood up in the wagon and took a shot at them. Too bad he proved a poor marksman! Fort Arbuckle, named for the general who built it, had been abandoned five years before. The Governor had fitted up the officer's quarters for school rooms and living rooms. This was the place they were to live. The place was left in a wretched state. Though the ceiling had been newly plastered, the old plaster was lying in lumps on the floor, and the whole place was covered with dust.

Not a very propitious beginning for a bride! Some ladies would have sat down and cried to see such a spectacle. Not Mother. She was made of sterner stuff. After sweeping a place for their trunks and for a bed on the floor, they fell to work to dust and to got supper in the fireplace. They ate the meal on one of the trunks on which they had spread a tablecloth. Tired out with their journey and the excitement of it all, they slept like logs and did not waken until the sun shone directly into their faces. Young and anxious to succeed, they tried to make the best of what they had and did not fret about what they did not have. In this way they began housekeeping, with contentment.

Among Father's papers was the following letter from the Indian Commissioner:

Department of the Interior
Office of Indian Affairs
Washington, D. C. Nov. 3, 1874

Sir:

I am in receipt of your communication of the 27th ultimo, respecting the opening of the Ft. Arbuckle School.

I trust you will realize all your anticipations in the work you have in hand. It is especially desirable that this school shall be made efficient, for its influence upon other educational work among the Chickasaws.

It is believed the demonstration within their observation of what children can accomplish in studies under proper tuition will act as a spur to their present sluggish and incompetent methods. I send you by mail today a permutation table, which you will find of assistance in teaching beginners.

Agent G. M. Ingalls has assumed his office. His address is Muskogee, Indian Territory. In order to furnish the necessary information to him as well as this office, you will please communicate through him sending a monthly report according to the blanks herewith furnished.

Very respectfully,
E. W. Phoust, Commissioner

Father drew the following plan of the Fort:

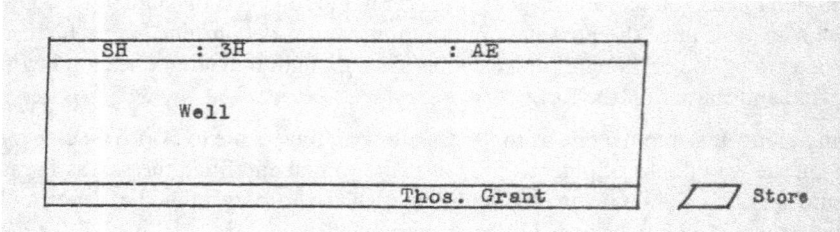

As soon as possible Father opened his school, but at once he decided that a day school was not sufficient. The pupils, having often no means of transportation, found it difficult to attend regularly. Therefore a boarding school was opened so that the pupils might have both the secular and religious training which they so earnestly desired. The drawing of the Fort shows the buildings which were occupied by the school. The first one was taken over for the use of the family; the rest belonged to the school proper. The well at one side of the parade ground furnished water for the school. The account which Father wrote follows:

"We began active work the first part of November 1874. Mrs. Ealy, having taught a number of school terms in Juniata County, Pa., could and did take an active part in organizing the school. Scholars are from North, South, East, and West, from the Canadian River section and from near the Red River, from 10 miles east and 10 miles west of Ft. Arbuckle."

"The parents of the pupils got busy, killed pork, and brought provisions to run our large boarding house. Several black women came in and cooked and took care of the rooming houses and the boarding house. All things however were not sweetness and light. Measles broke out in the school; and at one time 30 scholars were down with this disease. The people even brought fresh cows and left them to furnish milk. One evening when the students had finished milking, as was their custom, after the calves had taken some milk, and were being tied to the fence, a strange occurrence happened. Just as one of the boys was about to tie a calf to the rail of the fence, he noticed a very large rattlesnake stretched out on the other side of the fence. Nearly every man carried a revolver and knife in his belt. Fortunately, this student had one. He pulled his revolver quickly and had the snake killed before it had stopped rattling."

"I asked one of the men, George Loftus by name, how many panthers he had killed that year. His answer was, 'Well, me and the boys has killed six this fall.'"

"The poor Freedmen and their families were harassed not only by poisonous reptiles and by wild beasts but by mounted ruffians, who would ride into their camps when they were holding religious meetings and begin shooting right and left."

"Game was exceedingly plentiful. Wild pigeons (while flying over the house) often darkened the sun. As one rode down the road or trails he could see wild deer moving about among the trees and bushes. Wild turkeys of every size could be shot at any season of the year. Bears also were numerous and their meat is excellent. The pecan nuts fattened them, as also the hogs, turkeys, and deer. Once I had the pleasure of shooting turkeys by moonlight. It was a wonderful experience."

"Now everything has been changed. The county in which we taught is being cut up by railroads and is included in the State of Oklahoma."

"We worked hard and faithfully for the promotion of good citizenship while we were there. Our eldest daughter Anna [called 'Pearl'] was born at Ft. Arbuckle on Sept. 3, 1875. She became the wife of an attorney, C. W. Appleman, and died in Indianapolis, Indiana, in [December 29], 1908."

"We opened our school in an Indian reservation by Gov't. authority. I told the Freedmen that we would teach all who came, old and young, as long as we could accommodate them, every day in the week except Saturday. On Sabbath we worked about three hours teaching the Bible. Some of the scholars were over 70 years of age; in fact they ranged on down to four or five."

"The following list of pupils I furnish as a matter of history:"

"BOYS"
"Willie Jacobs"
"Lawrence Alexander"
"Chas. Harris"
"Geo. Williams"
"Robt. Ellis"
"Laurie Moor"
"Henry Taylor"
"Daniell Richards"
"Robt. Stevenson"
"Albert Stevenson"
"Alfred Franklin"
"James Young"
"Colbert Alexander"

"GIRLS"

"Minerva Freeman"
"Betsy Williams"
"Adelaide Colbert"
"Lizzie Harrison"
"Rachel Williams"
"Beatrice Alexander"
"Mary Stevenson"
"Lena Colbert"
"Louisa Hoppy"
"Mary Neadems"
"Mary McLaughlin"
"Iona J. Schell"
"Linda Williams"
"Dinah A. Freeman"

"The scope of the country from which we drew our scholars was very large as there was not any school like ours anywhere around. Some of my black men told me they were not allowed to read or even to have a Bible in their possession when they were slaves. One whose veracity I know told me he knew this statement to be literally true. He said his master told him how much he was worth to him and that he, the slave, had worked and made enough money to buy himself from his master, who then let him go free. The former slave's name was Galatan Freeman. Aunt Delphia, one of our workers and a scholar, told us that she had been with some other small girls playing on the beach in Africa. Before they were aware of anyone's being near them, a rowboat rounded the point and she was caught, carried to the boat, rowed to a vessel, and then brought to this country. They landed in Virginia and she was sold as a slave. She never heard a word from her home after that incident. Think of the loss of a kidnapped child among ourselves! The whole country is set in commotion; the whole police and detective force are on the lookout. Would anyone dare to assert that the grief of black parents is not so great as that of the white? Black people were even at times sold to the Indians. Of course they ware all liberated in 1863."

"I had some correspondence with Mr. Brown Peters, a former scholar who is now preaching, and he referred to those school days as 'the golden days.' We gave them spiritual uplift such as they had never had before. Some of the men to whom we gave books in our Sabbath School – those who could read – would start off on horseback, reading as they went with their bridle reins hanging on the saddle and the horse sauntering slowly along."

"The white people kept telling the Freedmen that they could not stay in the territory; that the Gov't. was going to move them somewhere else. Such uncertainty about their homes kept the people from building anything but shacks. I know that if they have a chance they will buy sewing machines, pianos, organs, and will show thrift and industry equal that of their white neighbors. Let us treat all men everywhere as we would have them treat us."

"Often in the midst of a religious meeting in the open air, men whose skins were white would ride into the meeting of the black folks and begin to shoot right and left in order to break up the meeting. The more worthless a man is the more likely he is to hate his fellow men. Wholesome law should cause such barbarity to cease so that the black man can sit down under his own vine and fig tree to worship God, none daring to molest him or make him afraid."

"It was our custom to assemble the school and all our help in the evening about the time the sun went down for chapel services. To hear those old women start off on the familiar hymns was sublime. Their voices were like the sound of a bugle. I do not think there was a single scholar or teacher who did not join heartily in the singing. We shall always remember those pleasant evening chapel services."

"Thos. Grant and family lived across the parade ground to the north. Our singing must often have attracted their attention. They were my good neighbors. I often went to the woods to hunt with Mr. Grant's oldest son Calvin, who was a young man of fifteen. We would take a small dog and go into the woods, and soon the dog would run into a flock of young turkeys. They would all fly up on the trees with their wings spread out, making an easy mark for the hunters. A few shots and we had enough game."

"Just a short time before our arrival in Ft. Arbuckle, Dr. Happy had been shot by some men who were robbing the store at Paul's Valley. All hands had been ordered up and everyone was to remained seated. Dr. Happy started to run back into the warehouse; as he ran he was shot. He was then taken to Ft. Sill, where he died in the hospital. That left Ft. Arbuckle without a physician."

"When the people learned that I was a doctor, I found it impossible not to practice medicine. My father had sent me a box of drugs. So outside of school I was kept busy."

"Miss Rebecca Forbes, our assistant teacher, bought a horse in order to ride with me for exercise but she soon gave it up, as my visits were too long and far and fast for her to go on horseback. Once as I was riding on a lope my horse struck the hitching strap, which was tied to a ring in the saddle. It was so unexpected that it jerked her head between her legs and she turned a complete somersault. I lit on my feet and took several quick steps to get out of the way, but for all that her hind feet hit me squarely in the back. I was not disabled fortunately and so got back on the horse; from then on I rode more carefully."

"The assistant we had had before Miss Forbes proved to be a dark horse. She was married to a doctor shortly after she began her school duties. They soon got up a paper behind my back, asking for me to leave Ft. Arbuckle, got the Freedmen to sign it, and sent it to the Sec. of the Board of Freedmen. Dr. McClelland, at Pittsburgh, Pa. not understanding the meaning of the paper, forthwith sent it back to me with the request that I explain the matter. Our teacher got her discharge at once when I wrote that it was done while I was away and I did not know anything about it."

"Previous to this the Dr. and his wife had tried another scheme to get rid of us. They fixed up two steaks of venison, large and well-buttered and broiled. Unsuspectingly we took their gift with pleasure and at once sat down and ate every bite. We finished at the same time. I said 'I am sick,' my wife said 'So am I!' We realized then that we had been poisoned. Fortunately God intervened and our lives were saved because we vomited until all the meat was out of our stomachs. The great amount of butter, too, helped. We gave God the praise for our speedy relief. When we returned the plates, we spoke of the delicious meat and did not even hint that we had any suspicion of poison."

"You can imagine how glad we were when Miss Forbes came to replace the former teacher. In her we had a lady of the first magnitude. She was as brave as they find them. She was obliged to show her bravery on her way up from Caddo to Ft. Arbuckle. I had sent a trusty man with a light two-horse spring wagon to meet the stage. When he reached the Wild Horse Creek, it was brimming over. He unhitched and got his horses across and borrowed a wagon on the other side, but when he returned to the area with Miss Forbes at dark, he drove to the bank of the angry stream. At once he understood it was far from safe to try to cross in the darkness and Miss Forbes declared she would not cross that river until daylight. She ordered him to drive up onto the prairie, and there in the open prairie in the rain she slept in the wagon while the driver slept on the ground underneath."

"In the morning the still swollen angry water had to be crossed. So without supper and without breakfast they went down to try the stream. He rode one horse to show her how deep the water was. Then she said that if he could get her trunk over the stream she would ride behind him on his horse. As he was a blacksmith and very strong, he took her trunk on his shoulders and rode across; then he returned for her. She climbed up behind him, and, though the water was up to the horse's back, they crossed in safety. When they

Mission House at Fort Arbuckle. Taylor and Mary Ealy on porch. Undated photo. Image from book.

reached Ft. Arbuckle, she said never before was so glad to see the face of a friend. 'Brave lady!' So she proved to be from first to last."

"Our retiring from that mission field was due to an arrangement of the Board and the Government by which the country was divided up among the various churches for Christian work so that one would not overlap the other. This section fell to the Baptists and on that account I thought it only fair to resign. Afterwards the Indian Agent wrote to ask me to return to Ft. Arbuckle and take over the school. By that time I was established in another place and so answered his invitation in the negative."

"When I returned to Ft. Arbuckle in 1876 after we had gone east to the Centennial, I found a man had moved into my house. But the Lord looked out for me then as he did at other times. I know a number of times we were in great danger but He protected us."

The rest of their stories about Fort Arbuckle is told in letters to their respective homes. Father mentions pictures of their house and of the swollen water where Miss Rebecca Forbes camped in the rain. These pictures have not yet turned up. Miss Forbes had come out in August 1875 to assist with the teaching.

In a letter of August 18, 1875, Rev. McClelland, Secretary for the Presbyterian Committee of Missions for Freedmen, states concerning Miss Forbes that she was a well recommended teacher of much experience in public schools. She was really sent as a substitute for Mrs. Lizzie D. Scott, who could not go out at that particular time, and asked the Board to take Miss Forbes as her substitute. Father and Mother found her an excellent teacher and she soon became a personal friend. They always spoke of her with great affection.

Father also mentions pictures of the school rooms and the boarding houses, of their exhibition booth and festival, of people coming to be married, two on one horse. He speaks of their day school as well as their Sabbath School. Everything seemed to be moving along smoothly and nicely. He even hunted up scholars across the Canadian River and down near the Red River on the border of Texas. He also must have had some recreation, for at different times he talked about hunting bears, panthers, wild turkeys, pigeons, and deer. The rich soil, the good crops, and beautiful scenery all came in for their share of his enthusiasm. Finally, when he was able to give books to the people, both they and he felt that golden days had come indeed.

In one old book I have run across a list of the pupils in that Fort Arbuckle school with the record of attendance. There were 58 in all on the rolls with a fair record for most of them. The books mentioned were Sanders' Readers, Union Spelling Book, and Testaments. Supplies, such as slates, pencils and paper, were given to the children. These were not free, for I find the cost of each entered in a book with a record. A slate cost 20 cents; a Union speller 20 cents; a Testament 90 cents. The Government, I suppose, paid the bill. After a great success and pleasant experience, they left Fort Arbuckle for a visit to the East.

It was June 5, 1876 when Father, Mother, and Pearl arrived in Schellsburg rather unexpectedly although Father had written that they intended to come back soon for a visit. They saw the friends and relatives in Schellsburg before they left for East Waterford, Mother's home in Juniata County, on June 28. The next item concerning the travelers comes from Aunt Mary's diary for July 3, when she said that Taylor intended to meet his two sisters Corrie and Anna at Harrisburg on their way to the Centennial. As a child I marveled at some of the wonders Father told about their visit to the Centennial, especially the beginning of the telephone when a man actually could speak to some one in a different part of the huge building. I wondered how such a marvel could happen:

By July 19 they were all back in Schellsburg, preparing for the return trip to Fort Arbuckle. Having learned that the Indian Territory field had been assigned to the Baptist Church, by the decision of the various churches to divide the mission fields, Father decided to send in his resignation; he preferred to work for the Presbyterian Board. Meanwhile he felt it necessary to return and close up the work in Fort Arbuckle. They left Schellsburg the last of July and returned there on October 2. All were suffering from ague [fever], Pearl worst of all.

A letter from Mr. McClelland, Secretary of the Board, mentions that fact and also states that A. G. Galpin, Acting Commissioner of Indian Affairs, had offered Father $900.00 and Mother $600.00 for the ensuing year but no assistant as the funds would not allow it. He wished to know whether Father would consider the offer on the terms proposed. He said likely Father had heard from the Commissioner himself and urged a speedy reply.

On October 18, sad news came to Mother. Her brother had died of typhoid fever. His death was attributed to the hazing of his roommate and the fact the boys slept in a damp bed. Jimmie was an unusually brilliant student; his death brought great sorrow to Mother. She immediately went to East Waterford where Father joined her on December 1, 1876.

Father had not yet fully decided what to do about Fort Arbuckle. So in January 1877 he returned to Schellsburg with the intention of going back to Fort Arbuckle to stay or to pack up his books and other possessions that had been left behind. He soon returned from Fort Arbuckle to Schellsburg where he was joined by Mother and Pearl, both looking very well.

In the summer of 1877 the whole family was in East Waterford, Pennsylvania, on a visit to Mother's parents. My sister, Anna Margarette or Pearl as she was called, had been born in 1875 in Indian Territory. In October [15], 1877 I came to join her.

Father had been asked to take a post in New Mexico and at once he began to make arrangements about that trip. It involved a trip to New York which he took in November. He had to consider now not only his wife but two small children as well, who would need much care during the long journey. Besides it was winter and an unusually cold one and that fact had to be taken into account. Finally the last of January he and his group were able to get off.

Chapter 2 | Lincoln

In his diary of January 7, 1878, Father speaks of a letter from the B. & O. about [railroad] tickets.

The tickets he mentions have to do with his plans to go to his pastorate in New Mexico. By this time the family had gone to Schellsburg again to visit the Ealy relatives, and Father was waiting to be sent to his new charge. It was to be in Lincoln, New Mexico.

The call to Lincoln came because Mr. Alexander McSween, a Scotch lawyer of that town and an ardent Presbyterian, realizing the lawless state of that place, had written to the Presbyterian Church asking for a young missionary to be sent to them. McSween felt that the ennobling and refining influence of the Christian Church would be of inestimable value in raising the standards of all those who came into contact with it. Hence Father was given the call.

Travel to New Mexico in 1878 was an unusual experience. As a result Father left an account in his diary, and both he and Mother wrote at length concerning the journey. As these various reports have sufficient difference to make them both interesting and valuable, I shall include them all. First we have the diary reports, which necessarily had to be brief.

Father records in his diary on January 28 that he had received a check from 23 Center Street, New York City, for $250.00 and that they expected to start for Lincoln in the morning. The following items come directly from the diary:

Jan. 29. T. F. Ealy, Mrs. T. F. Ealy, Susan Gates and our two little girls, Pearl and Ruth, left Schellsburg for New Mexico via Huntington and Broad Top R.R. for first Pittsburgh and then St. Louis.

Susan Gates went along as an assistant. I cannot imagine what Mother would have done without her.

Jan. 30. Reached St. Louis at 9:15 P.M. All well. Took private room with board and remained over night to rest.

Jan. 31. Left St. Louis 9:45 P.M. for Denver. The tickets from Mann's Choice (nearest railroad point to Schellsburg) were $41.00. Pearl and Ruth well.

Feb. 1. Kansas City 11:14 A.M. Changed cars. Good weather. All well.

Feb. 2. Denver, Colorado. Stopped at the Wentworth House. $2.00 per day. Baptists. I am very sick with bile colic [gallstones].

Here for the first time Father speaks of the recurring sicknesses, which seemed to plague him all the time during his ministry.

Feb. 3. Denver, Colorado. Wentworth House. Am very much better. Dr. Bancroft came to see me. Went to hear Dr. Read preach in the evening.

Feb. 4. Denver. Mrs. Sheldon Jackson (wife of the prominent Presbyterian Divine) called; also Mr. Walsh.

Las Vegas. Photo circa 1880. Courtesy Maurice G. Fulton Papers, Special Collections, UA.

Andres Nelson & Co. General Store/Hotel, Anton Chico. 1875-1906 photo. Courtesy Palace of the Governors Photo Archives (NMHM/DCA), 091340.

Feb. 5. Left Denver at 7:00 A.M. on Monday; got to El Moro [The name El Moro is a derivative spelling of El Morro, which is Spanish for "Moor"] at 6:00 P.M. New State House. All well except for colds.

Feb. 6. Left El Moro at 5:30 A.M. in stage coach. Took break fast at Trinidad; left at 7:00 A.M. Rode all day and all night in stage. Met Mr. Howard.

Feb. 7. Las Vegas, New Mexico. Arrived at 8:00 A.M. Stopped with Rev. Mr. [John A.] Annin. All well. One trunk not received.

Rev: Mr. Annin had come to Las Vegas in October 1869, where he had established both a mission church and school. It was there that the family first met Mr. [José Ynes] Perea. When they [Ealy and family] later settled in Zuni, Mr. Perea had preceded them in order to help with the work there.

Feb. 8. Las Vegas. All well. Telegraphed to Trinidad for missing trunk. Will be on next coach.

Feb. 9. Las Vegas. No trunk. Snow on the ground. Cool. Drew some money from the bank and changed from Valley Bank to this bank $200.00.

Feb. 10. Las Vegas. Preached at 10:00 A.M. and 7:00 P.M. to about 18 at each service on "Paul and Barnabas," morning; "We are saved by hope," evening.

Feb. 11. Las Vegas still. No word of trunk – dispatched again.

Feb. 13. Left Las Vegas with two mules; and a driver. $5.00 per day and all expenses. Drove to Anton Chico 27 miles. Stopped at [Andres] Nelson's [Hotel], Catholic; bill $5.00.

Three things are frequently mentioned in the diary; the health of the family, the price paid for everything, and (along with his preaching) religion or lack of it of those with whom he stayed.

Feb. 14. Left Anton Chico about 10:00 P.M. Cold – snow on the ground. Camped in the evening. Melted snow for coffee. Kept the children warm.

Feb. 15. Left camp early. Drove all day – cold. Melted snow to water mules 4 miles south of Perdenal [Cerro Pedernal, "Flint Mountain"].

Feb. 16. Left camp after sun-up. Getting warmer. Drove late to get good camp – 21 miles south of water hole. Bought water for mules and filled a 5 gal. keg.

Feb. 17. Sabbath. Left camp at sun-up. A wolf came within ten steps of the wagon. Camped early. Melted snow for mules.

Feb. 18. Broke camp early. Wolves barked in the night. At noon ate at Patos Springs. Reached Fort Stanton 18 minutes after dark. Stopped with Mary Donley – fine entertainment.

Feb. 19. Left Fort Stanton early. Bands out; soldiers on parade. Reached Lincoln at 11:00 A.M., 9 miles from Ft. Stanton. Found [John Henry] Tunstall had just been murdered. McSween and Shield's house full of armed men. Guard on housetop.

(Mother's account of the same journey differs slightly but is more detailed.)

JOURNEY OF A HOME MISSIONARY TO NEW MEXICO
By Mrs. T. F. Ealy

"Leaving Schellsburg, a small village near the Bedford Springs, Pa., January 29, 1878, we were carried by the great iron horse westward to the Rocky Mountains. After passing through several large cities in the different states, and by many friends, whom we would have rejoiced to see, we left the thickly settled portions to span the plains beyond the Missouri."

"After a monotonous ride over the plains, we were growing tired when about three o'clock Saturday snow-capped peaks of the Rocky Mountains appeared. Dr. Ealy, catching sight of them, exclaimed, 'The mountains! The mountains!' But as we sped toward them they seemed to recede and nine hours elapsed before we were carried into the Denver City depot. We remained in that city over Sabbath. Tuesday morning we took the train over the Denver and Rio Grande (narrow-gauge) road, passed through Colorado Springs and Pueblo, thence to El Moro, where we remained all night."

"In the morning we took the coach for Las Vegas, a distance of 150 miles. We crossed the Raton Mountains, from the summit of which Pike's Peak can be clearly seen in the distance. Ten o'clock found us at the ranch (farm) of old Mr. [Thomas O.] Boggs, one of the western pioneers. The hours passed pleasantly during the day, but night found us longing for the morning, and the first sight of Las Vegas was a feast to our eyes, though the adobe buildings contrasted strangely with our eastern towns."

"Rev. Mr. Annin, Presbyterian missionary at Las Vegas (the meadows), kindly entertained us several days. A very encouraging school was in session, conducted by his daughter, and the mission church and school building are a credit to him. A week's rest prepared us to travel ere our missionary home was reached."

"Feb. 13 found us on the road to Lincoln in an ambulance driven by two mules, with a Mexican driver who did not speak English. Evening found us in Anton Chico (Little Anthony) 27 miles on our way. Though we slept in an adobe house with dirt floor, our sleep was sweet. In the morning our hostess supplied us with two bottles of milk. Here too, we bought a five-gallon keg and filled it with water, as many miles were to pass over before we could reach a dwelling, and water was very scarce. The morning was very cold, and as our course faced the wind, which was blowing a perfect gale; we suffered much from the cold, not being as well supplied with wraps as we should have been, owing to the fact that one of our trunks had been lost on the Denver and Rio Grande Road. Our little ones began crying and we feared they would freeze, but seeing a camp fire ahead some distance, we hastened to it, and after warming our almost frozen babes, and partaking of the nice lunch put up for us by Mrs. Annin the morning before, we continued our journey, and night found us twenty-five miles nearer Lincoln."

"We felt much disheartened; night was on us, snow all around us, two little babes exposed to the fold with insufficient clothing, but God protected us. Our Mexican friend fixed a nice camp for us out of cedar boughs. After a supper of bacon, tortillas (flat cakes), and coffee made of snow water, we laid our little ones to rest; the ground for a bed, the sky above them and sat down to keep watch. Morning found us all alive, and though but little refreshed by sleep, we were anxious to resume our journey."

"Though we traveled all day, hoping the wind would fall, night found us crossing the Perdenal [Cerro Pedernal] (a very high peak) with neither wood nor water to be found. Fortunately we met some teamsters, who directed us to a little strip of woods three miles beyond. When we reached the woods we found a camp prepared for us. Pearl wanted to know if we were going to sleep on the ground again. Supper over, we took our little ones in our arms, asked God's protection, and lay down to rest. The wind howled around our camp, but God saved us from its severity."

"Saturday noon we reached Alkali Holes, the first dwelling since we left Anton Chico. Finding the inmates all drunk, both men and women, we did not remain over Sabbath as we first intended to do, but pushed onto the mountains, which we reached some time after dark. Again we found a camp in readiness; cold prevented us from sleeping, though Pearl and Ruth slept sweetly. In the morning we saw a hungry wolf prowling around our camp and from all appearances there must have been a den beneath us, as sounds proceeded from under the ground."

"Sabbath morning found us suffering from cold, our mules without water, and none to be found anywhere. So in mercy we traveled part of the day to find water for our thirsty animals and to get our babes into a warmer climate. We camped early, melted snow for our mules, as we could find no water, built three fires, and lay down to sleep."

"Monday morning we continued our journey and crossed the Gallinas and Jicarilla (Hickorea) Mountains, reaching the Patos Springs at noon. Night found us in Fort Stanton, where we were kindly entertained by Major [Paul] Dowlin [post trader]."

"Tuesday noon [February 19] we reached Lincoln, our home, but such an excitement prevailed, and still prevails, that we have not been able to accomplish much, though we have succeeded in establishing the first Sabbath School ever held here."

"Our work will be among Americans and Mexicans. We are anxious to begin. We feel hopeful. Desperadoes throng the country, seven men killed in three weeks. Mr. Ealy's first duty was to preach the funeral sermon for a member of the Episcopal Church [John Henry Tunstall], who had been brutally murdered by these desperadoes. May they be speedily brought to justice:"

"Lincoln, New Mexico, March 16, 1878."

FATHER WRITES OF HIS TRIP

"I answered a call from the Rocky Mountain Presbytery for medical missionaries in 1878 and was assigned to Lincoln, Lincoln County, New Mexico. I did not know who the people in Lincoln were, nor did I know how warlike or peaceful they were. I knew only call from that quarter and I answered it."

"On Jan. 29, 1878 with my faithful wife, two little girls, one-half years, and the other not yet four months old, and a lady friend, I set out from Schellsburg, Pa. upon an overland journey to an unknown part of our country to live among entire strangers. We traveled via Huntington, Vandalia, St. Louis, Kansas City, Denver, Las Vegas, Anton Chico, Alkali Holes, Patos Springs, Ft. Stanton to Lincoln, a distance of about 3000 miles. Sailors who think nothing of crossing the Atlantic would grumble at making this journey, especially the latter part beyond the railroad."

"At 9:15 on Jan. 30 we reached St. Louis; at 9:45 we left for Denver, which we reached Feb. 2. The long run through Kansas was extremely tedious. The older little girl when told to look out said, 'Pearl did see out.' A Chinamen would have said, 'Prairie all the sames.' Long before we reached Denver, however, the snow capped Rocky Mountains loomed up high into the heavens, breaking the monotony we had endured so long.

At Denver the hackman were more boisterous than any I had heard in St. Louis, New York, or Philadelphia."

"After spending a quiet Sabbath in Denver, we arranged on Monday for our journey south. Then on Tuesday we set out at 7 A.M. on the cute little cars of the Denver and Rio Grande R.R., a narrow gauge road. It seemed as if the engineers had taken some road wagon trail for their grade, but we were not tired riding at six that evening when we came to El Moro (The Strawberry) [the name El Moro is a derivative spelling of El Morro, which is Spanish for 'Moor'], the terminus of the railroad near the border of New Mexico."

"We were hurried out of El Moro at 5:30 A.M. on Feb. 6 before breakfast, which we ate at Trinidad (Trinity), a distance of two miles. Now we began to realize the rough part of the trip was just beginning. We pulled out of Trinidad at 7 A.M. with the Raton [Mouse] Mountains to cross. Six horses pulled us over. All day and all night we rolled on passing Ft. Union of noted fame at 2 or 3 o'clock in the morning. By 8 o'clock A.M. we came to Las Vegas, a town of possibly 3500 inhabitants. Here we lingered several days because, a trunk was lost somewhere between Denver and El Moro. When it arrived in Lincoln exactly three months and four days later, it had been robbed of most of its contents. People had better leave valuables in a safe deposit box in the East. One has not time to look out for such things on the frontier."

"By Feb. 13 we decided to start on our trip south to Lincoln and not wait any longer for the trunk. Since by this time our plans had been completed and a kind and patient driver, a Mexican, had been secured, this little company of five set out in a spring wagon, drawn by two mules. Our first stop was at Anton Chico, 27 miles away. Here we stayed at [Andres] Nelson's Hotel. The next morning we left at 10 to face a bitterly cold wind. We could not have endured the cold had we not tied up a quilt to break the force of the wind. Mr. Nelson had advised me to take along some water. It seemed strange advice to me but I was surely glad that I had added a 5 gallon keg of water to our wagon when we reached the long stretch of country without any water. Had there not been snow on the ground, without hauling water, traveling by wagon would nave been impossible. As it was, all the water our mules got for two days was that which we obtained by melting snow."

"On the 15th we camped four miles south of Perdenal [Cerro Pedernal], an elevation of queer looking rocks full of seams. I felt like starting a mineral exploring camp here. From this elevation one has a view of a broad expanse as far as the eye can see of a shallow basin with here and there salt lakes and antelopes in abundance."

"The next morning we left at sun-up aiming to reach Alkali Holes by night in order to lodge in a house. Here there were two houses and two holes bored by the U.S. Government. By traveling hard all day, we reached these wells about three P.M. I hurried to the first house, knocked, but no response came. We opened the door and went in. I said, 'We'll stay here all night.' I went around to the other shack, knocked, but there again was no response. When I opened the door, there stood three people full of smallpox! They were also half intoxicated. We hastily bought water for the mules and left precipitously."

"Twelve miles away we reached the timber where we could find a wind break. We always tried to camp where campers had been before. It was late before we pitched our camp on a knoll under a bushy cedar. Our camp was made where later Gov. Lew Wallace shot a bear. With the children in our arms we lay down to sleep about half lest some harm should come to them. Usually I awoke about the time the morning stars appeared. This Sabbath morning I well remember when I looked around, lo and behold! Close by my side stood a long-jawed coyote (a small prairie wolf). The driver and I set to work to chase her away. I threw afire brand at her but she merely evaded the brand and got behind a cedar tree. We did not have a gun. With fire we chased her a little farther away and got breakfast. When all became quiet, we heard the cries of her young beneath the place where we had made our beds. Her claim had been made before ours and so we did not dispute it further."

"Houseless, unarmed, lightly clad for the time of year, we felt it our duty to push on south even though it the Sabbath as a ship would plod on toward port not thinking of anchoring in mid-ocean until the Sabbath was over. It was through a mountainous gorge without human habitation. On account of the day we camped early and melted snow to water our poor mules. That night we heard many barking wolves."

"On the 18th we arrived at Patos Springs at noon and here ate our lunch. Just before we came to the Springs we witnessed a total eclipse of the sun. It must not have seemed darker when Pompeii was covered with ashes from Vesuvius. After dark we drove into Ft. Stanton. Here we stopped at Major Dowlin's sutler store and hotel. We were not even stopped by a guard. The next morning when I asked for our team to go to Lincoln, Major Dowlin asked me if I did not think I would strike a pretty rough place. I told him that I had been in rough places before. I did not know than that a war was raging. Lincoln was 9 miles away east of Ft. Stanton and the county capital."

The following is a paper written by Father at the time, but not incorporated in his diary. It was written at Lincoln:

"We live in a canyon. It is said to be very healthful here; none scarcely die a natural death. They do not get an opportunity because there is too much lead in the air."

"We reached Ft. Stanton in the evening of the 18th and left early the next morning for Lincoln, 9 miles away. Since our arrival there have been five deaths from shooting. No one would care to say where their souls are today."

"I had brought my family from Las Vegas (The Meadows) in a private wagon nearly 200 miles with nothing but a pen knife with its point broken off for defense. We leaned on the strong arms for protection, which is far better than trusting solely to carnal weapons."

"Camping out was no novelty to Mrs. E. nor to me and my older little girl, but to our lady friend [Susan Gates] it was something new. None of us, however, could quite enjoy the camps except our driver, who no doubt had shivered many times in the night air."

"With two little girls, one two and a half years old and the other nearly five months, snow on the ground, one trunk lost on the Rio Grande R.R., much discomfort in our traveling, we still feel extremely grateful to have been protected and kept a safe until we reached Lincoln, where we have found kind hearts."

"The winds here are so high at times that if one should lose his hat he might have occasion to look for it in Texas or the. 'Indian Territory.'"

Fort Stanton. 1898 photo. Courtesy Archives and Special Collections, NMSU.

Aerial view of Lincoln. The two story structure in the center is the Murphy-Dolan store, later the LIncoln County Courthouse. Undated photo. Courtesy Center for Southwest Research and Special Collections, UNM.

Parenthetically, I might add that when we grew older my sister and I often discussed what might have been in the lost trunk, which finally showed up minus most of its contents. We know Mother's jewelry and silver were there, but by the time we were old enough to question her, she had forgotten much that the trunk contained.

Now I shall return to the diary, which deals with the exciting times of what is known in history as the Lincoln County War.

Feb. 20, '78. Lincoln, Lincoln County, N. M. This is truly a frontier town – warlike. Soldiers and citizens armed! Great danger of being shot.

Feb. 21. Lincoln. Funeral of John H. Tunstall of London, England took place at 3 P.M. My remarks interpreted into Spanish. Good attendance. (We learned that Juan Patron, Lieut. Gov. of New Mexico, was present.)

Feb. 22. Lincoln. Wife, two children, Miss Gates and I all well. God is guarding us from death. Many of the citizens are returning to their ranches.

Feb. 23. Lincoln. All seems quiet. Three soldiers in the house all the time.

Feb. 24. Sabbath. Today organized the first Sabbath School ever held in Lincoln; 20 present. Meeting held in A. A. McSween's parlor.

Feb. 25. Mail three times a week.

Feb. 26. Boarded one week and two days with Mrs. Shield [Elizabeth Hummer, sister of Susan Ellen Hummer, Alexander A. McSween's wife].

Feb. 27. Lincoln. Heard from Albert (brother). Letter written February 14th.

Feb. 28. After breakfast took possession of Mrs. McSween's end of house. Wiederman [Robert A. Widenmann] and [Sam] Corbet boarding.

March 1. Lincoln, N. M. Left Schellsburg, Pa. a month and three days ago today. Received a letter from Mother Ealy dated Feb. 18th. Snow on the hills.

At this point I wish to introduce some family letters, written during these days of dread that have been preserved. They were all written stationery with the heading:

Office of John H. Tunstall
Lincoln, Lincoln Co., New Mexico
Lincoln, N. M. Feb. 25, 1878

Dear Father:
You will be asked how we are pleased with the town and country.

Have been here only one-week today and are yet boarding. We are in a narrow valley with very high mountains rising on both sides. The river is very clear and cold and all the ground tilled is irrigated. As there are late frosts, we cannot venture yet to plant much in the garden – all stock must be herded. There are some small fish in the stream. The nights are cool all the year around.

Pearl seems well-contented. Mrs. Shield has a little boy with whom she plays nearly all the time.

There have been soldiers in the town every day since we came. We are 9 miles from Ft. Stanton. Yesterday one boy shot another in the leg. This is frontier life.

We have organized the first Sabbath School ever held in Lincoln – I suppose in the County too.

There are two lawyers here, both Presbyterians [McSween and Shield]. We are comfortable, sheltered, and cared for by them for the present, but I am eager to get into my own quarters.

We need a blacksmith and a wagon maker. We have a carpenter. There are three stores. Eggs 50 cents, better 50, beef and pork is scarce.

I am greatly encouraged because there is such a vast field for usefulness, if the enemies of Christianity only allow us to live.

We are all well except for colds. We slept out four nights – melted snow to water our mules. Water is very scarce. You may travel two or three days and not see enough to water a prairie dog. One place I paid 60 cents to water two mules and fill a five gal. keg.

We have had some ugly nights since coming here but were very much favored while on our trip. Everybody says this is a healthful country. All the American women here are married, Susan [Gates] excepted.

The trip west about $315 for all of us.

U. S. Wiederman [R. A. Widenmann], U. S. Deputy Marshall, was poisoned here but recovered. He is a German, well-educated. He makes his headquarters in this house.

Love from all to all. Have not heard yet from our lost trunk. The watch was in it.

T. F. Ealy

Office of John H. Tunstall
Lincoln, Lincoln County, New Mexico
Lincoln, N. M.
March 1, 1878

Dear Mother:

Your letter dated February 18 came to hand this morning. It finds us keeping house. Mr. McSween, a lawyer whose wife is at present in St. Louis, has kindly allowed us to occupy his house for the present – and in meantime we may get one in readiness. Think we will like it here better than we thought. At present we have all kinds of furniture – but of course it is not our own.

Mr. McSween has about 70 chickens. We live with Mr. [David P.] Shield, his partner-in-law (Mrs. McSween and Mrs. Shield are sisters). Mr. McSween had an interest in a store here, but Mr. Tunstall his partner in the store was shot by men who do not want anybody to do business but themselves. The store may be auctioned or retailed out, or it may run on we do not know yet. There is not any [news]paper printed here yet but I have no doubt in another year there will be.

The county I believe numbers about two-thirds American. Indians and Mexicans are not troublesome; it is the whites – one party trying to elbow the other out of the county.

T. F. Ealy

The next two letters are dated March 4, but were evidently sent at the same time as the former one. They follow:

Dear Mary:

I think you would like this country. The roads are good of themselves without any work. Onions grow as large as the crown of my hat. Potatoes grow in some parts of the country. The Mexicans get plenty of salt 3 miles from here – shovel it out of the ground.

Mr. McSween is very kind to us. Gives us the use of his whole house. His parlor is elegantly furnished. His wife will be back in a month or so.

Dear little Pearl is not well but I think it is a shock produced by the cold air from the mountains. We have seen snow every day yet on the mountains a few miles off. We will watch her very closely. I think she will be well in a day or so. Today had a call from Dr. Apell [Daniel M. Appel] and Major Dowlin of the Post. Major took dinner with us.

The days are generally warm but ice forms every night. Meat keeps without any salt. The Mexicans are very slow. They tramp out wheat with sheep or goats, fan it by the wind; plow with a stick, keep their guns tied to the beam; reap with a sickle. They take pride in doing as the ancients did.

T. F. E.

Dear Corrie,

As I am writing to the whole family, will put in a slice for you. Dr. Apell said he would take me down to the Apache Agency some day [at Blazer's Mill]. It is about 40 miles from here. He is from Philadelphia; is a very nice young man. The Apaches are the most incorrigible of any of the tribes.

We have not been up to the Fort [Stanton] since we came down but now as times are good we will go up.

We burn cedar wood altogether. It costs $2.00 per load. We live in a canon [canyon] about a rifle shot wide. The mountains are very high on either side. I have not ventured up yet although they look so tempting to climb. There is very much talk of building the Denver and Rio Grande R.R. down throughout the territory. If they do, a trip out here will not lake many days.

Pearl is very much better; I gave her quinine and podophyllum [used as an emetic to induce vomiting].

Write often. Have you a minister yet? Is my house rented?

We ought to have an editor to publish a paper here.

Love from all to all

Your loving brother:
T. F. Ealy

Let us return now to the diary:

March 2. A little warmer today – not so much high wind. Every night ice is formed.

March 3. Sabbath. Held Sabbath School after dark in McSween's parlor – 15 present, 10 of them adults. Lesson first chapter of Acts. Read in concert.

March 4. Call from Dr. Apell and Major Dowlin of Ft. Stanton. Major took dinner with us. Pearl not well – mountain fever [headache, chills, muscle pain, high fever].

March 5. McSween and Shield take about 15 papers. I have an opportunity to read them all. Mail comes tri-weekly.

March 6. Wrote to Ft. Arbuckle, Indian Territory. Pearl much better. Ham and eggs for supper. Molasses 25 cents per quart.

(In this letter Father told the Indian Agent [Sylvester W. Marston] that he preferred to stay where he was. This statement seems to show that he was greatly pleased with the climate and his surroundings in Lincoln.)

March 7. Mail comes from Las Vegas via Ft. Sumner and Roswell on buckboard. We buy our goods at [Isaac] Ellis's store. Calico 10 1/2 per yard; butter 50 cents.

March 8. Very windy and cold. Nobody out any more than duty requires. McSween is having a wall 12 feet high built of stone and adobe around his house.

(The fact that McSween was having a high wall built around his house proves the critical condition of affairs.)

March 9. Governor [Samuel B.] Axtell and Colonel [George A.] Purington came in. Governor is a native of Ohio.

March 10. J. J. Dolan broke his leg by a fall from his horse in the street of Lincoln at the middle of the fences. Pulled a tooth which was very loose – received a $1.00.

March 11. Went to the woods 8 miles for a load of wood – cost nothing but my time. 12 soldiers in town. Widderman [Widenmann] left for Ft. Stanton.

Another family letter also seems pertinent to this time. It is written on letter paper headed so:

John H. Chisum, Pres't. Alex. A. McSween, Vice-Pres't.
John H. Tunstall, Cashier
LINCOLN COUNTY BANK
Lincoln, N. M.
3-13-1878

Dear Brother:

We rec'd. Mary's letter yesterday containing receipt for box of books. I have not heard of the box yet but it will likely come soon.

Yesterday a man introduced himself to me as Jack Long – he was very drunk; said he helped hang a preacher in Arizona.

One of the worst men in this county [James J. Dolan] broke his leg while trying to shoot an unarmed man in the street of Lincoln. Jumped from his horse before stopping him [Dolan was drunk]. I am careful to keep in at night and am out very little in daylight. Many men in town will soon kill themselves drinking whiskey.

Yesterday I got a letter, forwarded to me from Schellsburg – it was from the Indian Agent. He asked me if I would entertain an idea of going back, in July, to Arbuckle. Told him I would stay where I am.

We are all well and happy. There are many things going on here which I may speak of in the future. Write often. Get a renter for my house.

Tell Father I said he should pay you the hundred dollars he promised for me.

Ever your aff. brother,
T. F. Ealy

The diary goes on:

March 15. Time to make good in this place. Bought ham for 25 cents a lb. and beef for 10 cents a lb. Received 20 papers in one mail.

March 14. Heard of two men having been killed [three men – William Morton, Frank Baker, and William McCloskey]. The town is quiet. Pearl is a little better.

March 15. Ruth is 5 months-old. Visited Jesus' baby.

March 16. Sick baby is no better. Met Leviston [Montague Richard Leverson], Ph.D., an Englishman who expects to make a colony in New Mexico.

Mr. Maurice Fulton, who wrote to Mother in later years, said in a letter to her this about a man he called Dr. Leverson, possibly the same man: "Dr. Leverson apparently had influence with President Hayes, for it was his correspondence directly with the President that started the investigation that led to the recall of Governor Axtell. But I can find no one who can tell me much about this man Leverson. About all that is obtainable is that he was down seeking land for a colonization scheme he was fathering." He also has this to say about Leverson in the same letter: "A rather new episode came out connected with the first of April in which Brady was killed. It seems there came along with McSween, John S. Chisum, and others who came to Lincoln that day from Chisum's ranch, a gentleman by the name of Leverson, who was a prominent man and one active in this section for several months. When Leverson discovered that Col. Purington was letting Peppin, who was acting as sheriff, do some high-handed things, such as searching McSween's house without a warrant, he got very much excited and harangued the soldiers and the populace about the violation of the constitution, etc. Col. Purington treated him rather contemptuously and seems to have insulted Dr. Ealy also."

March 17. Sabbath. Citizens of Lincoln met to transact secular business about the acequia [irrigation ditch]. Held Sabbath school and lectured after night. About 18 present.

March 19. Cleared up in the evening. 6 men came in the night and ate their supper. We did not get out of bed. Mail came in before dark.

The following letter was sent to Dr. Sheldon Jackson at this time:

Lincoln, New Mexico
March 19, 1878

Sheldon Jackson, D. D.
Editor of the Rocky Mountain

Dear Brother:

Yours of March 6th received last mail. Our mail from Las Vegas, via Ft. Sumner, on the buckboard, comes twice weekly. I have access to McSween and Shield's Office [in Tunstall's store] where they receive about twenty-five secular newspapers from all over the country. Many of them the County papers of the Territory. I read them in order to post up on affairs of the Territory. Seventy-five miles east of us there will be quite a town [Roswell]. I will visit it, if spared, before long and see who lives there.

Some think this County (Lincoln) will be divided soon, and that will be one of the County towns. Roswell is the name of the town. There are some good families there now. I expect to preach at Fort Stanton soon.

A book came to Lincoln by mail for Mr. J. H. Tunstall, from his mother of London, England, I suppose, title "Meditations on Death and Eternity" [by Johann Heinrich Daniel Zschokke, translated from German to English in 1862]. Alas! his clothes were at this time lying in the back yard, pierced by bullet holes, and his body had just been buried in the grave. Mr. Tunstall was a young man, and carried on an extensive business. Had just drawn on a bank of London for several thousand pounds, which had not reached here at the time of his death.

Met Dr. Leverson of Colorado, says he will bring down a small colony, if the County becomes peaceful again. They will come, some from Colorado and some from New England. Did I tell you about Jack Long? Said he helped hang a preacher in Arizona. Do you know anything about a minister being hung in Arizona? Thought, as he was drunk, perhaps he might have been telling the truth.

Received the religious papers which you sent me. What suggestion would you make in reference to building a school-room, which for the present will answer for a Chapel? Mr. McSween thinks it would be better to build a school-room. Say nothing about a church, and let all the town help; but I am afraid that there might be trouble in the future. Think I can get one man to give one hundred dollars, whether it is denominational or not. Yes, two men can be found who will give that much.

The news here can be told in a few words, and yet to understand it thoroughly, it would require volumes.

Mr. McSween was administrator of the [Emil] Fritz estate. He performed his duty, and two or three here wanted to make him pay it over to them, when he knows and they know that there are five heirs in Germany. He refuses, and they want to kill him. So far as I know him, he is a noble man, and would have done well to have belonged to the Covenanters. They are prosecuting him partly because he is a Presbyterian. He has been arrested and has offered bail; but they refuse it, just because they want to get him out of Lincoln. He refused to go to jail, because they have threatened his life. He is now a refugee. I can see no dishonor in it. They drink whiskey, gamble, and nothing is too bad for them. Mr. McSween carries nothing to defend himself, threatens no one, is dangerous to no one. God save him.

We are all well,

Robert Adolph Widenmann. Undated photo. Courtesy Maurice G. Fulton Papers, Special Collections, UA.

William Brady. Undated photo. Courtesy Maurice G. Fulton Papers, Special Collections, UA.

Yours,
T. F. Ealy, M. D.

March 20. Five men came in this morning to eat breakfast. Our scanty meals will not last long at this rate. The demonstrations which they made we did not sanction.

March 21. The weather is good. People are plowing and making gardens. Wiederman [Widenmann] and [Sam] Corbet are boarding with us yet.

March 22. Looking for Mrs. McSween home soon. I look for slates; then will open school as soon as I can get a room.

March 23. Mrs. E. went calling; I kept baby and Pearl. Susan [Gates] and Mrs. Shield went with her.

March 24. Sabbath S. in evening, ten present. The day has been quieter than any other since we came to Lincoln.

March 25. Mrs. E., Susan, and Mrs. Shield made 4 calls this afternoon. I kept the babies. Have one patient opposite the house – old woman. Prescribed for a blind woman – no charge.

March 26. Mail comes before dark on Tues. from Tract Society in New York some hymns and tracts in Spanish. $3.00 for the postage.

March 27. Wed. Wind high yesterday and today. People do not go out much on windy days.

By March 28 the feud had broken out again. Firing could be heard down town. Father went to the top of the house to see what was happening and was shot at for his pains.

He felt that he knew who had done the shooting [this person has never been identified]. Then on March 30, there were 20 or more shots fired in the street near his house. He got out of bed expecting trouble but nothing developed. He decided the shooting had been done for effect. The next day, Sabbath, eight Cavalrymen and the sheriff passed through town at noon.

In spite of the tense feeling that pervaded the whole town and in spite of a cold rain which turned to snow, Father held Sabbath School in the evening. He made Acts IV the basis for his remarks.

On April 1, at 9 A. M., the firing began near Tunstall's store. This time two men, [Sheriff William] Brady and [Deputy] George Hindman, were killed. A company of cavalry, led by [Colonel] Purington and Capt. [George W.] Smith, came from Ft. Stanton and arrested five men [McSween, Widenmann, Shield, George Washington, and George S. Robinson]. The following day and night the town was unusually quiet. Everyone was sad because of the situation. Father said, "May God speed the day of peace."

Let us return to the diary.

April 3. Mrs. McSween went with her husband to the Fort. She returned last night. We are glad Mr. [John S.] Chisum and Mr. [Calvin] Samson are here.

April 4. It was quiet all day, very quiet, but like an earthquake, quiet, then war! war! war!

April 5. We got news that Dick Brewer was killed yesterday; Jno. Middleton wounded in the lung; [Andrew "buckshot"] Roberts shot in the stomach; [Frank] Coe wounded. [Roberts died from his wound.]

April 6. A dozen men have been shot since we came to Lincoln in Lincoln County. I helped make a strawberry bed. Chisum, Samson, Corbet, and I worked.

April 7. Sabbath. Rained, good rain. Held S. S. after dark – 12 present; Mrs. McSween for the first time. Lesson Acts V, The Lie.

April 8. Court week. We have a great many to stop with us. Shield and Wiederman here from Ft. Stanton.

From the Pioneer Presbyterian Mission publication of 1879 we note a letter from Father to Dr. Sheldon Jackson at Denver, Colo. was written on April 9. Father mentioned the fact that Dr. Jackson was being blamed by the Territorial papers of New Mexico and suggested that he himself would be the next target. He also stated that he found it difficult to do much Christian work in Lincoln because of conditions. Fifteen people had been shot since his arrival.

On the same date he speaks of meeting several strangers and of the fact that [John] Copeland was appointed sheriff. He says also that Mrs. E. got a letter from her sister Sarah.

On April 10, for the first time he speaks of the Zunis; that there was a court suit for some new man on this tribe. Since Lincoln was the county seat, court convened there. On the morrow no court was to be held, for the town was entirely too lively. It was necessary to have a guard from the Fort. The Judges were [William L.] Rynerson and [Warren H.]

Bristol. [Rynerson was not a judge. He was the District Attorney for the Third Judicial District.]

Let us again take some items directly from the diary:

April 11. Geo. Robinson and Geo. Washington are helping in the kitchen. Met Mr. [Thomas] Conway, lawyer.

April 12. Rocky Mt. Presbyterian contains a letter by me. Worked in the garden. Got seeds in mails from home. All the ground must be irrigated. A gentleman came to settle Tunstall's estate.

April 13. Court adjourned at noon to meet on Tues. They did nothing to change the jurors. I subscribed for 5 copies of "Rocky Mt. Presbyterian" $2.50.

April 14. Quiet. Held S. S. after dark – read in concert Acts VI; 30 present. Afterwards I preached on the text, "What is a man profited if he gain the whole world and lose his own soul?"

April 15. Court week. Made garden. Ruth six months old.

April 16. Court. Working some in garden. "The News and Press and Trinidad Chronicle" contain some articles on the county troubles.

April 17. Court Judge Bristol, noteworthy, stays at Ft. Stanton.

April 18. Met Indian Agent Godfrey [Frederick Godfroy]. Walked to top of the canon [canyon] hill about 500 feet with Lawyer Conway – took us half hour to come down.

By April 19 Father felt that he could not endure the inactivity any longer. The town of Lincoln was too much disturbed for him to be able to do much Christian work; the idea came to him that a trip throughout the country round about might result in greater soul saving. He might find another place to which he could go, a place which was not so filled with apprehension. That morning he took a buckboard for Roswell, 75 miles east of Lincoln, which he reached in safety at 2:00 A.M. After breakfast he secured a mule for further trips.

On the 21st he rode to Chisum's Ranch where he preached at 2:00 P.M. to a group of twenty, two of them ladies. He took for his text <u>Paul and Silas at Philippi</u>. The next morning was calm and clear. He was much attracted by the watermelons and the beautiful gardens (while he was walking around). So impressed was he with the beauty and quiet of the country, that he selected a section of land, 640 acres, section 30, south of section 19. It is possible that he was thinking of a suitable plot on which to build a church and the minister's home. That same evening he preached to some cowboys from Arizona at the Ranch. As before, two ladles were present. He spent a little time in fishing. The acequias [irrigation ditches], which be found three to five miles long, amazed him.

Having stayed all night with Capt. Lee [Joseph C. Lea] [in Roswell], he was ready by sunrise April 25th to return home. Again he took the buckboard and rode 75 miles back to Lincoln, where he arrived at dusk.

That same evening he wrote a letter to Dr. Jackson at Denver, Colo.

George W. Coe showing missing "trigger" finger, standing in front of his Glencoe store. 1934 photo. Wikipedia.

Roswell, Lincoln County, New Mexico
April 25, 1878.
Rev. Sheldon Jackson, D. D.,
Denver, Colo.

Dear Doctor:

I am happy to be able to communicate to you from this point. Am spending a week in this section, and have preached twice, once on Sabbath and last night to some cowboys who just returned from Arizona. I find one of them was at school at Elder's Ridge where I was once a student.

Thought I would call your attention to Lincoln now, so that you might have a little time to look up another man for Lincoln. I find so much to do since coming down here, and the people so anxious to have me settle in this neighborhood, that I feel certain they will do much to help on the cause of Christ. They are about to start a settlement, and they say the first thing to go up is a school and church house. <u>Good</u>. I can get a Sunday School as large as I now have in Lincoln right here. They are anxious for books and papers. There are about twenty children of Sunday School age right here, most of them Americans. Some have not been to Church for ten or fifteen years. If I live will visit them in August.

If they will stop shooting men in Lincoln I will try to open a school right away. I think the Court which is now in session will regulate affairs some. But it is very hard for me to say, because I don't know; the war may go on after the Court adjours [sic]. I see all the newspapers in the Territory have become slanderous.

I can make it next year if I come down here without help from the Board, I think. There are three brothers here, who will see that I do not suffer [John, James, and Pitser Chisum]. The Lord has given them abundance of this world's goods. They are the sons of pious parents, who were members of the Cumberland Presbytery Church.

I have not preached at Fort Stanton yet, although I have no doubt the black soldiers would like to have a minister come and preach to them. The officers have not much desire for any thing but cards, billiards, and whiskey. At least it appears so from observation. About fifteen men have been killed or wounded since we came to Lincoln. It is even dangerous to hold religious meetings in the town for if they are public and both parties come, there is the greatest danger of shooting.

If another man would go there, it would be company for me, and in a year more, I think we could find fields for three or more men to form a Presbytery. There is a place below here called "The Seven Rivers;" it is a bad place, but there is a store there now, and it is well known by everybody. People are taking up ranches there, also; the Feliz River is being settled upon.

I received another lot of religious papers from you, I suppose. Excuse paper, adios.

Will write soon again if I live. Oh! for a thousand tongues to preach the Gospel.

T. F. Ealy

By April 26 the family was able to move into the building in which the Tunstall store was [from Shield's house]. Here they occupied three large rooms; the front one was to be used as a school room and as a place for holding church services; the whole three formed part of the living quarters. It was a great relief for the family at last to have a place of their own. They hoped now to be free to carry out their mission to Lincoln and to be quite separate from the feuds and fighting.

The next day they were kept busy putting up two stoves and arranging the few possessions they had so that the place would be livable. The floors were good ones and the windows were large. It was indeed a nice place and they were all happy.

By Sabbath April 28 Father was able to hold Sabbath School at 10:00 A.M. and preach at 4:00 P.M. He was delighted to find a whole roomful of people for the church service. The meetings still had to be held in McSween's parlor because there were not yet seats in his house for the people who came.

The next morning five pupils showed up at the house for school with a promise of others. One man, who at first said that his children could come if they were not taught any religion, later changed his mind and told his children to secure all the Bible teaching they could. That decision proved to Father that this teaching was bearing fruit.

By the last of April there was a great amount of fighting outside of the town. As a result George Coe had to have his finger amputated; Father performed that operation. One man, McKnabt [Francis MacNab] was killed. The whole town was in a great state of anxiety. It was rumored that Ab Sanders [James Albert Saunders] was killed but he was merely wounded.

Father gives in his diary for May 1 the following: "No school today. Great danger rests on the town. God save us: Soldiers came into town in the evening and about twenty men surrendered and were taken to the Fort. McKnabt was buried the next day."

By May 3 matters had reached such a state in Lincoln that McSween, [Isaac] Ellis, and others were arrested and taken to the Fort for a trial by Col. Dudley. There both parties were to be examined. Meanwhile the whole town was quiet, awaiting breathlessly the result of the investigation. It appeared later that nothing much happened because the following day both sides returned home.

On Sabbath, May 5, Father held a service as usual at 4:00 P.M. The whole town was quiet but tense. He even was able to visit a patient whom he calls old Juniata [Juanita]. Indeed he was able to hold services all the rest of the time he was in Lincoln even though conditions at times were bad. Sabbath School was held at 10:00 A.M. and preaching at 4:00 P.M. On May 26 he records with gladness that the room was overflowing and that more ladies than usual were present.

For the rest of May, June and up until July 1 Father speaks very little about the feud. He is interested in his school, which had grown gradually to the number of twenty, half Mexican and half American. He liked the work and took great pride in it. All the pupils were studying English and learning well. School took up at 8 o'clock and ended at 4:00 P.M. He talked especially about the nice room in which he did his teaching, a room 12 feet high, 18 feet long, and 18 feet wide, with a huge window and a door with a large glass in it.

Another common subject was his garden which he began on May 11. That day he worked in it the entire day. Afterwards, he mentions at different times that he was working in his garden on a particular day. By May 25 he had his potatoes hoed before sun up; on May 29 he exults in the fact that the "radishes are good and the strawberries are ripe." His diary for May 31 reads: "Peas and other things are getting ripe. I have some garden." This enthusiasm for gardening became a life-long interest. On June 7 and 8 some additional garden was planted and on June 15 he irrigated the whole plot.

The Probate Court on May 6 appointed Wiederman [Widenmann] to settle Tunstall's estate. This action seemed to be satisfactory to both sides. Matters were not entirely quiet because on May 11 Father records that he had heard 100 of Chisum's cattle were stolen and on May 19 that Wiederman was killed. The latter rumor fortunately proved false, for he returned to town the next day and brought Dick Brewer's cattle with him.

Some family affairs are at this time introduced. The missing trunk, which finally turned out to be two, came on May 10. One had been opened with most of its contents missing. It had been shipped from El Moro, and three months and four days later it reached the folks at Lincoln. The town was so lacking in excitement that on May 18 the whole family felt it safe to call on Mr. and Mrs. [Isaac] Ellis in the evening. It meant going down to the other end of town. Mail, which came three times a week from Roswell and three from Santa Fe, was most important to people so far away from their own folks. On May 9 a letter came from Mother's brother and on May 28 Father was delighted to receive one from his own Mother, and on June 26 a letter from Father Ramsey. By this time the folks knew without question that the mail was being tampered with and so were very cautious what they wrote. They did not write many letters. On May 16 two letters were returned; one to Father's favorite sister Corrie, and the other by Mother to Father's cousin Rush Clark. Many people called; on June 1, two men from New York, Mr. [Frank Warner] Angel and a companion. The same day three others, Allen, Apell, and Sargeant.

Father constantly hoped that peace would come and he could go on with his work.

The weather and the climate are common topics. On May 7, it was extremely warm; on May 13 there was a small shower and on the 24th another one. In June there were two hail storms, one extremely severe. On the 15th of June a good shower visited the section. Though Father had irrigated his garden that day, he rejoiced greatly in the rain. By June 20 it rained nearly every day. Rain is one of the greatest blessings of such a dry climate as New Mexico. The climate he found most healthful.

Father's letter of June 15 shows his plans:

OFFICE OF John H. Tunstall
Lincoln, Lincoln County, New Mexico

Lincoln, N.M., June 15th, 1879

Rev. Dr. Jackson:

Our work here is encouraging. We greatly need a house to hold our services in. There is a property here [Tunstall's store] in the center of town – containing a room large enough to hold three hundred people. I tried to buy it & was asked $2,000 for it – now I am offered the same for $700 and a span of mules. The property contains about five acres of fenced land. I will give $50 of my salary towards purchasing it for the Church. I can have all the papers drawn up, etc. by a lawyer here who will give his services. I will agree to raise something in addition to what I offer of my salary – from the people, but how much cannot say. I find Presbyterians scattered up and down this canon & we in a private house; people will not come to a parlor as they would to a Church. I have a small school of 20 scholars half Americana half Mexicans. They do not pay me any money but give a little of such as they have. Let met hear from you at once on the subject of purchasing the property. Court is held in a house for which they pay $5 per day rent. I want to keep up the school & the lot I have mentioned is the best place in town for it; we can get it for $700 cash, I know. Write soon & oblige:

Your Obedt. Seryt.
T. F. Ealy, M.D.

As a carpenter needs the tools with which to work, so a preacher needs his books. Father had sent his at the time he left for Lincoln. Four months later, when he had almost given up hope, they came without being impaired in any way. To say he was delighted is putting the case very mildly. He needed as well, the medical works which came at the same time.

There of course were some sick people who required medical attention. As the only doctor in the town Father was kept relatively busy. One he mentions particularly on May 24 was a man by the name of [Daniel] Huff. This man found a dead man buried in his yard that day. Was there, some connection between his illness and the new grave? Possibly he felt the implied threat. The town was a healthful place so far as climate is concerned, and most of the work Father did was along the line of surgery on account of the shooting which kept up more or less constantly.

Meanwhile, the family remained fairly well. On May 23 Father speaks of his sore gums, which he at first attributes to the fact that he has to talk too much, but later agrees that he has two sore teeth. At this time he mentions the fact that he was not well; again he says on June 29 that he does not feel well.

A few references here and there were made to the county troubles. On May 12 the diary explains that the boys left town at dark. Up to that time everything had been quiet. On May 18 the town was still quiet.

Nearly all the fighters had left town. On June 12 they were to go to Mesilla for a fair trial. Four soldiers escorted them. The diary proceeds:

June 16. S. S. at 10 A.M. – 15 present. We expect an organ soon. Preaching at 4 in my schoolroom.

June 17. [John B.] Wilson wanted to sell me his house and about 8 acres in the center of town – asked $2,000 at first.

June 18. [Sheriff George] Peppin in town – came in the night; soldiers with him. All the men left town.

An extract from a letter of Mr. Maurice Fulton to Mother speaks of Peppin (Mr. Fulton has made a thorough study of this period): "Dudley is a puzzle – His coming down with soldiers did give moral support to Peppin and his crowd, without which I feel sure they would never have resorted to the extreme measure of burning McSween's house."

June 23. S. S. at 10 A.M., preaching at 4 P.M. Marion Turner, Billy [Jacob] Mathews, and others at preaching. "Ye must be born again."

June 24. School until noon. St. John's Day. Mexicans ride horseback and while riding full speed grab at a rooster buried in the ground.

June 25. Fighting on the Ruidoso. Sheriff's posse came in at dark.

June 27. 19 scholars. Last night Sheriff Peppin and man went out to the Ruidoso.

June 26. Today ends the second month of my school in Lincoln. I like it very much.

It was May 25 when McSween returned to Lincoln, after having [been] gone two weeks; again on June 26 he went off east. Beginning with July 1, Father has more to say about the fight. He states that [John] Copeland is prisoner; that the men had gone out to his ranch to take him. He was brought to Lincoln. The critical state of affairs is reflected in the diary and in some letters which were written at this time.

July 3. Sheriff's posse has gone to San Patricia to capture some men.

July 5. Very dangerous. One party in town, another out. People will not come to buy or bring anything to market.

July 6. It is too dangerous to go about in the country.

July 7. S. S. at 9 A.M. Preaching at 4 P.M. Had the use of Mrs. McSween's organ.

July 8. Beans can be planted on the 15th of this month. Great fear rests on the county; there will be more fighting.

July 9. All quiet in town although some feared there would be fighting. Mr. [William Harrison] Johnston called on us. Lives 60 miles below Spring River.

On this day Mother wrote the following letter to Rev. Jackson:

Lincoln, N. M. July 9th, 1878
Rev. Sheldon Jackson D.D.

Dear Sir:

We have organized a Sabbath school here, and it is very encouraging, but have scarcely any books. Bibles are very short and also music-books. Will you please send us one dozen Lot and Sanky [Sankey] No. 1 (small size) without music and two books with music, also one dozen of Testaments by mail. We will pay for them as soon as we can. Do not wish our work kept back for the want of these books. Have four pupils studying the

Shorter Catechism. In three week will close our first quarter of school and the progress our pupils have made is very encouraging.

Mr. Ealy is very busy, has very little time for writing.

Very respectfully,
Mrs. T. F. Ealy

July 10. A company of soldiers and 20 Navajos passed through town east.

(No entries for 3 days.)

July 14. McSween and about 40 men came in just after dark. S. S. at 10 A.M. Preached at 4 P.M. Paul and Silas sermon repeated.

July 15. Dolan's men came in from the west about dark. Yelling and shooting – about 100 shots fired. [This is the first day of the 5-day shootout in Lincoln.]

July 16. Firing all day and after dark. Two of McSween's windows were shot to pieces.

July 17. Not much firing. People in their houses in the dark and afraid to look out. I was shot at after night 4 times.

Father had gone out to see a man who had been shot [Daniel Huff]. He finally had to return without having seen him. He was shot at just as he reached the door of our home and dropped against it. Of course Mother expected to find him dead when she opened the door.

July 18. Ben Ellis was shot last night in the neck. I could not go to see him – was shot at trying to do so.

July 19. About noon Lt. Col. [Nathan A. M.] Dudley came into town with troops and two pieces of artillery; camped near center of town. McSween's house was burned and he was killed. [This is the last day of the 5-day shootout in Lincoln.]

At this point I wish to introduce the copies of some notes written by Mother and Father.

July 19, 1878
Lieut. Col. Dudley:

Please give us a guard of soldiers from this building. We have no place to go. We ask your protection.

Yours respectfully,
Mrs. T. F. Ealy

(This building is the Tunstall home.)

(No date)
Lieut. Col. Dudley,

We respectfully ask you to take Mrs. Shield and five children together with Miss Gates, Mrs. Ealy, my two children, and myself to the Fort for protection.

Very respectfully,
T. F. Ealy

Father kept notes of happenings during the time he was in Lincoln. These notes were later expanded. I am going to give them now practically as he wrote them.

When we first entered Lincoln some men in full fighting trim with double belts, one for revolvers and one for Winchester rifles, stopped us. After they had satisfied their curiosity by peering into the wagon and counting the women and children, they said they were looking for a man who might be getting away in our prairie schooner. I told them we expected to stop right here with lawyer Shield and family. Lawyer McSween and wife occupied the west end of a long house and the Shield's the eastern end. They proved to be exceedingly pleasant company of refined people. Just east of this large building Mr. McSween had erected a much larger building which contained a store, a bank, a large library, a law office, and a room for a drug store [Tunstall's residence/store, built and owned by Tunstall].

The news came that same day that Mr. John H. Tunstall had been run down, and shot in the woods as he was on his way home from his cattle ranch, 25 miles east of Lincoln, and that his body would be brought into McSween's home that night. So after dark his body was brought in on Feb. 20, 1878. A coroner's inquest was held and as I was present, I saw that he had been shot in the back. He was buried by a black fellow named [Sebrian] Bates at the eastern end of the bank building. Tunstall was from London, England, where his father still lived. Afterwards Mr. Wiederman, a deputy U.S. Marshal, went to Europe and visited Mr. Tunstall's father, whom he told all about the untimely death. Tunstall at the time of his death was 25 years old.

There was great danger every day on account of the war. Any day or night a fight might take place; in fact, these fights often did take place right near our house and on the main street. In spite of everything I tried to carry out my mission in Lincoln, namely, to preach Christ. Services were held each Sabbath. Of course the war kept away many who would have come. During all this time, from Feb. until July, we worked against great odds.

Sometimes we could not even go outside of our house for water for fear of being shot. Pearl kept her dolls on the floor under the windows, as she said, so that they would not get shot. One day a bullet came flying through our kitchen. I was shot at frequently. I wanted to remain perfectly neutral, and in order to do so, moved my family from the Shield house to the drug store end of the large building [Tunstall's store].

Before that change happened a death occurred which had serious repercussions. I saw some men pass our house, and just opposite the house Sheriff [William] Brady stopped to talk to a woman; I took it to be Mrs. Ham Mills. He was laughing and then he hurried up to overtake the posse. At the eastern end of the large house, which then was unoccupied – the house with the bank, law office, store, and drug room [Tunstall's residence/store] – but where we afterwards lived, a wide door into the corral swung open, a shot rang out, and the sheriff fell mortally wounded. [Juan Peppin's account says the men fired through portholes cut in the corral wall.] I did not hear him groaning but the women said they did. At the same time Geo. Hindman fell. He called for water and someone helped him up and as he was being helped toward Stocton's [Ike Stockton's] Saloon, he received another wound and fell dead. One of the men in the corral [Jim French – the other man was

William Henry McCarty, "Billy the Kid"], who ran out to pick up Hindman's or Brady's gun was shot as he stooped over, likely by [Jacob B.] Mathews.

The report was that he [French] was shot through the bowels but it was a mistake, as I dressed the wound when he came walking in our back door. The ball passed through his left thigh. I drew a silk handkerchief through the wound and bound it up. He was taken in charge by Sam Corbet. The Murphy-Dolan men were soon hunting for the wounded man. They searched the house, for they said they tracked him by the blood. I learned later that Sam Corbet had sawed a hole through the floor under a bed, and as there was not a cellar, had laid the wounded man under there on a blanket with a revolver in his hands. These shootings aroused everybody.

A messenger flew off to Ft. Stanton with the news of Sheriff Brady's death and in the quickest possible time Col. Geo. A. Purington and Capt. [George W.] Smith dashed into town and halted in front of our house. Col. Purington called me out and in the presence of the black soldiers and Capt. Smith said, "I believe you know all about this murder." My answer was that I did not, and that I was as innocent of it as the little babe in my wife's arms. They arrested five men [McSween, Widenmann, Shield, G. Washington, and G. Robinson]. We were left unguarded while the innocent ones were taken to Ft. Stanton. The guilty ones rode off leisurely to the hills. One of the men, John Middleton, while riding away, deliberately got off his horse, rested his gun on his knee and fired at the crowd, which were firing at him and his companions.

Being on the ground, I got but one story on the death of Brady. I will tell it as I heard it. Sheriff Brady went after A. A. McSween, 80 miles east of Lincoln, with a large posse of soldiers to bring him to court. McSween had heard that Sheriff Brady had made threats that he was going to put McSween into the jail, which was a hole in the ground with a watch-tower over it, and that he was going to run the water into the jail and drown him. So McSween promised before the men that he would be in town at sunup in plenty of time for court, and according to his promise he came.

The sheriff had everything timed so well that had Brady not been killed he would have met McSween just in front of the jail, which was a few feet from the place Brady fell mortally wounded. A man who helped to carry Brady past the house to the Murphy, Dolan and Reilly [Riley] headquarters told me that the sheriff had handcuffs in his pockets. It looks as if he were ready to carry out his threat to put McSween handcuffed into jail. These men did not believe Brady when he promised on the Pecos River not to put McSween into jail and so had stationed themselves in the, corral to enact vengeance on Brady.

Even before Jno. H. Tunstall was killed, a letter had come from a District Attorney officer [William L. Rynerson] telling the Murphy, Dolan, Reilly [Riley] men to "shake up" the McSween outfit. When news came that Tunstall had been killed, Reilly ran down to the McSween house, pulled off his coat, took out his letters, threw them on the table and said in a very excited manner, "Search me; I am innocent of Tunstall's death." McSween picked up the letters and put them back into his pocket all except one letter. That told the tale; it unlocked the secret. [See Appendix B for a copy of this letter.]

It was a trying matter for others as well as for me to go for our mail to the Dolan-Reilly headquarters, since the post office was full of men, either standing or sitting, with revolvers, a fact which seemed quite out of place in a U.S. Post Office. Yet this was a daily occurrence and, as there seemed to be no stop to it, after a time I quit going for my mail. McSween's mail came in a brass-locked private mail sack from Roswell and I received permission to have my mail put in with his. After his death it was said there was a half bushel of mail found. It had been buried in an arroyo and had been uncovered by a high wind. As it was not found in one place it could not have leaked out of the mail sack.

The county was in such a state of turmoil that Lawyer Shield walked the floor and kept saying, "Oh: this is terrible!" I think he acted the part of a man when he withdrew from the town [he moved to Las Vegas]. I also had a chance to study McSween and I know his death was a great loss to New Mexico. He did not have any use for a gun or pistol. Such a man as that cannot be very dangerous, except to evil doers. His great library showed that he was a thinker. The treatment he received savored of the inquisition. A good man was not wanted in Lincoln. He wanted to live and let live; his opponents wanted to live and destroy all who were friendly to McSween. The money that McSween and Tunstall were spending in Lincoln was a bonanza to the Mexican people, for previous to this time the people were mere peons.

Whenever the fighting ceased, my wife and I were busy teaching the young people English. If only the Government had stretched out her strong arm and stopped the jealousy and fighting, but alas, the army on the ground merely winked at what was going on. I had an Uncle, Rush Clark, in Congress, to whom I wrote, but he kept writing to me to keep neutral. So I did not dare tell the whole truth.

One day the Dolan and Reilly men, two to one, came upon some ranchers from Spring Meadow who were coming up to Lincoln. [Frank] Coe was hit; McKnabt [Francis MacNab], about 27 years old, was killed; and Sanderson [James A. Saunders] was hit as he ran down into a hole. The ball struck him in the pelvic bone from behind, glanced; and made his heel sore. There it was located. The hospital records at Ft. Stanton I think will show that fact. I was told by one who was present at the fight when Dick Brewer was killed that the ball made only a little spot at the corner of his eye, but the back of his head showed a large hole: The fighting when [Buckshot] Roberts was shot occurred near the Indian Agency, 50 miles from Lincoln [at Blazer's Mill]. It was the same day Dick Brewer was killed. When Geo. Coe was hit, the bullet hit his gun and glanced. As a result of that accident, I took off a thumb and finger for him. When it was quiet a few days in Lincoln, then we knew war clouds were gathering.

An unpleasant incident occurred one day to me. A man by the name of Jack Long met me as I was going to [Isaac] Ellis' Store. This was almost the last house east on the left-hand side of the street. Long tried to pull me to the right side of the street – he seemed to be under the influence of liquor. He had a revolver in his belt. I told him I was going to the store for my wife and must hurry. On our way down he had my arm – he said, "I helped hang a Methodist preacher in Arizona but I won't hang you." We reached the store, Long ordered the proprietor to go out, that he wanted to talk to Ben, his son. Mr. Ellis walked behind the counter, picked up his revolver, faced about, and said, "Is there anything you want, Mr. Long?" I hurried out the door not stopping for what I went after, but I got away from Long. Later, he was made a [deputy] sheriff by the Murphy, Dolan, Reilly outfit.

Mr. McSween had offered me some ground in the corner of his garden to make a strawberry bed. I had worked for some time in the garden when one day old Mr. Carter, cook at the Mescalero Indian Agency, asked me to extract a tooth. He told me at that time what he had heard at the Dolan and Reilly house, that if I did not get out of that garden they would put a ball through me. I believe that God sent Mr. Carter as a messenger to warn me and that He took care of me all the seven years I was in the west. The night before McSween was murdered, a messenger came to warn him that people were coming to kill him. Had he taken the warning, his life would have been saved.

The fighting kept up now and then all through March. On Mar. 30 we were aroused by rapid firing, 20 or more shots, followed by yells and groans as if men were being hit by every shot. It was enough to distract the calmest mind.

Early in April court convened and the 5 men who had been taken to Ft. Stanton were brought to Lincoln for trial. On April 9 [John N.] Copeland was appointed Sheriff. The judges, Bristol and Rynerson [Rynerson was not a judge, he was the district attorney], had guards from Ft. Stanton. Court adjourned after five days with nothing done but a charge to the jury. By May 1st 20 men surrendered to the soldiers and were taken to the Fort. By May 3 McSween; Ellis, and others were taken to Ft. Stanton for a trial before Col. [N. A. M.] Dudley, Commander at the Fort. U. S. Wiederman [Widenmann] was to settle Tunstall's estate.

Most of this time I was busy healing the sick, teaching both day school and Sabbath School. In spite of the wretched conditions of the county my school celebrated July 4 by a picnic at the side of the canon [canyon].

Meanwhile McSween, who had been absent from town for two weeks, returned on May 25. The boys who had surrendered were ordered to Mesilla to secure an impartial trial. This was June 10. By July 14, 40 armed men stole quietly into town. The next day, Dolan's men of about the same number came into town about dark, whooping and firing shots to the number of about 100. The next day there was firing all day. Two of McSween's windows were shot to pieces. On both July 17 and 18 the people remained in their homes, afraid to look out. About noon July 19 Col. Dudley brought his entire command to Lincoln, as well as a Gatling gun and a cannon which had been repaired for the occasion. He camped a little east of the center of town and said there should be no firing over his camp or he would turn his guns on the house whence the firing came.

While this order seemed good, it should have been more general and peace should have been ordered all along the line. The result was that those back of Col. Dudley were frightened away while those in front were allowed to run at large, for it was plain that McSween's house was to be the target. McSween was a man who never used a weapon to defend himself. He was not a fighting man. He was a scholar and a Christian gentleman. His library was the second best in the territory. He died without a friend to stand by him. Even his wife had fled for her life.

At 3 P.M. then the incendiaries set fire to his house after gasoline [it was coal oil] had been poured around it. While it was burning men stood off and shot into the burning building. This fiendish work kept up until about 9 P.M. when two or three men in the house with McSween said, "Now we must break and run for our lives!" McSween answered, "Boys, I have lost my mind!" He did however step across the doorstep and sit down while the others with him ran. His enemies came up quickly and shot the poor man several times. There in the morning he lay mangled. Two black men [George Robinson and Sebrian Bates] wrapped him in a sheet furnished by my wife from our scanty supply. His advice all the time was "don't kill anyone."

About 4 P.M. we, Miss Gates, Mrs. Shield and family, and my family, were taken to Ft. Stanton and in about 8 days sent to Las Vegas. I must say that while I appreciate the kindness of the military I must not let that kindness affect my honest judgment, viz., that McSween was wantonly murdered and for fear I would tell the story before the officers fixed it up and the public find out the situation. I was ordered <u>not</u> to communicate with the outside world unless my communication first went through the adjutant's office for inspection. I shall now give the official document:

Headquarters
Ft. Stanton, N. M.
July 21, 1878

Rev. Mr. Ealy,

Sir, I am directed by the Commanding Officer to state to you that while you are enjoying the protection and courtesies this Post, that under no circumstances will you be allowed to keep up any correspondence, either verbal or in writing, with the parties who are considered under resistance to the Territorial or U.S. Authorities, neither will you be allowed to correspond with newspapers or other parties on the condition of affairs in Lincoln County, except your letters are sent through the adjutant's office for inspection.

Yours respectfully,
Your Obedient Servant,
M. [Millard] J. Goodwin
2 Lieut. 9th Cavalry
Post Adjutant

The diary for:

July 20. At 4 P.M. Mrs. Shield and her children, my family, Miss Gates, and I were taken to the Fort by Gov. ambulance.

July 21. Fort Stanton, N. Mex. Sabbath. Was not able to preach. We are very much worn out and need rest. Thank the Lord that we are quiet.

Father's anxiety is reflected in this letter:

Fort Stanton, New Mexico, July 21st, 1878

Dear Jackson:

I am in Stanton awaiting an opportunity to get north – what shall I do? The plaza will be broken up at Lincoln. McSween was killed yesterday (19th) in his own yard, and we cannot remain there under any consideration. He would have supported the Gospel to the amount of $100 per year.

His property was burned over his head and when he came out, he was shot five times.

Answer me here immediately, and also at Vegas for I may start before your letter reaches me. I would preach in Colorado or Kansas.

T. F. Ealy

Mrs. McSween, later Mrs. Barber, in a letter to Mother in 1927, referred to the three days fight in these words: "No one who was in the three days' siege can ever forget it. It was dreadful and uncalled for."

Mr. Maurice Fulton spoke of this war as "the most stupendous of the West's feuds and fightings."

Mother, in later years, at my request put down her recollections of that time. I shall give her clear and unbiased testimony of what happened, as follows:

MRS. T. F. EALY'S RECOLLECTIONS OF LINCOLN IN 1878

It was after dark on the evening of Feb. 16, 1878 that we reached Ft. Stanton. The trip from Trinidad, where we left the railroad, had been long and tiresome – five days of weary travel. Our new home at Lincoln was still ten miles away. How eager we were to reach the end: Then came the distressing news. Mr. Tunstall had been killed; two gangs were in the midst of deadly warfare, and the whole of Lincoln County was rocked to its foundation by the contest. Lincoln was the center of the disturbance and it was to Lincoln we had been sent by the Presbyterian Board. Should we go on in spite of the terrifying rumors? Major Dowlin at Ft. Stanton insisted that it was sheer madness to venture into that seething town. But what else was there to do? Dr. Ealy, my husband, Miss Gates, my two small children and I had just gone through a trip wearisome in the extreme, and the very thought of a return without days, yes months of rest, was unthinkable. Besides, Dr. Ealy was a missionary and had no connection with any feud. Surely he could go in to Lincoln undisturbed by the thought of the two forces that were dominating that whole region. That decision then he reached and both Miss Gates and I were glad to support him in it oven though shivers of apprehension chased one another up and down our spines when we thought of encountering any of those western ruffians.

We had not long to wait for just such an encounter, for the next morning, as we were driving into the town of Lincoln, three men, [Lawrence] Murphy, [James] Dolan, and Reilly [John Riley] stopped the wagon and began to search through all our belongings. Their excuse was that they were searching for bandits and firearms. It was a stormy entrance into our field of work. Dr. Ealy protested that his sole object in coming to Lincoln was to teach, preach, and practice medicine. His explanation did not seem to meet with any favor in the eyes of these desperadoes and they looked at him and even at us with scornful eyes. At that look the thought passed through my mind that likely soon their hostility would take a more active form, and just then I would have been willing to start back along the tiresome journey to Trinidad without a moment's delay. When Dr. Ealy further explained that he was coming at the invitation of Mr. McSween, who had asked Santa Presbytery for a minister, the look of scorn in the eyes of the men became one of active hate. The whole truth came to us in a flash – it was McSween against whom their most deadly hatred was directed and we were now in the feud willy-nilly.

On we went, though, to McSween's, following the direction given sarcastically by Murphy. Mr. McSween came out of his house and greeted us kindly but very sadly. He told us about Tunstall's death, how he had been shot down in cold blood not far from his ranch by the friends of the three men up the street, merely because he objected to their stealing his cattle and was about to take the matter to law. The easiest way, they thought, to settle the matter was to silence Tunstall once for all. Mr. McSween invited us into the house and took us into that part of the house where Mr. and Mrs. Shield and family lived. (Mrs. Shield was Mrs. McSween's sister, while Mr. Shield was Mr. McSween's law partner.) Here we were made welcome, although we could see that everyone was very uneasy.

The following night Tunstall's body was brought to the house of McSween. Tunstall was vice-president of a bank started by Chisum, McSween, and Tunstall. Among those who attended the body were Billy the Kid, Dick Brewer, and Fred White [Waite], men who herded the cattle of Tunstall. They were all good friends of Tunstall and were ready to take the executing of vengeance into their own hands. A clash was inevitable. Tunstall's body was in bad shape as he had been shot and then beaten until his forehead was battered very badly. Dr. Ealy embalmed the body, which was put into a metal coffin. As Tunstall was an Englishman it was thought that his friends there might wish the body sent to England. Until such a time the body was to be buried at the east side of what was intended at the time to be Tunstall's home, the building where we afterwards lived while in Lincoln. It contained a law office, a bank, a private office, a store, and three rooms. The funeral of Mr. Tunstall was held the next morning. As Mrs. McSween was away from home, I was asked to play two or three hymns. Beside the organ, on which I played, stood Billy the Kid and his cowboy friends armed to the teeth. No one knew when hostilities between the two factions would be resumed and almost everyone connected with the feud was ready to use his gun at a moment's warning. Juan Patron, Lieutenant Governor of New Mexico, was present at the funeral to show his sympathy for the Tunstall faction.

A week or so later Mr. McSween told us that we might use the Tunstall rooms. There we began housekeeping and in the front room conducted a school through the week and on Sabbath had church services. A number of pupils began to attend school and we were beginning to feel safe once more.

Meanwhile war parties were moving in and out of town. One week one faction seemed to be in control, and the next week the other. At McSween's all was quiet, as he and Mrs. McSween had gone away for awhile. Then one day Colonel Dudley, a Lieutenant, and a, number of the soldiers suddenly appeared. They had come down from the fort to see what was going on. The Lieutenant came to see us; I think he was a Presbyterian. As he left he handed me $5.00, saying he knew the Missionaries weren't well off.

Lieutenant Axtell was Governor of New Mexico at that time, and he came to see us for a few minutes; he said very little about the feud. Things seemed to be pretty quiet for some time; occasionally we would hear of the parties clashing and of one or another being killed.

As far as I know the feud was caused, partly by a 10,000 life insurance. One of the Fritz brothers [Emil] had died and the sister and brother left wished McSween to collect and divide the money. There were some heirs in Germany, and McSween asked the Doctor if he would write for him. He told McSween I would write for him. I wrote, but I don't think more than one or two letters, but he wanted them to add their request to those living here, near Lincoln, to have him attend to their affairs. He didn't receive any reply as far as I knew while we were in Lincoln and I suppose Mrs. McSween never received any letter, as the mails were intercepted so much at that time. The mail was distributed from the Murphy-Dolan Store.

Just a month before Mr. McSween was killed he left for somewhere, and either at that time or before, Mr. Shield left and went to Las Vegas; he felt it was dangerous there for anyone, as there was so much fighting.

I know Dr. Ealy preached funeral sermons for the killed of both parties. In the short time we were there he conducted thirty funerals and only one died a natural death. We had church every Sabbath and sometimes some of one party would be present and sometimes the other party. The ones who came helped with the singing and were quite reverent.

Sometimes one or two of the cowboys would come in and ask me to play, and how they did sing. They came with their guns and belts full of cartridges. I guess I was off the tune as often as I was on it as they stood behind me and I felt very nervous, though they behaved very well and left when we were through.

Then came the week of the three days' fight. On Monday morning just as the Doctor was opening the shutters and preparing for school, one of the Shield boys came in and said, "There will be no school today as both parties are in town." He told us the Murphy-Dolan party were divided, part at a tower [Torreón] just east of where we lived, and the other at the Murphy place. The McSween party were at his house, and at [José F.] Montaño's and [Isaac] Ellis's at the far end of town.

There was a lot of shooting that day, but I don't think anyone was killed; that evening or sometime in the night a Mr. Green [John B. Wilson] who lived close to us came to the window and called the Doctor saying, "There is a man over here dying," and asked him to go to see him; they started off and immediately those in the tower [Torreón] began shooting. Wilson, or Green, called to them, "Don't shoot, I am taking the Doctor to see a dying man [Daniel Huff]." It was sometime before the Doctor came home. The house where the man lived was just beside the tower, and the man told the Doctor the cursing and swearing was awful. The man was very low and died before morning. The Doctor went back as soon as it was light and found him dead. Arrangements were made to bury him that same evening. Two men, Bates and Washington, dug a grave along side where Tunstall was buried and about the time they were lowering the body into the grave, the desperadoes from the tower opened fire and frightened them so much that they dropped the body into the grave and ran for their lives. In a short time the widow and two children came and stayed – until sometime the next day. She couldn't talk English, so it was hard for us to talk to her. We all sat up as it would have been impossible to sleep. The shooting, yelling, and screaming were distressing.

We got all our drinking water from the neighbors, but all the other water for cooking, etc. [came] from the river at the foot of a little hill back of our corral. The children and all of us were suffering for water; Susan said, "If we don't get water we will die anyway." So we started and were not molested. We carried several buckets of water which lasted while we were in Lincoln. At the same time, the lady, Mrs. Huff, whose husband had just died, went home with her children. We told her to come back again, but the shooting began so fiercely I suppose she went somewhere else or someone got her.

I never saw Mr. McSween after he left home a month before. Wednesday night was worse and worse. We barricaded our windows with our trunks and laid our beds on the floor. That night Ben Ellis was shot while looking after his horses. A couple of men from their place waded up the river until they reached where we were living; then they crawled up to the corral and managed to reach our door, although many shots were fired at them from the tower. The Doctor went with them and tried and tried to reach Ellis' but he was not able to wade the river and could not get there. It was a long time before he came back. He tapped on the door; I asked who was there, then I let him in. He waited until morning; when he took the baby in his arms and led our little Pearl and we all walked down the street to Ellis'. The wound was a bad one and the man had lost much blood. As the Doctor dressed the wound, we learned how he happened to be shot. We went back home and the first thing we knew, Col. Dudley and a corps of soldiers had come from the Fort and were stationed opposite the McSween house. I opened the door and stood outside and saw the Murphy men carrying oil and pouring it around the windows of the McSween house. I think before this McSween had some conversation with Dudley, but I am not sure. Jack Long, one of the Murphy men, came lounging around our house. I asked him if they were going to burn us out. He said, "We will if any of the McSween party are in there." I said there were none in the part we were living in, and we had nothing to do with the rest of the house.

In a short time Col. Dudley marched his soldiers past our house, down in front of Lieutenant Governor Patron's, where he went into camp. He came up to our house; we went to the door, when he said, as nearly as I can remember, "A terrible state of affairs:" Then the Doctor said something about the Government ought to stop this fighting and give citizens a chance. Col. Dudley wheeled around and marched back to his camp. The McSween house was on fire and I didn't know what might happen. Miss Gates said, "If you will write a note to Col. Dudley, I will carry it to him." McSween had written a note to Dudley, which he sent with his [servant] Bates. He (Bates) come in to our house on his way back, saying the Murphy party were watching to get the note from him. He asked someone to read it to him. He said if it were read to him he could remember it and he would leave the note there. As I read the note, I know well the contents of Col. Dudley's reply. "I don't wish any communications with you whatever, and if one shot is fired from that house, I will open fire from the cannon."

I wrote a note to him as courteously as I could, asking for protection. Then he brought a wagon and took us all down to Lieut. Patron's. There were with us Mrs. Shield and four children [all other sources say five] and Mrs. McSween. He told us to keep below the windows as he could not prevent the shooting. It was about dark or nearly so when we got fixed there. The yelling and shooting were terrific. We couldn't see what it looked like towards our home as we were cautioned to keep low. It must have been about ten o'clock when the McSween party tried to escape from the house; five of their number were shot [McSween, Harvey Morris, Vincente Romero, Francisco Zamora, and Robert Beckwith – Beckwith was with the Dolan side]. In the morning everyone was anxious to know if there were many killed and who had escaped.

We soon learned McSween was among the killed, and that there were five corpses lying in the McSween yard [four corpses – Beckwith's body had been removed to Fort Stanton during the night]. None of us went to see the terrible scene except Miss Gates. She described it as being so horrible I stayed away. I gave her a [bed] sheet and [Bates and Washington] before mentioned made a rude coffin and buried McSween in the same place Tunstall was buried. One other of the bodies was buried there at the same time [Harvey Morris], and one had been buried there before, so the plot contained six graves.

That evening Col. Dudley said; "I will take you all up to the Fort, and from there to Las Vegas." He added, "No use trying to live here, as times won't be much better for awhile." I thought he would have felt some shame for his part in the holocaust; but he was as pompous as ever. I was polite to him and took all the favors he gave us gratefully, as we were in a strange country without money and without friends.

We stayed at the Fort until Monday when we started to Las Vegas. When we reached there Dr. Ealy had an offer to do some teaching at Anton Chico, so we went back there and remained while Dr. Ealy communicated with our Board. We were there at least a month when we received a commission to go to Zuni, an Indian Village in the western part of New Mexico. We stayed there several years and then came east.

I do not think Mr. McSween was anything of a fanatic. I think he was a whole-souled Christian gentleman, working for the good of the people among whom he lived. I wrote to Germany for him and everything in his letter was simply a request for permission to divide the money among those here and there, if any were living. I think he was driven so quickly from one place to another that he had hardly time to do anything. I don't see why Tunstall's life and property had to be sacrificed for the money anyway.

He, Tunstall, owned the store and ranch. After the fire had destroyed McSween and his property, the ruffians came to where we had been living and literally robbed the store and cut the locks in a hundred places. I saw McSween just a month before he was killed. He was Scotch and had some of their superstitions. He said there was no way for him to escape as he didn't know where he wouldn't be followed. I don't now where Walter Noble Burns [author of *The Saga of Billy the Kid*, Grosset & Dunlap, 1926] got his information about him in his home during the three days' war. Mr. McSween seemed to have all the best people of the town with him, Juan Patron, the Montaño's, Ellis's, etc. I don't know whether Sam Corbet is living or not; he was in Tunstall's store up until the last week of the fighting, when he left and went up the country. U. S. Wiederman [Widenmann] was at McSween's for a while after we reached Lincoln, and he talked as if he was a friend of McSween's. He was suddenly called away, by whom I do not know.

Now as to Col. Dudley, I never like to talk about one who has been kind to me, but I cannot tell or give my opinion of him without saying what I think about him. If he came to Lincoln to protect lives and property, why did he stand a short distance from the McSween home and permit those Murphy men to carry oil and saturate the doors and windows of the house. Mrs. Shield was in McSween's house with four children and he never offered them any protection. They came to our house and I included them in the note I wrote him. He didn't want anyone at Lincoln like a minister, and as McSween had asked for a man to teach and preach, it didn't agree with his notion of things. His writing that note to McSween, in which he said, "I won't hold any communication with you whatever, and if one shot is fired from your house I will turn my cannon on it," is proof of his character.

Besides, why did he allow those ruffians to destroy everything in Tunstall's house?

The connection of my family with Billy the Kid came at the time of the Lincoln County War. Billy had a prominent part in that war. He became involved in it through his friendship for Mr. Tunstall, the man who had been killed the day before my parents entered Lincoln.

The war was really one between rival cattle interests. Mr. Tunstall, who was one of the cattle barons, had among his cowboys Billy the Kid. He had won Billy's unending friendship by presenting him with a horse and a lovely saddle. So when Tunstall was killed, Billy vowed vengeance upon the enemies of Tunstall and joined the friends of Tunstall. Many people who had no connection with the war suffered death because it was a ruthless affair.

Mother always had a soft spot in her heart for Billy the Kid. It was the story of New Mexico that we children liked best of all. According to Mother he was a charming-looking chap with splendid manners. He loved to sing in a beautiful tenor voice when he came to Sunday School, as be did when he, happened to be in Lincoln.

Finally affairs became so bad in Lincoln County that the people insisted upon a change and petitioned the U. S. Government to do something. Governor Axtell was asked to resign and in his place Lew Wallace was appointed [Axtell was fired by President Rutherford B. Hayes because of his actions during the Lincoln County War]. He tried to win Billy to the side of law and order but Billy the Kid had gone too far to retreat. He went on with his course of robbing and rustling cattle. He was shot to death by Sheriff Garrett in 1881.

Billy the Kid's story has always seemed a sad one to me. Dead at twenty-one with twenty-one murders to his credit! When one thinks of the possibilities of that lad, he wonders who will be taken to task for his life. His intelligence, his courtesy, his love for beauty, his capacity for leadership, his acceptance without fear and without complaint of the rough as well as, the smooth in life, and his great capacity for making friends – all characteristics which people admire, Billy had in a marked degree. Billy's friends in the Southwest were and are still numerous! They tell us he was a brave, fine lad. From my childhood on I have always felt sorry for Billy the Kid and have felt that somehow he did not have a square deal.

Father, much later (I believe about 1914) wrote this about the war as he observed it:

On the morning of July 19, 1878 Turner [it was Deputy Peppin] decided to go to the house of McSween and demand the surrender of Billy the Kid and others against whom he had a warrant. He was accompanied by John A. Jones and eight or ten others.

Turner [Peppin] talked, at the house of McSween, to Wm. H. Bonney, Billy the Kid; soon the fight began in earnest. It was at this time that Col. Dudley of the 9th Cavalry arrived from Stanton, 9 miles distant, with his whole command. He camped in a hollow between the two forces and ordered no one to fire or he would turn his cannon on them.

Trader store at Fort Stanton owned by Paul Dowlin. 1870s photo. Courtesy Maurice G. Fulton Papers, Special Collections, UA.

The war had been brewing, according to Pat Garrett, since the summer of 1878, but commenced in earnest the following year in the spring and continued for nearly two years. On the one side was John Chisum, called "The Cattle King of New Mexico" with Alex. McSween and John Tunstall as important allies. On the other side were Murphy, Dolan, and Reilly, merchants of Lincoln and extensive cattle owners. These latter people were supported by Hon. Thos. B. Catron, a U.S. Attorney for New Mexico, and a resident of Santa Fe. [Catron was fired as U.S. Attorney because of his actions during the Lincoln County War.] He later represented New Mexico in the U. S. Congress.

McSween was a successful lawyer at Lincoln. The war grew out of the argument that Chisum's herds, about 40,000 to 80,000 head, were monopolizing the grazing along the Pecos River. The other side also claimed that he had driven off cattle that did not belong to him. He in turn blamed the Murphy, Dolan, and Reilly outfit for driving off his cattle. The District Attorney at Santa Fe [Rynerson] advised the Murphy crowd to shake up the McSween crowd and if necessary kill them. McSween told me he had seen the letter [see Appendix B for a copy of the letter].

Col. Dudley refused to protect McSween and ordered his men not to fire over Dudley's camp or he would turn the cannon on them. My wife read his note in reply to McSween's request for protection. McSween's house, where his party had taken refuge, was deliberately set on fire. About 2:00 P.M. the flames burst forth from the doors and windows. This was after three days of sporadic firing.

On McSween's side, besides McSween, Henry [Harvey] Morris and three [two] Mexicans were killed [Vincente Romero and Francisco Zamora]; Turner's [Peppin's] party, which numbered 40 men, and the soldiers, lost but one man, besides Beckwith [Charlie "Lallacooler" Crawford]. Billy the Kid's party numbered only 19 aside from McSween.

Mrs. McSween hired a lawyer by the name of [Huston] Chapman to settle the estate of her murdered husband in the month of February, 1879. [William W.] Campbell shot him. Campbell was arrested. Dolan and Mathews were also arrested. The object of this procedure was to smother out any attempt to ferret out the killing of this great and noble man McSween. Campbell was taken to the guard house at Ft. Stanton and then let go as were others. The trial was a mere farce.

During the days we were compelled to remain at Ft. Stanton we were looked upon with contempt, at least by Col. Dudley and the officers. As I walked out one day the black soldiers gathered around me and asked if I would preach to them on Sabbath. I said I would be glad to do so if they got permission from Commander Dudley. When they asked Col. Dudley, he said "<u>No</u>." There we were for a week treated as if we were culprits. I was not allowed to preach nor to write any communication for publication unless it went first through the adjutant's office. I wrote a polite note to the Colonel and asked for an axe and also for a soldier to shorten some wood we had which would not go into the stove. This is the answer I received:

Headquarters, Ft. Stanton, New Mexico
July 23, 1878

Rev. T. F. Ealy

Under the protection of the Garrison at Ft. Stanton, New Mexico.

Sir: I am in receipt of your note of this evening and in reply have to say, I have ordered an axe to be sent you for the purpose of shortening the wood to suit your fire place or stove referred to by you, which you will be required to use or go without wood. Soldiers at present have more important duties to attend to than waiting on parties holding your position.

If these views do not meet your expectations, the sooner you leave the post the better I shall be pleased. I am surprised that a Minister of the Gospel should be so indolent as to be unable to cut a few sticks of wood to aid his wife in cooking for himself and small family at a time when you have nothing in the world to do besides.

Very Respectfully,
Your Obedient Servant,
N. A.M. Dudley
Lieut. Col. 9th Cavalry Commanding

I shall be happy to do anything in my power to contribute to the comfort of your wife and children. In which desire I believe I am joined by every officer and lady at the Post.

N. A. M. D.

The great sympathy for my wife and children stopped right there. It is true Capt. [Edward] Ball showed it by dropping into my wife's hand a $5 bill saying that he knew missionaries need money. Think of the depression on our minds – out of friends – out of money – out of a home. I can sympathize with the Jews when they hung their harps upon the willows by the river of Babylon.

Then let us note a few items in the diary, items which deal with the time in Ft. Stanton.

July 22. The officer's [sic] wives have been calling on us.

July 23. A man dying in the hospital, named [Charles] Crawford, called Lallacooler.

July 24. Preached his [Crawford's] funeral sermon. 27 years old–wounded in the spinal column. His mother lives in Iowa, Text Ecc. last Chap. 16 vs.

July 25. A gentleman called on us. Visited the hospital. Saw Al Sanders.

July 26. Ft. Stanton, N. Mex. We are preparing to go north; do not know where, perhaps to Pa. Col. Dudley says he will send us to Las Vegas.

A copy of a note Father wrote to Col. Dudley at this time has come into my hands:

Ft. Stanton, N. M.
7, 26, '78

Lieut. Col. N. A. M. Dudley:

Hon. Sir: Having fled to the Post in time of great danger occasioned by the Lincoln County Feudal War, and having found within your Garrison great sympathy and kindness shown us by yourself, all your officers, their wives and the men in the ranks; we take this opportunity to express our hearty thanks; and yet feeling ourselves unable to meet the demands which will be made upon us, as our exit from the County at this time is sudden and unexpected, and feeling afraid that something might happen to us in a private conveyance, we still beg one more favor from your Excellency, the Comd. at the Post, begging you to furnish us transportation to Las Vegas, where we can communicate with our friends and secure aid.

We remain very respectfully your
Obedient Servants,
T. F. Ealy, M.D.,
Mrs. Mary R. Ealy,
Mrs. D. P. Shield

July 27. Wrote a communication to Col. Dudley. This morning answered by Col.

July 28. Did not preach – was not asked by any of the officers of the Post to preach. No encouragement is given to us.

The folks were in a quandary; where they should go and what they should do was the question which occupied their minds. Mother was sick over the excitement and she didn't look with much favor upon the long trip back to Las Vegas. There would be two improvements over the trip south though: it was summer and therefore the weather was much warmer and their conveyance was much better than the one in which they traveled before. On July 29 they started from Ft. Stanton. The first day they were able to go forty miles because they had a government ambulance and a six-mule team. They stopped for the first night at Jiconas J. Hoerade's.

On the way from the Fort to Las Vegas, Father and Mother slept one night in the ambulance thirty miles north of Perdenal [Cerro Pedernal]. That was August 1. The next day they reached Anton Chico at 11:00 A.M. By this time Mother was extremely unwell because of various things that had occurred; the fighting, the attitude of the military at Fort Stanton, the lack of money, her fear for the safety of her little ones, and the inconveniences of the journey, and the anxiety about their future. Father in his diary attributes her sickness to the sleeping out. When they reached Las Vegas on August 3, they went at once to the [R. J.] Hamilton Kap Hotel. There they saw Mrs. Shield and took dinner with her. Soon their friends the Annins came to ask them to be their guests until they found what to do.

Father preached twice on August 4; his texts were "As for God His Way is Perfect" and "Prayer to Trinity." On Monday he wrote to Col. Dudley, Dr. Jackson, Dr. [Henry] Kendall, and also to the railroad for reservations as he thought they would be compelled to go back to the East.

His letters to Dr. Jackson and Lieut. Col. Dudley follow:

Las Vegas, New Mexico
August 5, 1878

Reverend Dr. Jackson,

Dear Brother:

I have read your letter to me at this point and am not able to say yet what I will do. Have written to Cimarron, think it would be a good field together with Elizabethtown about fifteen or twenty miles off to the West of C.

Have written to Mr. [Frank] Springer, a prominent lawyer of that place for information. Hope to hear from him by Wednesday morning.

I was in Lincoln and saw more than anyone could have persuaded me I would see. Did not think that U.S. Troops would be allowed to lie on their backs and let houses be burned and men be burned also and shot down. That was the case in Lincoln. If troops had not gone to Lincoln, Mr. McSween would not have been killed, I firmly believe. We were between the firing and were not offered protection until we at great danger went and asked them to send an escort to take us out of danger. They did so and the next day took us to the Fort (Stanton) and in a week sent us free to Las Vegas.

The last day (6 days) coming Mrs. E. was, quite sick, but she is improving. However, I do not think at present she would be able to go on much of a journey.

Miss. Gates is along with us, and thinks, of teaching in the mountains 40 miles north of here at Agua Negro [Agua Negra, Black Water] – I want to take her out tomorrow.

Preached twice for Brother Annin yesterday. As the railroad is expected by next April this town will certainly receive its share of Presbyterians. I hope we may remain here until we decide where we will go. I want to be at Presbytery 29th of August which meets in Santa Fe.

If I remain in the Presbytery or Territory rather, I will not decide about any other point until I hear from Cimarron.

Your Brother in Christ,
T. F. Ealy

Las Vegas, N. M.
Aug. 5, 1878

To Lieut. Col. N. A. M. Dudley
Com. at Fort Stanton

Dear Sir:

I have the honor of thanking you for the safe, comfortable, and gratuitous transportation you gave us to Las Vegas from Ft. Stanton. The drivers conducted themselves very well all the way.

Very respectfully,
Your obedient servant,
Rev. T. F. Ealy, M.D.

Three days after the family reached Las Vegas, Father started on a trip with Mr. Perea, Miss Rebecca Annin, and Miss Susan Gates to Agua Negro, to see if he could find a place for Susan to teach and to look over the field for himself. There he ran into an evangelist, Mr. R. [Rafael] G. Gallegos.

While in Agua Negro Father found time to write a promised letter for "The Rocky Mountain Presbyterian." This is it:

TO THE ROCKY MOUNTAIN PRESBYTERIAN,

I promised that if I lived I would write again from Lincoln. Well, thanks to our Father I have lived and have been permitted to labor there in a quiet way from February 18th to July 14th when I preached my last sermon there. The next Sabbath I was in Fort Stanton and August 4th I preached in Bro. Annin's pulpit, Las Vegas. Now I am writing from a point 40 miles north of Las Vegas where I can see snow on the mountains, wheat, corn, and oats growing in the valley. The crops look very promising. There has been a very good rain today. It will be of great benefit to the corn and oats which are just filling out their ears.

My mission up in the mountains is to bring Miss Susie Gates to Agua Negro for the purpose of opening a school. Many of the Mexican people have expressed themselves as being well pleased that she has come and promise her scholars and support. God bless her in her work. She need not be lonely or discouraged if "Thou art near."

Bro. Annin preaches here about once a month and R. C. Gallegos, an evangelist, is stationed here. "But what about Lincoln?" you say. Well we just remained there as long as we could tough it out. Bullets were flying through town, through and around our house, and we labored and prayed and waited for quieter days but they did not come. The quieter days did not come at Lincoln and the day before we left we witnessed what we never believed would be tolerated in a Christian Nation, like our own, especially when the U.S. Troops were present. We saw two houses burned to ashes while there were eleven men inside. Next morning we saw some of those men carried through the town on stretchers who had been shot down while they attempted to escape from the last room where they had taken refuge, to await the approach of night, hoping that then they might escape being murdered when they ran from the flames. An elegant piano, Brussels carpet – costly furniture – rich curtains – fine pictures, etc. all destroyed in the flames – but what are they to the lives lost. We left the country with many others who did not wish to take up arms.

T. F. Ealy

After settling Susan at Agua Negro, Father rode on horseback fifty-four miles farther to see if he might find a suitable place to preach at Cimarron. For some reason he went on twenty-five miles to Ocata. There he met Bro. [Hilario] Romero of Taos. He stayed all night with Felix Moss, and the next morning at 10:00 A.M. preached on the subject "Give us this day our daily bread." Leaving Ocate [between Las Vegas and Taos] at noon he rode through a gentle rain for part of the afternoon, reaching Cimarron at dusk.

Father was thinking of Cimarron as a likely spot but for some reason he returned to Las Vegas and on August 12 preached there for Rev. Mr. Annin. The following day, August 13, he went to Anton Chico, with which place he was somewhat acquainted. The diary records his decision.

What Father needed was to recuperate after his trying experience in Lincoln. A long period of rest would have been extremely beneficial. Instead we find him going from place to place trying to find one suitable for establishing his church, school, and home. How welcome a long rest would have been!

Aug. 10. Left [A. J.] Calhoun's [at Ocate] after calling on and talking to some people in the morning at 10 A.M. Rode 15 miles and ate lunch. Bro. Gallegos preached to some Mexicans by the wayside at Reciva Creek. Rode 32 miles.

Aug. 11. Calhoun's – 45 miles to Las Vegas. Passed Ft. Union at noon. Rained nearly all day. Reached Las Vegas late. Found wife and babies pretty well.

Aug. 12. Las Vegas. Preached yesterday for Bro. Annin at 10 A.M. Luke 2:11. At night Bro. Gallegos preached in Spanish. Cool audience.

Aug. 13. Tuesday Anton Chico. Reached here 3 P.M. Stopped at Mr. Hamilton's [Hotel]. Found many glad to see us.

Father wrote at once to Dr. Jackson:

Anton Chico, San Miguel Co., New Mex.
August 13th, 1878.

Rev. Doctor Jackson

Dear Sir:

We have anchored again. I left Mrs. E. at Vegas, while I took Miss Sue Gates to Agua Negro and from there I visited Cimarron in company with Brother Gallegos.

A reaction in the current caused my bark to drift back about 110 miles. When I came through here, the people who are interested in improvement wished me to stop. I thought little about it, but after we were gone there were some steps taken to call me back. There is great need of a school here, and they want two schools, one for boys and one for girls. There is no physician here, and they wish me to act as such.

Anton Chico is about 30 miles from Las Vegas, on the Pecos River, South East from Vegas.

We reached here an hour ago. They were still fighting in Lincoln Co. It is not my fight I shall inform Dr. K [Henry Kendall]. If I had been persecuted for righteousness sake I would have stood up to the torture. Will write him today. Find enclosed his letter. Have promise of twelve or thirteen scholars and all promise to pay.

I have written a short scribble for the "Rocky Mountain" – if you think it worthy of insertion. But should it not be, leave it out. Hope to be in Santa Fe at Presbytery 29th. I would say this in regard to Cimarron. There is no minister there of any denomination. They seem indifferent about going to preaching – although I did not preach to them. I was told only about four went to hear Mr. Harwood of La Junta; while there I met a member of a Congregational Church, one of the Presbyterian Church, one of the Methodist Church.

There is not a minister in the country, eighteen miles from C. is Elizabethtown, a mining, town, of how many people I did not learn. The station for the railroad will be about 20 miles East of Cimarron. That will be the nearest station to the town. I was in Lincoln when McSween was killed. Left next day at four P.M. Saw more then I ever thought could be tolerated in the U.S. or territories. That poor man was assassinated most barbarously. Perhaps you will be very anxious to know what things I saw. I will briefly state them to you.

July 14th. Mr. McSween and about 40 men came in to the town of Lincoln. There was not a shot fired. I, nor my family, did not know that they had entered. It was just as the moon rose after dark. Part of the Sheriff's posse were out of town. They were sent for the next day, and reached town about sun-set. Came in riding at full speed and yelling and before getting off their horses began firing at McSween's house. About 100 shots fired. And for five days firing was kept up in the town.

July 19th, Lieutenant Dudley and Command entered town about noon. Camped near center of town. All McSween's side withdrew except himself and ten men who remained with him in his own house. About two hours after the troops came in, Mrs. Shield's house, which adjoined McSween's, was fired, while she (Mrs. S.) and family were removing their property – her little girl stepping in the [coal] oil which was poured on the floor. About the same time, or shortly after, McSween's house was fired by means of coal oil. The Sheriff's posse were stationed around the house and kept firing all the time. Any attempt to escape would have been death. The eleven men inside were almost burnt alive and when about dark they attempted to escape from the last room yet remaining unconsumed by the flames – were shot! Not all. Some I believe got off – but the noble McSween was killed. Our house was between the firing and we were not offered protection until about dusk. Miss Gates want at the risk of her life and asked an escort of soldiers. The Col. immediately sent an escort.

T. F. Ealy

Aug. 14. Anton Chico. San Miguel Co., N. Mex. Up at 5 A.M. Rented a house at 8 dollars a month – 6 rooms. Floors in two rooms of pine.

Aug. 15. Mr. Nelson's little girl is very sick. I am not at all well. Mrs. E. and babies are well.

Aug. 16. Feel better – better yesterday. Great inducement to go to Zuni; a home, $1200.00, and expenses to field.

Mother wrote to Dr. Jackson:

Anton Chico, New Mexico, August 16, 78
Rev. Sheldon Jackson D.D.

Dear Sir:

As my husband is very sick he wishes me to answer your letter. Had your letter reached us while at Las Vegas before coming to this point, we might have gone to Zuni, since we know we would have a house, as we have been drifting hither and thither without comfortable quarters, exposed to hard-ships and danger. We were completely disheartened without money. We spent all our first quarter coming out, and have received nothing since; here we came Tuesday of this week, by the earnest request of a number of the citizens. Have rented a house for six months and are making preparations to open school the first of September. The people here are very ignorant and bigoted but seem to want Mr. Ealy to stay among them. His knowledge of medicine gives him more influence over the Mexicans than you can imagine. Miss Gates has gone to Agua Negro expecting to open school there the first of September.

If we were on the ground, I would like nothing better than to instruct those Indians, but neither Mr. Ealy nor myself are strong enough at present to undertake such a trip especially with two small children. If Mr. Ealy is able, will meet you at Presbytery; am so sorry we had to leave Lincoln, and would like to go back there if peace was only proclaimed; will try to get some of our most promising pupils there to come here if possible.

There are between 300 and 400 people here, and as the people, themselves, have expressed a desire for us to start a school, we have promised to remain six months, it would not be honorable to leave now. But if the Board at the end of that time, still wish us to go to Zuni, everything else being favorable we will try to go, provided our work here can be dropped end filled by others. Perhaps Mr. Ealy may write to you next week, says to tell you he acted on Mr. Kendall's suggestion viz, "If he is a skillful mariner he will find a harbor, sail in, then report."

Very respectfully,
Mrs. T. F. Ealy

Settled in Anton Chico in a house of six rooms, one 30 feet long, the folks were beginning to feel at home once more. It was a great satisfaction to be able to sleep without the anxiety of constant war which had plagued them during their whole stay in Lincoln. It is true they were in a Catholic town, but most of the people were very friendly. The little Nelson girl died and was buried with the Catholic rites, the priest officiating. Many candles were lighted for the occasion. The Americans especially were kind and helpful.

Father was planning to open a school by September 1. He had every intention of making Anton Chico his next place of residence even though on August 16 he had received an offer of a pastorate at Zuni. Mother's letter explains their reason for this decision. Father proceeded to order school books end other supplies in order to be ready for the opening of school. A check from New York for $250.00 and letters from home helped to crystallize his purpose. He knew now that he had contact both with his church and his home. His health as well as Mother's was much improved, a result of his mind being at rest.

Before that be had spoken of Las Vegas being 30 miles from a telegraph office. He was evidently thinking of the fact that he might need to communicate suddenly with his home people. Many miles from home as he was, a family to look after, not at all well, and few funds – all these matters brought home to him the fact that he was so far from a telegraph office.

Meanwhile rumors from Lincoln County came to them: [William Harrison] Johnston and his father-in-law were shot in Spring River. They had a shop together. Mr. [George L.] Barber and James Chisum passed through Anton Chico.

Pleased to be with his family again Father spent August 25, Sabbath, at home. He remarked there is no place like home. On August 26 the wonderful rain came and that same night another welcome one arrived. Melons were just ripe. In the mail a check for $72.00 came as a loan from Dr. Jackson, money which he felt he did not need and therefore planned to return to Presbytery at Santa Fe (Holy Faith). On August 27 Father started for Presbytery and rode thirteen miles on his way.

The following item from the October "The Rocky Mountain Presbytery" concerns the travels to Presbytery in those days.

The members of the Presbytery of Santa Fe all reached that body in wagons or on horseback, camping out by the way; some traveling three or four hundred miles. One evening, while a party of them sat around the camp fire at worship, the snap of the teeth of a mountain lion was heard in the dark thicket behind them. Rev. Dr. Ealy, who traveled alone on horseback, hung his hammock so high in the trees at night that the mountain lion could not reach him.

Another item tells of the large and enthusiastic meetings of the Santa Fe Presbytery.

Aug. 29. Rained all night. Last night ate green corn. No salt and much milk. Rode to Kosboski's. Met Mr. Annin 25 miles from Santa Fe. Rained in the night and during the day.

Aug. 29. Left Kosboski's for Santa Fe at S. Feel unwell. Reached Santa Fe at 3 P.M. Stopped at Exchange Hotel. Wrote to Mrs. E.

The statement in Father's diary for August 29, "feel unwell" is not surprising, after his diary record for August 28, "ate green corn." The amazing thing is that a doctor, who would know better, did not act upon his knowledge.

Aug. 30. Held an interesting session of Presbytery. I preached at 7:30; text Ga. 3:13. Wrote Dr. Beatty and sent $65. Sent $100 to Valley Bank.' T. F. Ealy, moderator.

Aug. 31. All the members of Presbytery present but Darby. Dr. Jackson was received and name enrolled from Presbytery of Utah. Darby not a member.

Sept. 1. Sermon by Dr. Sheldon Jackson, I Pet. 1:15. Mexican brethren held street meetings. Spanish preaching at Mrs. Griffith's rooms. Bro. Annin preached at 7:30 – Job 38:31,32.

Sept. 2. I was ordered by Presbytery to change from Anton Chico, N. Mex. to Zuni, N. M. Bro. Shield ordained at 7:30 P.M.

Father found that Presbytery would prefer that he go to Zuni rather than remain at Anton Chico. He was willing, but it must have been difficult to pull up stakes so soon again. As he had already ordered school books and other supplies he evidently planned to remain in Anton Chico.

Sept. 3. Gov. Atkinson provides for me at the Exchange Hotel. Left Santa Fe about 8 A.M. Slept on ground – rained a little. Raphael Gallegos along. Pearl's birthday – 3 years.

Sept. 4. Got into saddle at daylight. Breakfast at San Jose and reached Anton Chico at 5 P.M. Wrote 5 letters. Found all well. Miss Rebecca Annin teaching.

Anton Chico, New Mexico
September 4, 78

Rev. Dr. Jackson

Dear Brother:

I reached home today an hour before sun down. Found all well, and Miss Rebecca A [Annin]. here. The school members 7. My four scholars have not yet come from Fort Sumner.

Mrs. Ealy is willing to go to Zuni. Says she will take Miss Susan Gates along, if she will go. It will probably require your attention at Agua Negro to place another teacher there. We cannot start inside of two weeks. Give me your address at Zuni. Please send me check for $100.00 here at Anton Chico.

The team hire I will pay when I get to Zuni, or rather I will ask you to be prepared to pay it. Will let you know what it is, when we leave Albuquerque. You might send me $50.00 to Albuquerque if you think it would be safe. Mrs. E. likes Manual's plan of house with school house by its self.

Fraternally,
T. F. Ealy

Anton Chico, New Mexico
September 4/78

Rev. Dr. Shield

Dear Brother:

I reached home today. Found all well and our school going on. Mrs. Ealy is willing to go to Zuni. Tell Dr. J., if with you, to send $100.00 check to Anton Chico. I wrote him at Puerto [Puerto de Luna] – we hope to get off in about a fortnight.

Fraternally,
T. F. Ealy

Anton Chico, New Mexico
September 4/78

Dear Brother Jno:

I am home again. Got here early. Found all well. Mrs. Ealy will go to Zuni. Your plan of the house Mrs. Ealy likes better than Dr. J's. She thinks the S. R. ought to be a short distance from the dwelling.

In about two weeks we can perhaps get off. Tell Dr. J. to send me $100.00 check to Anton Chico.

I have written him to E. Puerto.

Fraternally,
T. F. Ealy

Sept. 5. School members 6. Many more wanting to come. Books coming, $25 worth. Must start for Zuni in two weeks, 250 miles.

Sept. 6. School numbers 9. We expect to start for Albuquerque on 23rd, about 200 miles.

Sept. 7. Wrote 4 letters, Charley Ramsey, Dr. Donaldson, Sister Mary, and Dr. Jackson, and 3 more after tea, Chisum, Spiegelburg, and D. [David] Eaton.

Father's letter to Dr. Jackson on Sept. 7th:

Anton Chico, New Mexico
September 7/78

Dr. Sheldon Jackson:

Dear Brother:

Instead of one hundred dollars ($100.00) I should have asked for two hundred ($200.00). If we take our assistant teacher along, it will increase the expenses very much.

We will leave here Monday, September 23rd. Expect to be in Albuquerque on the 25th or 26th. D. V. If you cannot communicate again at this point let us hear from you at Albuquerque. Do not forget this interesting point, scholars have been brought here to go to me from the convent at Vegas. I do hope a man can be sent soon. A man coming will find some warm friends to welcome him.

Upper Anton Chico – which is a mile above must have 200 of a population. Two men from Las Vegas are thinking of building a large grist mill here. The water power is excellent. Fish plenty. The A. T. and S. F. R. R. will come near the town, and any road from the East through the Indian Territory will strike very near here.

Fraternally,
T. F. Ealy

From September 8 to September 15 Father was quite ill. His physique, never particularly rugged, was feeling the effect of the busy worried life he had been leading. The severe nights in the open on the way down to Lincoln first weakened his resistance; then the anxiety in the town itself because of the almost constant fighting didn't help matters any, and his inability to carry out his mission to the people brought a sense of frustration. After he left Lincoln too he had no time to rest and collect his thoughts; instead he had to go from one place to another trying to find a place where he might work for the Lord. Now in Anton Chico the reaction came. Through the week beginning September 8, he records in his diary that he was quite sick. On September 12 he was 30 years old. The next day he was unable to be out of bed.

Meanwhile, in spite of his illness he practiced some at his medical profession. During that week he opened a foot which was greatly inflamed. He called his own trouble, inflammation of the stomach. For two or three days he was bedfast. Susan came to join the folks, intending to go with them to Zuni. Several persons, among them a priest, who said he regretted their going, and Mrs. Nelson came to call.

Father was too ill even to write and so I am including here a letter from Mother to Dr. Jackson:

Anton Chico, New Mexico
September 14/78

Rev. Sheldon Jackson

Dear Sir:

Mr. Ealy is very ill, suffering from cold and from riding so far from Santa Fe; I was very much alarmed about him and feel uneasy yet. We are anxious to get to our journey's end before the severe weather comes on.

Mr. Ealy thinks he is getting better, and if able will start soon; will try to reach Albuquerque about the 25th; would like to have some money there to lay in a supply for winter as well as to provide some things to make us comfortable. We have not succeeded in renting the house yet; we inferred from your letter Mr. Perea had gone in Mr. Serge's place. Are we correct?

Miss Susie Gates is here ready to go with us. Taught one month at Agua Negro but had but one pupil.

If nothing prevents, will see you soon Zuni.

We had a call from the priest yesterday, asking us to remain, and saying he is very sorry to have us leave. He says the school will not increase any, as he will not allow any of his pupils to go to Miss Annin. But I think very many of them will go without his permission.

Mr. Hollman says he does not wish a teacher at Agua Negro till spring; thinks Miss Gates may want to go back by that time.

Very respectfully,
Mrs. T. F. Ealy

P.S. Two checks received, one $100 and the other for $50.

By the 16th of September, Father was able to go around though somewhat weak. On that day he operated on a man for balanitis [swelling of the foreskin] – fee $10.00. He also treated a case of quinsy [tonsillitis].

The whole family now became busy with preparations for the trip to Zuni. They hoped to be able to start by September 23, for they didn't look forward with any pleasure to a trip after the cold weather set in. Some mountains still had to be crossed, and the memory of their trip to Lincoln was too recent for any of the hardships to have been effaced. They hired a man to take them to Zuni with four yoke of oxen for $125.00. Father bought a wagon for $50.00 and a stove for $30.00. Into this wagon were to go all their possessions as well as flour and groceries for six months. Of course the party of five fitted in somewhere. The result must have been similar to that of the migrants of the Southwest. I remember seeing such a family in Tucson several years ago. The conveyance there was an old truck instead of an oxen team; otherwise the effect must have been the same. One difference was that this party was made up of people unused to hardship.

I shall close the chapter with a letter from Father to Dr. Jackson:

Anton Chico, New Mexico
September 21/78

Dear Doctor:

We will start 23, D. V. Have hired an ox team, four yoke for $125 – to be paid when we reach Zuni. Please have some of our salary there when we reach Zuni.

We have bought nearly all our supplies here at Anton Chico. But there are some things which we will want to get at Albuquerque, and to buy them we will need about $50 more than we now have. I asked you before to have me a check for $50 at Albuquerque when I reached there; then I think we can get all we need for our winter supply. We will do our best to make 20 miles a day. All well.

You might ask if we can get carpet made in the Zuni village – if so, we need not buy it at Albuquerque.

Yours in the Lord,
T. F. Ealy

Probably we will camp over Sabbath at A [Anton Chico].

Chapter 3 | Zuni

It was the 23d of September [1878] when the five people started from Anton Chico to Zuni with a driver. Although not sufficiently cured of his cold and not entirely rested from traveling around, Father had youth in his favor and a naturally buoyant spirit to help him; so he looked eagerly forward to the next adventure. It was October 12th before the party arrived in the Indian Pueblo.[1] Of the trials and hardships of the trip, which must have been many, he does not speak. They went by the way of Albuquerque.

When the folks arrived in Zuni, a big dance was in progress. The hearts of the folks must have been filled with dismay to hear the odd calls of the dancers and to see their frightfully-painted faces. It was Saturday night and no house had been prepared for them. Mr. [José Ynes] Perea, who had gone ahead, had secured a temporary place in one of the Indian homes, where their beds must be placed on the stone floors; there no convenience of any kind could be found.

In order to understand the new life into which the family stepped, I am going to relate some characteristics of the tribe of Indians with which the family had close contact during the next few years.

The story of the Zunis shows that they have been independent during all their history. In all the clashes with the Spaniards, who came up from Mexico against them, they stood out among the Indian tribes. Even when they were conquered they still went on as far as possible in their old way. New Mexico was visited by Coronado [Francisco Vázquez de Coronado y Luján] as early as 1540 but it wasn't until 1598 that this section was colonized by Onate [Juan de Oñate]. In 1848 all New Mexico was ceded to the United States by Mexico [following the Mexican-American War], and two years later it was formed into a territory. At first the Government largely overlooked this section and it became a haven for those who were fleeing from law and order. It was made into a state in [January 6], 1912, the 47th. The population of Zuni when Father was there is given at 1617. It is about 5000 now. An extensive study of these Indians has been made by [Frank Hamilton] Cushing, Mrs. [Matilda Coxe] Stevenson, [Alfred] Kroeber, and others.

The social and religious life of the Zunis remained unchanged under the 350 years of Spanish rule. They still retained their ancient beliefs and ceremonies. The Zunis openly embraced the Christian religion but secretly practiced the religion that they had followed for centuries. They had a communal government; all were practically on the same level. It is true they had a governor and caciques or chiefs who had some authority over them. The Spanish had added to their staple corn, wheat, and many vegetables; they had also introduced the planting of peach orchards. The life in 1878 was practically the same as it was in those early days.

They were agriculturists. They cultivated arid regions. They also wove blankets and made a good bit of pottery. They have always practiced monogamy.

Dances held a great part in their religious life.

The following on Zuni Kachinas I have taken from records by the Smithsonian Institution. Miss Ruth L. Bunzel is responsible for the information

ZUNI KACHINAS

While the Zunis have had six major religious cults, the Kachina Cult seems to be the dominant one. The other cults in modern times are losing members, but it is said that the Kachinas are becoming more extensive and more active. Included in this cult are all the male members of the tribe, who are required to take part in its ceremonies. A few women were admitted from time to time. This cult is extremely spectacular and penetrating; in fact it penetrates every phase of the life of the Zunis.

It is built upon the worship of supernatural beings called Koko, who were brought to the Indians by means of impersonations in a series of dances. The Koko are supposed to live in the bottom of a lake west of Zuni at St. John's, Arizona [Lyman Lake]. They live on the spiritual essence of food offered to them in the river and clothe themselves with the feathers of prayer sticks.

The male members of the tribe dance when they wish to honor the Koko or when they wish them to grant some special favors. There are various types of dances, such as the rain dance, the corn dance, and the deer dance.

As a rule the dancers are masked. These masks are extremely important, since the power of the Kachinas resides in the mask; hence the Kachina whose representation is worn thus makes himself into a person. Zunis have special reverence for the mask and only the one who wears it may touch it. One must not don a mask unless he is taking part in a special ceremony. But then must not be touched. Spectators must be careful not to touch a masked dancer. The mask is really the bodily substance of its Kachina.

To secure the presence of the Kachinas at a dance the Indians must plant prayer sticks by the river side. The Kachinas have many human qualities. They like to sing and dance and also to wear pretty clothes. They are especially fond of the Zunis and gladly come when invited.

The masks are tribal property and are handed down from one generation to another. They are kept in sealed jars, which are looked after by the maternal part of the family, and when needed, are taken out of the jars with great care. The wearer must sacrifice food in the river before wearing a mask and plant prayer sticks. These masks are made of leather, earlier ones of elk-skin and buffalo hide. There is no attempt at realism in these masks. Feathers practically always form part of the mask.

As for the costume we find it varies. The breech cloth is worn by all. Over it is a hand-woven and embroidered white cotton kilt, which is fastened at the right side. With it is worn a belt or sash.

The Indians have always held the Kachinas in great veneration, even to the modern times. This incident, told by "Newsweek" in 1952 illustrates that fact. In that year, William Field, nineteen, a Harvard student of Santa Fe, New Mexico, brought great anger to both the Indians of Arizona and New Mexico when he dared to appear at a fiesta in the costume of a Kachina or Indian god. Oliver la Farge, an Indian authority, called it "a gross insult to the Indian religion." The Hopi and Pueblo chiefs called it degrading. Field apologized and offered to make amends.[2]

Dr. Henry Palmer speaks of the various Pueblo tribes and adds that "to anyone interested in the study of Indians, I commend the Zunis. They have always been remote from any other tribe; they held out long against the Spaniards, and are as bitter today in their hatred of Mexicans, as they could possibly have been two hundred years ago."

The following, taken from a paper published in Albuquerque on August 23, 1952 speaks of the language of the tribe: "Dr. [Stanley Stewart] Newman, a linguistics specialist claims the Zuni language stands alone – that is, so far no proved relative of it has been found in other Indian tongues."

He said, "Indian languages are not simple. In some cases, they are more complicated than English. While the Navajo, Laguna, Taos, and Apache languages are tone languages like Chinese – in which the pitch of the voice shows the meaning of a word – Zuni is not. It uses the pitch of the voice as in English."

"Dr. Newman's Zuni grammar which he is working on at present will describe the system of sounds, how they are pronounced and how they are combined. Then he will develop a system of prefixes, suffixes, and roots and show how they are combined."

"The grammar also will include syntax and illustrate how words are combined into sentences."

Father has given the following examples of Indian words:

North – Rah langue
South – Me Ka quire to ne
East – Ta wonque
West – Z na que

The diary reads:

Oct. 12. Arrived in Zuni, New Mexico. Big dance, Indians look frightful painted.

Dr. Jackson wrote thus about the beginning of the mission in Zuni:. "On Sabbath, October 13, about sixty came out to divine service and on Monday work commenced on the well, preparatory to the erection of a house. Good water was found at the depth of twenty-one feet. In a week the well was dug and stoned twenty-five feet deep, the trench for the foundation of the house dug, and the stone on the ground ready for the laying up. Some of the stone was hauled on carts, some carried in bags on the backs of burros, and some carried on the heads of men. The house is being pushed with great vigor."

Undaunted, Father called a meeting of the Indians the following morning to tell them of his hopes and plans. Many came and stayed very late. As he said, they smoked the family nearly out of the house.

On Monday he vigorously began work on a mission house a little distance from the town. He put four men at work digging a well; the following three days he and Mr. Perea helped with that work.

It was several days before Father had time to communicate with Dr. Jackson:

Zuni, Pueblo, New Mexico
Oct. 15, 78

Dear Dr. Jackson:

We arrived here all very well on Saturday last, Oct. 12th just at the closing exercises of a Devil's Dance. The noise was hideous. Perhaps there were one hundred people

Zuni Pueblo in 1878. Image from book.

Zuni Pueblo showing Dowa Yalanne ("Corn Mountain") in distance. Photo by John Karl Hillers, 1879. Courtesy National Anthropological Archives, Smithsonian Institution.

looking at us from the roofs. One of our drivers said he did not want to stay long is this town.

We got our stove up and got some tea, had four Indians to sup with us, and then being tired, we prepared our beds on the floor and lay down. All slept very well, did not feel afraid, and were not molested in the least.

Sabbath the 13th, called a meeting, about sixty came, we had our room well filled with souls, we thought they would stay all night. Monday the 14th, we put four Indians at the well. They dug all day, and the sweat rolled off them. Did not get water – we think water can be reached today. Four are just starting to dig. The governor says nothing will be done until water is found. Then plenty will go to work.

I had the honor to present the governor and Pedro Pino the cords and tassels. Some want money and some take goods for work or pay them a dollar a day, and they board themselves. Tomorrow I expect to put twenty to work if we find water today, but the supply will soon run out if we keep a strong force on the building. A box of soap, of chewing tobacco, of candles, and a sack of coffee, and one of sugar we could use for trade very well. Mrs. Ealy says if some church will send her a sewing machine and goods she will make all the children who come to school two suits. We have wool, sulphurina [yellow], but it is not the color we want. Scarlet cool they want. Red silk and cotton handkerchiefs pretty large, they want; a good pair of scales would be of great service to me, and they would think that I was dealing more fairly with them.

After studying about the house I have decided to build it well as I go; first dig out all the foundations so as to make a good cellar under the whole house – four rooms and hall on first floor, and four rooms and hall on second floor. I can get all the hands I want. My building the house two story of stone will give more room and take less roof. Do you not think a tin roof would be the best? It would be the most satisfactory and if the necessary tools are sent with the tin, Perea and I can put it on. The days are very fine for working now, we work early and late.

I will buy the groceries you forwarded for your own use and pay you as soon as I get the money; it will not be longer than spring, if so long.

We are making an inventory of your groceries, and will send you an order on Board before long. You ask for an order on Board for my transfer from Anton Chico to Zuni – that I cannot give, for you promised to pay my (our) expenses, which are $165.00.

The Indians want some money as well as goods and without money it will not be easy to get along. Almost all of those I have paid off have asked for money.

Today we have water at 25 feet, 17th. Tomorrow I will try to well up the well. The frame Perea & I put up. The rope wheel and buckets are doing good service. It is now about 20 ft. and we will sink it perhaps one foot more.

Met Dr. [James A.] Menaul just after we left Laguna [Puebla] in sight of the town. You told me that I would not need to bring any tools, that Dr. Menaul would lend me his, but he left nothing here. An augur, saw, drawing knife, chisel, stone-hammer, trowel, etc., we absolutely need. I have found pitched paper which I take is for the roof; if so, we need say nothing of the tin.

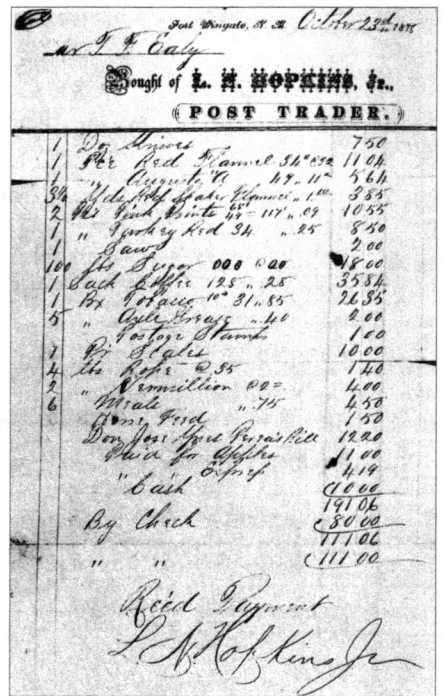

Bill of sale, L. N. Hopkins, Jr., Post Trader, Fort Wingate, October 23, 1878. Image from book.

18th. The foundation is dug out; we are ready for the masons. A great many stones are on the ground, hauled on wagons, burros, and carried on the men's backs; we will finish walling the well tomorrow, I am doing that. The water is very cool and good.

The Indians want light red flannel – want two yards for $1.00. Wish we had it now.

T. F. Ealy

While there is no entry for three days, I got a clue from an old account book as to what was going on during that time. On October 17th Father records that Juan Don Ducero brought five men and two wagons to haul stone. That day they hauled only one load for the munificent sum of three dollars. The next day the same number of men and wagons came, but this time each wagon brought two loads and the bill was six dollars. On October 18th, thirty-one men were at work and the next day $34. Evidently, each was paid one dollar a day for his work. On October 20th, the record states that $12.50 was paid for work. On October 29th Ducero's son-in-law was paid $2.00 for his wagon and help; $3.00 for horse hire, and corn for horses, and iron for a wagon tongue $1.50 more. Juan Ducero's entire bill was $10.30, which was paid for partly in sugar and partly in cash.

This same book gives a record, when the house was completed, of the money paid for labor, lumber, freight on door and windows, hauling of stone and lumber, yet I find it difficult to determine the exact cost of the house. For hauling stone the pay seems to have been $4.00; in all $96.30 was paid for the hauling of the stone. The well cost $36.40. The vigas or rafters, 41 in all, cost $41.00. What did the entire house cost? As nearly as I can compute it, I make the amount $373.95. I may be far off from the exact cost. The final bill proves that is the case.

The account was not complete until 1880. See the following bill:

Building account Zuni, New Mexico
Jan. 15, 1878

Handed over by J. Y. Perea, money left with him by Dr. Jackson:

For the building	266.00
Rec. of Dr. S. Jackson	51.75
	364.55
Total	602.30
Moving from Anton Chico to Zuni	125.00
Freight on doors and windows	105.00
Lot of thread	17.75
Two wagons bringing lumber	24.50
Hauling stone with wagons	86.00
Carrying stone on burro's and Indian's backs	60.00
Vigas	73.00
Attending masons	159.55
Cost of well	35.00
1 pr. counter scales	10.00
Total	697.40
Feb. 1879 Rec. from Dr. Jackson	150.00
May 27, 1879 – Hauling stone	12.00
June 17, 1879 – Carpenter 60 days work	80.86
June 17, 1879 – Boarding carpenter	32.00
Aug. 4, 1879 – Indians hauling stones	15.00
Aug. 17, 1879 – Paid Dubois for trees	5.00
Aug. 17, 1879 – Fencing lot	354.00
Ceo. for three months work	36.00
Two bills lumber	152.00
Oct. 1879, Rec'd from Dr. Jackson	551.96
Grand total	1,384.28

An item from the diary:

Oct. 21. Susan [Gates] began school – very poor room. Dirt floors – fireplace, 6 desks, no windows & hole in the wall and roof. People living overhead. 22 present, all boys. I think we will have no difficulty in getting the girls into school in a little while.

Zuni, Pueblo, New Mexico
Oct. 21, 78

Dr. Jackson:

I have been so busy since arriving, that I did not go to the office. To send anyone I am not able as an Indian wants $5.00. We have some little prospect of getting the Post Office in Zuni. Tomorrow I am going to the Ft. and P.O. Wish I could hear from you soon.

Am sorry you, Menaul, and Perea all could not get a few adobes made while here; you two weeks, Maneul three, and Perea nearly four. In a week I got the well finished, and the foundation dug out and stone enough for the masons to begin work. Now I must start on the hunt of masons. But remember, we need help soon. The Indians want to go for the lumber and I am not willing to pay the price they ask, $36.00, for three wagons. Perhaps I can get wagons cheaper at [William] Crane's or over in that region. I will try tomorrow, and if I cannot, then will start the wagons immediately on my return. It will take four days to go, and four to come. They want seven yards of muslin for a dollar. We traded off that which was left here to divide the rooms.

Today we opened school with 20 present, all 30. Miss Gates taught. I will not be able to go to teach the school for a while. The girls and women often come into our house.

Think I can easily get them into school. It will cost 20 for stone as nearly as I can get at it. It took a great many stones to wall up the well, about 25 ft. in depth. I will add about 34.00 for lumber for a box. The well must be covered. Just now the thought struck me that I could make a box and cover out of a store box which would answer very well for the use until I get a team sawmill.

Well, for stones	20.00
Labor	15.50
Total	36.50

P.S. If I can't get masons, will buy a trowel and stone hammer, and try my hand at it. Let us hear from you, Good night.

T. F. Ealy

A bill of goods found with Father's papers shows that he had to ride to Ft. Wingate for supplies:

Fort Wingate, N.M.
Oct. 23, 1878
Mr. T. F. Ealy
Bought of L. N. Hopkins, Jr, Post Trader

1 doz. Knives	7.50
1 pc. Red Flannel 342 @ 0.38	11.04
1 pc. Augusta Flannel 49 @ 0.11 ½	5.64
3 ½ yds. Red Shaker Flannel @ 1.10	3.88
2 pcs. Pink Points Flannel	10.55
1 pc. Turkey Red Flannel	8.50
1 Saw	2.00
100 lbs. sugar	15.00
1 Sack coffee	35.94
1 Box tobacco	26.35
5 Boxes Axle Grease	2.00
Postage Stamps	1.00
1 Pr. Scales	10.00
4 lbs rope	1.40
Vermillion	4.00

6 Yeals	4.50
Horse feed	1.50
Don José Ynes Perea's bill	12.20
Paid for Apples	11.00
Paid for Apples	4.12
Cash	10.00
By check	90.00
By check	111.06

Oct. 27. Working as hard as we can work at the stone house.

Nov. 3. My hands have to be tied up in the morning with grease on them so that I can work.

Nov. 8. I am working harder then I have ever worked in my life.

On November 9th walls of two rooms were completed; walls of stone. Up to that time Father had done all the masonry himself. He was finding it hard since he had never learned the trade. He says, though, that he was rather proud of the walls. By the 17th two rooms were finished and the family moved into them rather than stay in the Indian Village any longer.

Two letters were written to Dr. Jackson close together:

Zuni Pueblo, New Mexico
November 9th, 1878

To Dr. Sheldon Jackson

Dear Bro.

Yours of the 22nd inst. received from Wingate a week ago when the Indians came with the lumber from Crane's; they agreed to go for twelve dollars, each (two wagons). When they came back, brought a bill for $21 dollars and wanted the $24 dollars besides – finally we got it settled and now we are good friends again. The large box at the Hospital I did not get yet. But the bale I got, containing the carpet and rugs. Mr. Crane said the organ was not to be moved until the new house was completed.

If I have three weeks of good weather yet I think I can get into the house. Have now decided to put roof on if I can complete the first story, and in case we decide to run it another in the spring, can easily remove the roof and the stone will not be many, for the wall will not be so thick. The first story I am building two feet thick or wide. All the masonry which is done, I think is pretty well put up. Of course it is not my trade, neither do I care to spend my precious time in this way, but I will not trust any traveling pretender who comes along hunting for work. We have to pay for those days of the men, not very hard work; then this house in which we now live leaks in many places. I do not care to live in it a day longer than necessary. Altogether have spent about two hundred dollars on the building, leaving out the well. By next Saturday a week from today all the doors and windows will be set in. About thirty-five more dollars will get enough stone in for the first story. The Indians want warm clothes for the winter. They do not care for beads and gold rings; very many of them ask for money. Perea and I went to Wingate and bought

House Dr. Ealy built in Zuni. Taylor and Mary Ealy standing in front of the house. Image from book.

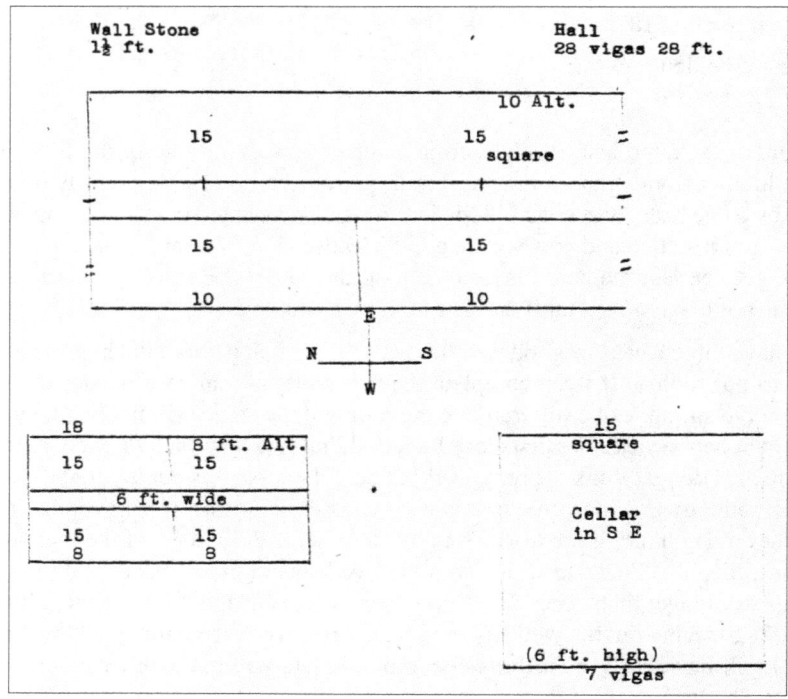

Drawing of plans for house at Zuni by Taylor Ealy. Image from book.

axle grease, muslin, sugar, etc. We did not go to Crane's, met him at the Fort. They have the steam saw mill running by this time.

I sent an order to the Board for $200.00. Will not forward another until I hear from that. We are all well, in good hopes of getting into the new house. Pedro Pino says two teachers will not be able to teach all the scholars when they all start. But when there isn't the room, we mean to rent our quarters for school if we can not get into the new (school) house; otherwise, I do not see how we can do any teaching. We pay 50 cents every week for rent of School House. Ought we to pay it?

The check for $51.75 I will need; send Nov. 12th more of the same kind. About twenty days more will see the wall of our house completed. Perea and I are both at it now. We got the men started a month ago today, and nearly a week of the time we lost going to the Fort and getting off the trails; each time I chop my wood before daylight and we have breakfast by sun up. Mrs. E. cooks and Susan (Miss G.) teaches. All have plenty to do and time rolls by rapidly.

Today the 12th, Burgess went to Albuquerque and sent your box by Pottinz; he was empty and said that he would charge two cents per pound. I will pay him when he returns: Told him to leave them at Banning's. Hope you got your fur robe. Sent it with Charley Bell of Anton Chico, said he would leave the box at Albuquerque Express Office. Mr. Perea would like for me to ask for the extension of his time. He (this is a secret) expects to be married to Miss Gates at Christmas. Then the winter will not be too severe for them to go off, and before that time I can not spare them.

As soon as spring opens some steps ought to be taken for a chapel: we have no place to meet. P. sends regards.

Respectfully and truly,
Your humble servant,

T. F. Ealy
Zuni, Pueblo, New Mexico
November 15, 1878

Dear Brother Jackson:

Your last letter of November 6th came through in short order as Mr. P. was at Bennett's when it arrived. They have a daily mail now. I am trying to get a mail route to Defiance from here. Your letter containing check for $364.55 came also. I am building by faith pretty much, depending upon the Lord to supply when necessary. We are pegging away at the wall. Tonight we got some help. Tomorrow two wagons haul stone. They come from the Mormon settlement. Brought 31 vigas [rafters]. I pay a dollar apiece. Some days it is a little cold. But so far we have not been hindered much.

Yours in Christ,
T. F. Ealy

This paper, taken from the "Rocky Mountain Presbyterian," describes a dance my father saw.

THE GREAT DANCE OF THE ZUNI
By Rev. T. F. Ealy

It began on Sabbath, November 15, and continued all Week. This is the Mas Major sacred dance, or best dance. Connected with it are a great many ceremonies which no one can ferret out unless he can talk the language. For the time everything is given up. It is a general relaxation to all the town. The scholars are not expected to go to school.

Seven distinct sets are dancing at the same time.

Today I saw perhaps one hundred women come into the placita with large baskets upon their heads filled with corn meal, bread, melons, etc. etc.; also several burros loaded with mutton. All these things were laid down at the feet of the dancers. I suppose to feed them.

Corn meal was sprinkled upon the dancers. The women and little girls would stand at the tops of ladders, waiting to sprinkle corn meal upon them as they passed up.

This evening I got there just in tine to see a very strange performance, as the performers were about to enter the "estufa" or room which is set apart for meetings of a sacred character. There are six of these in town: all of them are entered by ladders from the top. There are no doors in them. Before going down into this particular estufa, or sacred room, one at a time would go one corner of the housetop and stand as if in prayer. After a few minutes a men, painted all over, came up out of the room, walked silently towards him, and, with a feather in hand, touched him on the sides, at the same time making a noise like some little animal squealing when it is fast – a little louder than a mouse when it is held and pinched. Then the one would turn around twice and go to another corner. This was repeated at each corner.

Then the Cacique [Chief] came up out of the room, sprinkled meal upon the man, took a basket from his head filled with corn, melons, etc. This basket he passed down himself, when the man from whom he took the basket went to the front of the ladder, and as he stooped to put his hands upon the sides of the opening through which the ladder came, he was touched on the sides again by the painted man, still keeping behind him, and the same kind of nose was made. Then he swung his feet down upon one of the rounds of the ladder and passed out of sight. The man having the feathers also went down after each one. In the midst of all this two men came out of the room; one had a stick with a little fire on the end, and with a piece of shingle tied to a string made a noise like the wind blowing through a crevice. Then they went down off of the house and passed out of sight.

Going through all these ceremonies required a long time, and the spectators, one by one, tiring, went down ladders and off in different directions, so that I, almost alone, was left sitting in the moonlight, eager to see more of the Indian's strange religion.

Zuni, Pueblo, Valencia Co., New Mex.

Nov. 17. (Next entry) Moved partly to our new house; only two rooms finished. Mr. Perea and I did all the work. Stone house.

Father was too busy to write and so Mother took over.

Zuni Pueblo, New Mexico
November 18, 1878

Reverend Sheldon Jackson, D.D.

Dear Sir:

I have been wanting to write a few lines to thank you for the shawl. I think it very pretty.

Mr. Ealy and Mr. Perea are busy building and have no time for writing except in the evenings. The house is going up slowly. I would be so glad if we could get into it this winter.

To-day I have been trying to teach some of the little girls to sew, but find I have no sewing implements, such as needles and thimbles.

If you are sending anything soon, please send some needles, thimbles, knitting needles, etc. I will do all I can to instruct them in housework and sewing, while the others do the head teaching.

Mr. Ealy's idea was to have two stories, not three; eight rooms. He did not or does not think of finishing but one story now, just board up the windows and doors for some time perhaps a year or more till it is convenient to finish it. Do you think the plan a good one?

We are so anxious to get out of these damp rooms. We are suffering from colds and the weather is not very cold yet. The children are coughing very much. I am afraid it will injure them should we stay here long.

Mr. Perea and Miss Gates expect to be married Christmas (that is if the new house is finished).

The Indians are willing to work but expect to be well paid; they will not work for less than a dollar a day in trade. I can buy eggs, beans, dried peaches, etc. from them very reasonable in trade. If they ask more than I think right, I say "No care" and go to work and they pretty generally say "Go care" and hand them over at my price.

To-day the Indians had a new dance quite different in dress from any that we have seen. These dances are becoming almost every day occurrences. I am tired hearing them tattoo.

Pedro Pino calls Mr. Ealy and me his son and daughter. Calls in occasionally for coffee and tobacco.

Mr. Ealy will likely write you soon again. We hope our labors here may be blessed. Remember us and our work always in your prayers. With regards to Mrs. Jackson, I remain,

Respectfully yours,
Mrs. T. F. Ealy

Four other letters were written at this time.

Dr. Sheldon Clinton Jackson. Undated photo. Courtesy Montana Historical Society.

Zuni Pueblo, New Mexico
November 28, 1878

Dear Brother Jackson:

An Indian tells me he is going to the store tomorrow. Am glad they call and tell me when they go to Bennett's. This is the second one who called before going. It saves us a trip and they do not get much from us for going.

Thought you would like to have a line from us. The mornings now are quite cold but from 9 until 3 we can work very well on the stone work of the house. Two rooms will be ready for the vigas in five or six days if we can work – have an Indian at it. He lays the stone well but not fast. Have only had him two days. We get all the help from them we want at a dollar per day and pay them in goods; muslin and calico are called for every day. We were obliged to trade off all we had for our ceiling; candles, soap, a barrel of cheap molasses, I think would sell. Cheap woolen goods would sell well to make them pants. Some of them have hats on. Ready-made clothing, if it were cheap, would be a fine thing for them. John Wanamaker, Philadelphia would be the best place to buy ready made clothing. But we could not get them for this winter.

One hundred and fifty dollars (150) would do me until spring for building. We are all well. Have just had a letter from Mrs. Menaul. Told us of Mrs. Dr. Shield's death. Poor Doctor: I feel so sorry for him.

Mrs. Ealy had a letter from Mrs. Sec. Partridge.

Yours in Christ,
T. F. Ealy

Fort Wingate, Yew Mexico
December, 1878

To Doctor Sheldon Jackson:

Dear Brother:

Mr. Perea and I have come to get the organ. Are this far on our return – were last night at Mr. Crane's; found them pretty well. Will now take the box from the hospital. And the bale which you have had sent from Denver. Mr. Crane sent it up to the Post not knowing that I would be down there. Mr. Perea will help me another month if the weather is not too inclement. We want to get the other two rooms up. He was married to Miss Susan E. Gates on Christmas Day in presence of Mrs. Ealy, two Indian women and three Indian men in the new house, which Mr. Perea and I built with our own hands.

I owe Mr. Perea eighty-five dollars which he loaned me to pay a bill on the house. He will want to go back to Vegas next month and asks me to pay him then if I can. He has been working for the mission – so has Mrs. P. Neither of them has paid me any boarding nor has a word been said about that matter. I know you have enough to look after. As I am trading goods to the Indians perhaps I am subject to a fine if no license is taken out. I do not know.

Do you think I ought to buy their wood in the Spring?

Your brother in Christ,
T. F. Ealy

Is Mr. Perea to pay any board or is he to be allowed $20 per month which you promised Vargas? He is helping me to do a great deal of work at the house. In a couple of days we will raise the vigas on two rooms.

Dec. 9th. The vigas are on two rooms. We expect to move Monday next (16th). The nights are quite cool now. We did not alter Pino's house any. I thought it would not pay if we moved. Have an opportunity to send this to Wingate. Good night. A happy Christmas.

T. F. Ealy

Zuni Pueblo, December 20, 1878

Dear Mr., Jackson:

We are now living in our new house; will send you a sketch taken from in front of Pedro Pino's house by Perea. We feel better than living in the old dark rooms. Think I will rent the front room of Pino's house for school if he will not charge too much. He seemed very sorry to have us go from his house; calls us his children. Or house is warmer than upon the hills in town. The bluff behind the house two miles off shelters us from the Northers. The wood is very costly. They do not want to bring a burro load for less than a dollar. I will begin teaching January 2. We are all well and happy.

Yours in Christ,
T. F. Ealy

The lumber is nearly all used up. More will be needed.

Zuni Pueblo, New Mexico
December 3, 1878

Reverend Doctor Jackson

Dear Brother:

Today Zuni is full of visitors; Navajos; a great many, Isletas, a great many; Lagunas two; San Philipas several; Moquis six.

Tomorrow the big feast begins; will last four days. Zunis have made great preparations to entertain them.

Just now I have been interrupted. The Governor, Cacique (King) Pedro Pino, Alcade and others came in and sat quiet for a little time. I wrote on until Pedro spoke. They wanted to order Perea out of town for ten days. I objected; then they consented to allow him to remain shut up in the house. We consented to that. One good thing, a new Governor

Pedro Pino. Photo by John Karl Hillers, 1879. Courtesy Smithsonian Institution.

is to be appointed at Christmas [Patricio Pino, Pedro Pino's son]. Perhaps I will have a voice in that. I told them that Americans never shut up any man unless he has committed some crime. After that [Patricio] Pino withdrew by shaking hands. He had the most reason about him of any of them. Believe he will be the next Governor if I have any voice in it.

We have no trouble in getting Indians to work, but some complain that the other teacher paid in money but I do not, only in "good."

Dec. 5. Last night Mrs. E. and I went to see the minstrels or something. They danced, buried feathers, recited something like a creed; had an alter with pictures of sun, moon, stars, wolf, etc., etc. Six houses of the rich men are open to visits and have "muchas cosas" to look at, but I have neither the time nor am I willing to lose sleep at night running about sight seeing. Am so tired when night comes that a little writing – a short Spanish lesson, and some wood chopping are all that I can get done before bedtime.

Dec. 23. Building a wall at house.

Dec. 24. 20 miles to the P. O. Got mail tonight – 11 letters, some papers and things for Christmas from friends in the East.

Dec. 25. J. Y. Perea and Miss Susan Gates married. Two Indian women and four men present. 3 o'clock. Coffee and sugar for the Indians.

This note concerning Mr. Perea appeared in the October 1880 "Rocky Mountain Presbyterian."

"Fr. José Ynes Perea, a Mexican licentiate, was ordained to the full work of an evangelist by the Presbytery of Santa Fe at its recent meeting. Mr. Perea has had an eventful history. His father's family was the richest and most aristocratic in New Mexico. At an early age he was sent East to the School of Rev. Dr. Pingry, where he early imbibed Protestant views. Upon returning home he signalized his Protestantism by breaking the images in his father's house, for which he received a sound whipping. Upon the close of his school life he had become so profound a Protestant that he was not allowed to return to New Mexico and became an exile and wanderer for sixteen years. During this time he visited the principal seaports of Europe and Asia, and resided for a time in California.

After his return to New Mexico he was for several years a shepherd, with little companionship but his Bible and God. It was thus he was found waiting for the first Presbyterian missionaries that went to New Mexico. For several years past he has been doing a good work as licentiate evangelist and is now advanced to the full work of the ministry, the first from among the Mexicans of New Mexico."

Snow came in abundance on Christmas Day and that same night, but some of it melted the next day because of a warm sun. Father started for Ft. Wingate via Savoya on December 26 where he stayed all night with Bishop Teeny, a Mormon. December 26 he was ready to resume his journey to the Fort, which he reached at 4:00 P.M.; however, he did not stop there but went on to [William] Crane's at Bacon Springs. His purpose was to secure his organ. The next day he went to Ft. Wingate on his way home. There he stayed all night.

By December 30 he was able to leave for Zuni. Having reached Nutria [Las Nutrias, "the otters," a Zuni pueblo] 18 miles away with great difficulty on account of the snow, he camped in an old Indian house into which he had to go by the roof. The next morning at daybreak, tired after an almost sleepless night, he was ready to go the last eighteen miles to Zuni, happy indeed to arrive home once more.

José Ynes Perea. 1909 Photo. Courtesy Presbyterian Historical Society, Philadelphia, PA.

You can see from the entries in Father's diary how hard the life of a preacher was in those days. If one reads between the lines, one wonders how it was possible for him to carry on and for a young wife with two children to endure the lack of any sort of comforts and to keep up her spirit when separated from her young husband, as seemed frequently necessary. It amazed me in reading for the first time the diary, to learn how frequently Father had to fight sickness as well as other hardships of all sorts. He had gone out to spread the good news of the gospel and tried to keep anything from deterring him from carrying out that worthy aim. Rarely, though, one finds any note of discouragement in anything he says. It is no wonder that his life ended at 66 years.

By the end of the first year my parents were becoming accustomed to the strangeness of their lives in the Indian village. By this time, too, they were used to a school which numbered possibly 40 one day and 8 the next. They had learned somewhat the extent to which the dances pervaded the lives of their scholars and indeed the whole town. Father often talked with Pedro Pino about their customs and religion. The letter was quite frank with him and tried hard to make him understand their beliefs; and Father tried, in spite of his strict Puritan training to grasp the way the Indians looked at their religion. He had a great respect for Pedro Pino and he in his turn tried to get the Christian's points of view. He asked Father to read to him from the Bible at every opportunity he had. One day he said that he should like to have the young people of the town learn the Christian ideas but that he himself was too old to change.

Another matter that Father and Mother had to learn was that no matter how inconvenient it was, they must entertain all who came and asked for their hospitality. It had a good side, for in this way they met many of note and were brought into touch with matters of outside importance. Otherwise, they might have led too restricted a life.

Fort Wingate, NM. 1873 photo by T. H. O'Sullivan. Courtesy Library of Congress.

Chapter 4 | Second Year

A Christmas gift of a diary from Mother the last of 1878 seemed to put into Father the desire to continue his account of the daily happenings in his life. The necessity of building a home and of starting his work in a new field had kept him busy all fall so that it wasn't until January 19th that the first entry appears and this one is spread over three days.

Jan. 10, 20, 21. [1879] Zuni, N. Mex. Mr. Abraham L. Earle of New York[1] visited us to examine the progress of the Zuni Indians, and expressed himself much pleased with the result. He had been sent to report to Congress on all the various Indians; a report which is to be made to the Indian bureau since Congress is about to take a vote on whether or not to transfer all Indians to the War Department. Uncle Rush Clark is a member of Congress and I have written to him about the transfer. I am opposed to it.

Jan. 26. Zuni, New Mexico. One year ago we left Schellsburg, Pa. Here we live in a large city of Indians. Have two schools, one for boys, and one for girls.

The year just past had offered many new experiences to both my parents. They had endured the hardship of travel without modern conveniences, a civil war, which was the result of a feud, a transfer to a new and extremely strange field, and an introduction to a people with odd customs and language. Father at once began to study the Indian language, which at that time was not a written one.

Mail time is always an exciting and interesting time. A person is always expecting something unusual, something new. Then how much more provocative the coming of the mail must have been to those people living in an isolated mission station with no means of communicating with the outside world except by letter. 'Then someone brought the mail, for its delivery was dependent upon the good graces of any person who happened to come through Ft. Wingate, the expectancy was heightened. Each day might bring a letter or many of them.

At first there was not ever a stage route through the village, but the time came when mail was brought by stage each day. The route started at Ft. Wingate and went into Arizona to St. John's. It was not en easy trip to or from the Fort, for a mountain barred the way; the roads too were merely trails at first. Father spoke more than once of having missed the trail, but with the coming of the stage the roads were widened and the trip was not so harassing.

The coming of the stage had another effect in that many more people now came to the village or passed through it on their way some place.

Jan. 29. Mail. The Indians have agreed to carry my mail, 25 miles to the P.O., without charge. A letter from Sheldon Jackson and a check for $150 toward the house.

Jan. 30. Snow last night – very windy. Wrote to R. J. Hamilton in Anton Chico; to Dr. J. V. Launderdale, Genesee, N. Y.; and to B. M. Thomas, Indian Agent.

Jan. 31. Breakfast before daylight. Brought a load of stone before school. Average attendance at school; boys 20; girls 14. Number on roll 85 boys, 25 girls.

Two views of Zuni Pueblo. Photos by John Karl Hillers, 1879. Courtesy National Anthropological Archives, Smithsonian Institution.

Feb. 1. Perea and I hauled three loads of stone with his horses and my wagon. Wrote to Dr. J. to acknowledge receipt of check.

Zuni Pueblo, New Mexico
Feb. 1st, 1879

Dr. S. Jackson,

Dear Sir:

Your letter of 7th ult. is just rec'd., containing ck. for One Hundred and Fifty Dollars. It came on at the right time. If you are coming to Zuni perhaps I had just as well wait until you come, before I expend anything more than this which I have.

We will not teach another winter unless better rooms are furnished for the schools. Our average for boys this month (Jan.) is 30 and for girls 14. 85 boys on my roll. 25 girls on Mrs. Ealy's roll. Mr. and Mrs. Perea start for James on Monday (Feb. 3).

We need an assistant teacher. Mr. A. L. Earle has been here to visit the Zunis and is visiting, at the Pueblos. His address is care of Mr. E. S. Harras, 177 Broadway, N. Y. Enclosed please find an order on the Board for $31.37. This is the bill for the groceries which you had forwarded here for yourself. Everything was counted carefully at your own price and this is what it all amounted to; several things on the list were not in the boxes when we came.

We are well. The Indians have agreed to go for my mail once a week without charge.

Yours truly,
T. F. Ealy

Feb. 2. Held S. S. in Pedro Pino's House – 8 boys and 4 girls present. In evening read 2nd chapter of Genesis to adults. Pino said I should not miss a day reading to him. (Pedro Pino was the former governor of Zuni.)

Feb. 3. Bro. and. Mrs. Perea left for [St.] James. Mrs. E. moved her school to our house. School in the parsonage.

How delighted Mother must have been to be able to move her school to the parsonage! Enough of the house was now completed for her to have a room for her classes. She surely must have been relieved to have her school close at hand when she finished the house work, for she had to take two small children with her wherever she went. She also found it exceedingly difficult, I am sure, to go over to the town each day to hold classes. Possibly when she returned she would find someone there for a meal or to stay overnight.

Feb. 4. Very cold. High wind and snow. Bennett and Burgess came to Zuni. Brought our mail and a check from Gov. Sent it to the bank. Also brought one letter from home and one from Waterford. Albert (Brother) preparing to go to Dayton.

Feb. 5. Cold – snow on the Ground. Not many scholars. The Indians do not furnish enough wood to keep this house warm.

Feb. 6. Dance in Zuni – Navajos taking part. Mr. Perea came back from Savoya. His horse not able to travel – expects to start on Monday 10th.

February was occupied with pushing the work on the house with all speed possible. After school and on Saturday Father worked at the wall of the house. On February 12 a man was secured to dig at the foundation; Father worked all his spare time. On Saturday February 15, he was able to work all day. The Indians kept running in and out of the house until his patience was about exhausted. He needed more stones but found it hard to get them. Wood too was scarce and the weather cold.

During this month the Indians kept up their dancing. February 9, was the fourth day. On February 10 and 11 the dance continued. Then there were 51 in the dance. The fact that Pedro Pino was one of them amazed Father greatly. He not yet had come wholly to the realization that the Indian dances form a part of all their life. The fact that Pedro Pino was so interested in the Bible made Father feel that he would no longer care for the Indian ceremonies. He soon learned how strong a hold the dances have on the people. By February 12, with most of the dance over for the present, the pupils returned.

It was also during this month that rather began to work on his sermon for Presbytery in August, since he was moderator. He also reports that at noon on February 15 an American came to feed his horse. He had set a hen on February 7; not superstitious at all, for he set her on thirteen eggs.

In his account of religious work for 1879, Father reports on January 26 the Sunday School convened with 40 scholars; 32 boys, 8 girls: and 4 teachers. The songs were "There is a happy land," of which the pupils could sing one verse, and "Shall we gather at the River." That same evening Mr. Perea read the first chapter of Genesis in Spanish; Pedro Pino interpreted it to the Indians. There were 12 men present.

In February he had Sunday School at 11:00 A.M. and preaching at 7:00 P.M. On the 9th two Navajos were present. This was unusual. At this time only 8 Zunis came. At the service in the morning Father kept to the Bible story of Genesis. By this time he was able to read from the Spanish Bible. Pedro Pino interpreted what he read to the Indians. On February 16 he met the chief men in Pedro Pino's house.

Feb. 17. Feast among the Indians. Not many scholars at school. Cool last night. Quite a number of Navajos called on us today.

Feb. 18. Indians dancing – not many boys and girls in school. Worked on the wall. We are looking for the call.

Feb. 19. Mail came. I am appointed postmaster of Zuni. Received Anna and Elrood's photograph (sister and brother-in-law). A letter from Mother. Held a meeting with the Indians about going to Santa Fe.

Feb. 20. Bishop [Samuel B.] Tenney and wife came to see us or rather stopped on the route to see someone else.

Feb. 21. Wrote two letters. Mrs. E. teaches through the day and bakes at night. We are doing all we can for the Indians under the circumstances.

Feb. 22. Taught part of the day. The pupils form the habit of coming to school and do not understand "no school Saturday."

Feb. 23. Sabbath. Bishop Tenney and wife returned on their way home. We walked over to town to see the men, women and children dancing.

Feb. 24. Read every Sabbath after dark to as many men as I can get into my room. Started by trail to Ft. Wingate. Lost my way; rode all day, returned in evening.

The roads during the time Father was in New Mexico were largely non-existent. You note hat he speaks of riding the trail to Ft. Wingate and of becoming lost. However, each year he remained in the Territory many of the trails were widened to roads but at the beginning it was difficult for him to get around. By the time he left there was a regular stage coach connecting many of the towns and the railroad had come into the Territory.

One realizes that it was only after dark that he could get the men to be present at his services.

Feb. 25. Quite tired. Taught. Dancing in town. Many men take very little interest in school. Girls are learning. We are all fairly well.

Note the type of life Father and Mother led; while monotonous, was an extremely busy one.

Zuni, New Mexico
Feb. 25, 1879

Dr. Jackson

Dear Bro:

The bundle of clothes which you sent or caused to be sent to us from Denver we have not yet received. I went to Mr. [William] Crane's in regard to it and he said he had sent it to the Fort in care of one of the officers and while in the Fort I had a good deal of business. When we got partly up the mountain, I thought of it but could not go back. We ought to have had it for there were some very cold days. Our feet were frozen a little. I will go to the Fort in two days and will look after it.

Yours truly,
T. F. Ealy

Feb. 26. Taught today over 20 boys. Tomorrow another dance. I expect to go to Ft. Wingate.

Feb. 27. Left home for Ft. Wingate – got in before sundown. Read my mail and bought all I wanted from the store.

Zuni Pueblo
Feb. 27, 1879

Dear Dr. Jackson:

You talked of coming out to Zuni in the Spring. Did not designate the time. Do come. We are now alone, Mr. and Mrs. Perea having left for James two weeks ago. We will be glad when our assistant teacher comes. I am obliged to be away sometime; then it is very unpleasant to leave Mrs. Ealy alone.

Mrs. Perea was not paid anything while teaching, consequently we got nothing for board. She taught two months.

I am appointed Post Master in Zuni, Valencia Co, New Mexico. This is good news to us to think we are to have a post office.

T. F. Ealy

Feb. 28. Ft. Wingate, N. Mex. Went to Mr. Crane's [at Bacon Springs] 12 miles and returned. Went to the Hospital to a concert given by the brass band. Met Col. [Peter T.] Swaine and Lady.

This article taken from the "Home Mission Magazine" of the Presbyterian Church explains the statement by Father that he brought from Ft. Wingate needles, thread, and quilt patches.

"Mrs. Ealy writes from Zuni: I have been trying to teach some of the girls how to sew, but find I need more needles, thimbles, thread, patches, etc. Can you not find some missionary society which will be willing to send me some? If any society would furnish me with a sewing machine and the material I could make clothes for the needy, naked school children. Address, Mrs. T. F. Ealy, care of Messrs. Bennett and Peters, Ft. Wingate, N. Mexico."

March 3. Read to Pedro Pino in the evening about the bow in the cloud. Taught some of the pupils as they dropped in. Our little Ruth got full of lice from the Indians.

He was amazed to find his school room had been preempted by a trader [Douglas D. Graham] without his consent. He had been holding his school in Pedro Pino's house.

When Father found that his school room had been rented to a trader, he suddenly decided that he would teach at home. There on March 4 he had twenty boys to teach and in one corner of the room six little chickens, which had to be kept warm. It must have been interesting to hear the cheeps of the chickens in the midst of a lesson in combined English, Spanish, and Indian. In the report for February, which was made out on the same day, he found the average attendance was 20 boys and 14 girls.

The next day he spent the time in hauling five loads of stone and in getting his mail ready to send; among other letters he sent his salary to Fort Wingate.

By March 6 the weather had become warm enough for him to plow his lot and sow wheat. That same day he met three Moquis [Hopis], who attended a council which he had called the following day. It concerned some horses which the Zunis claimed the Moquis had taken. Father reported that the Moquis chief hugged him and Mother good before leaving. Evidently the result of the conference pleased the chief greatly.

March 8 was so windy and cold that Father could not do any work outside; therefore he spent most of the day in reading about diseases of the eye. Meanwhile the Indians began another dance which they kept up for five days.

March 9 (Sabbath) the folks spent a quiet day at home. Very few called, although some Navajos came to trade. Father told them that he did not trade on Sabbath. He read as usual to Pedro Pino from the Bible. He also wrote a short note to Dr. Jackson thanking him for the bundle that was sent to them from Denver because he did not know who sent it; he asked Dr. Jackson to thank the people. In this note he proposed the name of Miss Jennie [M.] Hammaker [his wife's cousin] of Schellsburg, Pa. for the vacancy for assistant teacher.

The next day, which was comparatively mild, he spent at washing walls, teaching, and planting cuttings of alamos or cottonwood trees. The following day he worked at the wall and taught from breakfast until dark.

Grinding grain at Zuni. "Zuni Breadstuff," by Frank Hamilton Cushing, 1920.

March 12. Got load of lumber and goods from Ft. Wingate by Tenney and George, the Laguna Indian. Up late – very tired.

The Indian agent had instructed Father to keep some things to sell to the Indians. On March 13 his diary records that he sold 17 hoes. That day he speaks of having 18 pupils in his classes and Mother's having 7 girls in addition. That number made up a fair-sized school. He was also made happy by a picture of his brother Albert and his wife Effie. It seemed to bring them closer.

As dancing was going on in the town, most pupils came in early on the 14th and then left early. That gave Father a chance to work at the wall almost to the point of exhaustion. You may be sure all went to bed early. The next day he was busy again and even was able to secure an Indian to work at the wall. Though Saturday, the Indians kept coming around and bothered the workers. That day among other duties Father packed a box of pottery for Mr. B. M. Leonard.

By keeping up assiduously his study of Spanish Father was able by March 16 to read the second Chapter of Matthew in Spanish. Pedro Pino did the translating into Indian. It is this same chapter which Father has left in the Indian language. I think he hoped in time to put the whole Bible into Indian, at least the Testament. I have in Father's handwriting the above chapter.

March 17. I pushed one Indian in the door head first and one out of the door. Worked at wall when not teaching. Indian mason.

March 18. Unusually busy. Tomorrow nearly all the Indians expect to go out to sow wheat. Indian working at well.

March 19. Up an hour before the sun. The wind blew very hard. Our house is drifted all around with sand. My Indian mason worked until noon.

The wind was so bad that the Indians were kept from starting out to sow wheat, but by March 23 they had practically all gone to their summer town and the folks at the mission were left practically alone. The weather was cloudy and cold. The day before Father had sacked four costals [costales – sacks in Spanish] or burley bags of wool, for he had a large number of skins and some wool to sale. He had secured some help from the Indians who were given their supper for working. On March 25 he sacked two costals.

As a result of his having no teaching to do Father was able to spend long hours at work on the house. He now put into the house the windows on the west side. Needing some stone because the well was not entirely finished, he went to the quarry on March 28 and hauled five loads and the next day six. On his last trip he was unfortunate enough to pull off one of his finger nails. Samuel Tenney now came to haul stones, for Father's sore finger kept him from working. Samuel Tinny hauled six loads one day and five loads for two days. By this time there were enough stones for them to finish the work on hand for the present.

George, a Laguna Indian who was helping with the masonry narrowly escaped being killed by an ox which belonged to Samuel Tenney. Father killed the ox. Mother was not at all well.

Since the Indians were away dong their spring sowing, Father did not hold religious services on March 30.

March 31. Started for Ft. Wingate very late. Got in after dark.

Apr. 1. Left Wingate for Crane's [at Bacon Springs] and returned after dark. Wrote 3 letters.

Apr. 2. Left the Fort at 3 A.M. for Zuni. Got home a little after sundown. At Nutria found the Zunis and Navajos jangling.

Apr. 3. Worked at wall; two Indians at corral.

Apr. 4. Worked at wall. Very windy. Two Indians working at corral wall. Young men here all night. Saw Tenney here.

Apr. 5. Dr. [Walter] Reed and family from Camp Apache all night. Very stormy. Could not work much.

Apr. 6. Dr. Reed and family left this morning. The wind blew hard all day. We held no services as it was vacation.

Apr. 7. School vacation is over. It was very short and we needed a longer one very much. Sam B. Tenney came to build wall. High wind.

All the rest of April Father's diary is full of references to work on the wall of the house and to teaching. He kept pressing the building with great vigor. He also had some people working on the corral. One day he had only two pupils, one of them came to work at the corral. On the 10th of April, at noon, he left eight men to work on the corral and rode 10 miles below Ojo Caliente ["Hot Springs," a Zuni pueblo] on some business and then back to the town, where he stayed all night. When he came back to Zuni he found only three men at work. The weather was extremely cold with snow. Most of the Indians were out of town sowing wheat. By April 14 the snow had ceased and rain had come.

One diversion came the next day when Lieutenant Stafford from Ft. Wingate sent word that he wanted Father to go over to the Fort. On April 18, though the weather was cold and snow had begun again, Father started for Ft. Wingate and reached there early. He was entertained by Lieutenant Stafford, who wished Father to marry him and Miss Alice M. Smith of Lockport, New York. He performed the ceremony at 2:00 PM the next evening. Meanwhile, in the morning he had gone over to see his friends the Cranes at Bacon Springs.

On April 18 Father left for Zuni in a buckboard which was drawn by four mules. He reached his home and family an hour before sundown. He found all well. As he had brought some mail, he and Mother sat down to answer some of the letters at once in order to send them back to Ft. Wingate with the driver.

During Father's absence the Indians had stopped work on the corral. The cold weather and their need to sow wheat and corn stopped them.

Apr. 19. Worked and taught. High wind part of the day. A man here all night – carpenter. I'll try to have him stay awhile and work.

Apr. 20. Sabbath. No services. Sam Tenney and the carpenter here all night. The highest wind I ever have seen in New Mexico, Zuni Pueblo.

Apr. 21. High wind and very cold. My wall is drifted two ft. deep with sand. Carpenter did not do any work – too cold. Gave him a dose of pills. Perea from Bernacia called.

Apr. 22. Cold. Carpenter covered the well. Put on three vigas (rafters).

Apr. 23. Burgess passed – home from Albuquerque. Brought some tools from Tenney's for me.

Apr. 24. Mrs. E. bathed Ruth – not well. I taught, built wall, and helped on the house. Carpenter at work.

Apr. 25. Carpenter at work. Ruth about the same – summer complaint. I taught and laid up wall.

Apr. 26. Indians planting corn. Not many came to school. Carpenter at work. I worked some at the wall. Ruthie about the same. Pearl is well.

Apr. 29. Got an Indian to haul stone. Went with him one load. Carpenter at work. I heard several boys their lessons. Indian hauled two loads.

Apr. 29. Indian hauled six loads of stone. Carpenter at work. I worked at wall a half day. Sacked some wool and rolled it out for shipment.

Apr. 30. Indians hauled three loads of stone. Indian mason at work on the wall. I worked hard laying up rock. Carpenter at work.

May 1. Sent off my freight this evening. Worked all day at the wall. Feel unwell. Col. Compton passed; will be back on the 11th. Carpenter today.

Sometimes Father speaks of sacking wool in burlap bags, which he calls costals [costales]. This was done at the suggestion of the Indian Agent. On April 29 he spoke of sacking some wool and here he speaks of sending off his freight. This wool was put into his schoolroom, which he still kept in the town, and sometimes he was almost suffocated with the wool, especially if many students elected to attend school the day the wool almost filled the room.

May 2. Wind very high. I worked all day on wall. Mrs. Ealy baked, taught school, and not well at the same time. Carpenter sick. Baby well.

May 3. Worked at wall. Carpenter at work. Expect the mail today. Patricio Pino (the son of Pedro Pino) building a house at Piscato.

May 4. Read three chapters of Matthew in Spanish. We have no place yet for S. S. or preaching.

May 5. Put up the vigas (rafters) on the west wide of the house. Carpenter at work.

May 6. Did not work at the house. Helped Mrs. E. – she is not well. Carpenter half day. Saw 100 or more Zunis on horseback. Dancing in town. Planting corn and melons.

May 7. Tenney came back from Ft. Wingate with lumber and goods. Carpenter at work – roofed the west side rooms. Coffee 12 cents per lb. in the East. Got large mail.

May 8. Planted some garden on the west side of the house in the rear; lettuce, cabbage, peas, tomatoes, melons, and one pumpkin. Carpenter at work.

May 9. Carpenter laid floor in west side of house. One side of the corral is up. Sam and Ammon Tenney working. I am putting on the tar paper and mud for roof over-boards.

May 10. Very windy. Col. Compton, wife and Dr. Reid [Reed] arrived enroute to Apache. Carpenter stopped work after dinner.

May 11. Very windy. Jenkins here. Did not read to Pino tonight—expect to tomorrow.

May 12. An officer arrived from Ft. Wingate with a subpoena for Mrs. E. and me on the Col. [Nathan A. M.] Dudley trial impending in Ft. Stanton. [They were wanted as witnesses for the prosecution.]

Father refused to allow Mother to accompany him on a trip as tiresome as the one to Ft. Stanton as he knew would prove to be. On the other hand, he was not satisfied to leave her and the children at Zuni all alone. He knew the Indians of the town were friendly, but he was affected in his decision by the fact that Mother was far from well; that some other Indians were to pass and take the opportunity to annoy an unguarded woman; that he might be gone for some time; and that the house was not directly in the town. Therefore, when he left Zuni on May 13 in answer to the summons, he had with him his wife and children. It was May 15 before he set out for Ft. Stanton. It took eleven days to reach the Fort. The account of his trip is recorded in his diary. It was June 2 before he was through with his testimony and was able to set out for home.

May 13. Left Zuni and reached Ft. Wingate two hours before sundown. Mrs. Ealy not well all day; ate neither dinner nor supper. I do not think under any circumstances she should go on so long a journey.

May 14. Left Wingate in morning – stopped over night at Bacon Springs. Mrs. Ealy and two babies along.

May 15. Went up to the Fort with Mr. Crane. Contracts taken today. Left Fort at 1 P.M. Drove 24 miles: Lieut. Major Jewett and I. Left Mrs. Ealy and babies at Crane's [at Bacon Springs].

May 16. San Antonio – 24 miles from Ft. Wingate. Got to San Mateo a little after noon.

May 17. Got to Rio Puerco at 3 P.M. 64 miles from San Mateo. Clark forage agent.

May 18. Sabbath. Got to San Ysedro at 12:15 P.M. 22 miles. Rode up to see Dr. Shield at James 3 miles. Took tea with him. Came back at dusk.

May 19. Left San Ysidro early and got to the Rio Grande at noon. I am writing this on an island in the River while the ambulance waits for the ferry. 2 ½ hours getting over. Drove 22 miles.

May 20. 26 miles to Santa Fe. Got in at 2:30 A.M. Stopped at the Exchange [Hotel]. $3 per day. After dinner changed to the Presbyterian parsonage. Mr. Smith at Saratoga, N.Y.

Then Dr. Jackson wrote to Father about the proposed change in the time of Presbytery, Mother answered the letter because Father was away.

Bacon Springs, New Mexico
May 20, 1879

Reverend Sheldon Jackson
Denver, Colorado

Dear Sir:

I presume Mr. Ealy will have no objection to having Presbytery meet in October instead of August as he does not expect to attend.

Mr. Ealy and I were subpoenaed by U.S. Court now convened at Fort Stanton as witnesses to some of the murders while we were in Lincoln County.

Very respectfully,
Mrs. T. F. Ealy

May 21. Santa Fe, N. Mex. Gov. Wallace just returned from Lincoln County. Met him. (Gov. Lew Wallace is best known for his book, Ben Hur.) Gen. Hatch returned. Am entertained at Mrs. Sharon's.

Santa Fe, N.M.
May 21, 1879

Dr. Sheldon Jackson

Dear Brother:

I am in Santa Fe on my way to Ft. Stanton. Am subpoenaed to the Court now. Session there. Mrs. Ealy was also called, but I did not get her farther then Mr. Crane's at

Bacon Springs. Her questions will be given her by the Commander, Col. Swaine of Fort Wingate.

I start for Stanton tomorrow in a government ambulance. Whether my life is in danger I do not know. I would rather a thousand times not go.

We left our house in charge of Mr. Raher Dawson, a carpenter from Ft. Scott [Texas]. He is a very good workman. I am having him do a lot of work on the house; such as flooring, putting in partitions, etc. If only arrangements were made to build a chapel, he would take the contract. I think the Lord sent him ahead to be of service to us. Do try to give me some idea of what is the prospect of a chapel, if any, as I can secure his services.

Think he would take a contract or work by the day for $2.50 and board. In order to get my house at all comfortable and fenced I will be out about $500. Dr. Reid [Reed] who passed through from Apache said it was as good a house as any from Apache to Santa Fe and had better windows than any, Apache not excepted. I have a large corral fenced in and the fence around the front is now going up. Saw Dr. Shield at James; he needs a housekeeper; next thing you hear there will be a sick man there.

I cannot write for the Rocky Mountain until vacation; think I will now write to Miss Hammaker to meet me on my return from Stanton. We need her.

Your obedient Servant,
T. F. Ealy

Mr. Fulton speaks of a great amount of material that has come to light in the papers of Gen. Lew Wallace, who supplanted Axtell as governor of New Mexico. He was not yet governor when Father was at Lincoln though he was still in New Mexico. The papers contain some letters from Bonney (Billy the Kid) which show him an intelligent person.

An interesting recent fictionized biography of Billy the Kid is that of Edwin Corle.[2]

May 22. Left Galestio 26 miles from Santa Fe early for Perdenal [Cerro Pedernal] on my way to Stanton. Lieut. [Samuel S.] Pague along.

May 23. Perdenal 50 miles. Dave Montgomery keeps ranch.

May 24. Left Perdenal – reached Alkali Holes 3 P.M. Saw lots of antelope about 40 miles.

May 25. Sabbath. Left Alkali Holes soon after sun-up. Reached Jickorria [Jicarilla], Jenny Hoerade keeps ranch 48 miles.

May 26. Left Jickorria [Jicarrilla] at 5 P.M. for Stanton. Arrived at Fort Stanton at 1:30 A.M. Took dinner at Dowlin's.

May 27. Ft. Stanton awaiting to be called up in court. Met a number of persons from Lincoln.

May 28. Judge Leonard and Judge [Henry] L. Waldo are the two attorneys employed in the Dudley trial. Hon. Ira E. Leonard.

May 29. Nothing to do but wait. The Sheriff arrested two men and upon Judge Waldo's reading the law to him released them.

May 30. Friday. Was not called up today. Wrote to Mr. Earle, 177 Broadway, N. Y.

May 31. Saturday. Not yet called and perhaps will not be called at all. Mr. Roberts is teaching in the school at Lincoln.

June 1. Sabbath. Last night Geo. Washington accidentally shot his wife and child.[3] There is not much Sabbath in Ft. Stanton or Lincoln.

June 2. Monday. Applied this morning, to Col. G. A. Purington for transportation. My organ is at Carson's ranch 30 miles northwest of Lincoln. I was before the court from 1 to 4 P.M. [According to the official court records, Taylor asked to amend his June 2 testimony and did so the next morning, June 3. See Appendix A.]

Father gave the following account of the trial. (If the part he didn't hear was as much of a farce as his part, it is no wonder that Lieutenant Colonel Dudley was acquitted.)

"A government ambulance and an officer, Lieut. Prague of Ft. Wingate, suddenly appeared at Zuni Pueblo, where I was at work and subpoenaed me and took me along to Ft. Stanton. Mrs. Ealy and the children were left behind at Bacon Springs. Both Mrs. Ealy and Mrs. Perea (Susan Gates) would have been splendid witnesses. Mrs. Ealy was ill and Susan was not asked to go."

"We were days getting there. When we arrived at Ft. Stanton I was shown to a room by Major Dowlin. This room contained two beds with a table in the center, on which were three revolvers. I did not set down my grip but walked in one door and out the other. I hunted up Ben Ellis, whose wound in the neck I had sewed up when I lived at Lincoln. He and Judge Leonard roomed together; I told them I would not room with men armed to the teeth but if they would share their room I would gladly sleep on the floor. They consented and I felt safe." [4]

"When I was sworn in, I was asked to tell the truth, the whole truth and nothing but the truth. Dudley sat in front of me when I was to testify and sat with his thumbs in his vest armholes as he looked me directly in the eyes. Judge Waldo his lawyer, said, "You were a missionary to Lincoln; were you?"

"Ans. 'Yes, sir.'"

"Judge Waldo, 'Don't you know where the Bible speaks of ingratitude, sharper than a serpent's fang?'"

"Ans. 'The Bible does not say that. You are quoting from a Book with which you are not familiar.'"

"Waldo, 'That will do sir!'" [See Appendix A for Ealy's testimony.]

"I was dismissed, I was informed when I went to the ambulance that the seat I occupied coming would be given to another. It was intended that I be left over 400 miles from Zuni so that I would be killed before I got out of the country. I ran from the court to dinner and caught the buckboard starting to Roswell, 80 miles east. I told the driver I wanted to go along. He said, 'I am too full to take you today but will tomorrow.' I replied, 'You take off that quarter of beef. I must leave today and will go along. I have a wife and children among the Indians.'" So I left Ft. Stanton and the farcical trial."

"I got off so quickly that no one saw me go or even suspected that I would do what I did. I rode day and night to get around to Santa Fe. The ambulance which left Ft. Stanton reached Santa Fe at the same time I did and Lieut. Prague, ,who came on it, said 'Why!

Top: A Zuni cornfield with its scarecrows. Bottom: Detail showing shelter in corn field. "Zuni Breadstuff," by Frank Hamilton Cushing, 1920.

where did you come from?' The day end night trip as so hard on me that when I had a chance to relax I slept so soundly that it was with difficulty that I was awakened by the driver to eat and be ready to go on. I really seemed to die and come alive again."

"I left the buckboard at Las Vegas and met the stage there with Miss Hammaker and two ladies. Miss Hammaker was going to Zuni to assist us and the other two ladies to the Mission at James to reinforce it."

"Mr. and Mrs. Crane at Bacon Springs were unusually kind to me as to everybody else. There I was reunited with my wife, who was much better, and my family. We drove back to Zuni. You can image there was a glad and thankful and tired man when I reached my home in Zuni."

Mr. Maurice Fulton's notes of Father's testimony are as follows, as Mr. Fulton told them to Mother in a letter:

"Appel told him (Dr. Ealy) that Dudley would not receive a note from Ealy but would from Mrs. Ealy; he saw Dudley go toward McSween's house late in the evening while it was burning; he spoke to Dudley in camp, since he understood the Tunstall building was to be burned and he wished to remove his personal property, but Dudley ordered him from the camp – used violent language in the interview. He agreed that Dudley finally furnished transpiration to Las Vegas."

In regard to the final point, when Father was asked if he did not remember where it said in the Bible, "Ingratitude, thou marble-hearted friend!" his reply was, "Sir, I feel you are quoting from a Book about which you know nothing.

Father felt that Colonel Dudley had done nothing to prevent the shooting of McSween and others in the Lincoln County War. As a result, after his testimony, he was threatened with death. Warned of a threat to his life by a note which suggested that he return to Zuni in a round-about way, he heeded the warning and so when he left Fort Stanton he started in the opposite direction from Zuni.

June 2. Voucher made out for cost of transportation. $93.75, 28 days en route at $4 cost $112. Nine days in attendance $36. Left at noon. [As noted already, Taylor could not have left on June 2 as he appeared at his request June 3 to amend his prior testimony. So he left on June 3. See Appendix A.]

June 4. In Roswell at daylight. Took breakfast at Supt. Lee's 75 miles from Ft. Stanton. Bosque Grande at 2 P.M. All night 18 miles north. Cost to Roswell, $6.

June 5. Left Ft. Sumner, N. Mex. At 1 P.M. 82 miles from Roswell, $8.

June 6. Friday. Whitemore's at 1 P.M. about 40 miles from Puerto de Luna.

June 7. Las Vegas. From [Fort] Sumner to Las Vegas $11.25. Met Jennie Hammaker, Miss S., and Miss Leach. Left at 8 A.M. [with Jennie]. Reached Santa Fe at 7:30. Paid $12 from Las Vegas to Santa Fe.

June 8. Have been riding 5 days and nights, about 400 miles. Slept until noon. At Santa Fe.

So by a circuitous route, by way of Roswell and Fort Sumner, Father was able, by almost super human effort, to reach Las Vegas on June 7. There he met Miss Jennie

Hammaker, who was related to Mother and had agreed to go to Zuni to help with the teaching and to lift a few of the burdens from Mother's shoulders. Father's statement for June 9 shows that he was completely exhausted. The next item, though, proves his resilient nature. He arose the next morning shortly after six. Jennie and he went directly to Bacon Springs, which they reached June 11 in time for breakfast. It was almost a month since he had gone to the trial. He had left Mother ill and therefore was greatly worried all the time he was gone about her condition. He was exceedingly delighted to find her all right once more. He was always, throughout his life, dependent upon her level head and her wise counsel. It would have been a great advantage to him to have had her with him at the time of the trial, but as a physician he said that she should not go. In this statement he made a great sacrifice.

June 11. Dinner at Ft. Wingate and supper at Zuni 10:30 P.M. Found all well. Since 9 A.M. traveled 57 miles.

June 12. Zuni Indians dancing for rain. Very dry. One month ago I received my subpoena.

June 13. Left Zuni for Wingate and Mr. Crane's. I expect to get in tonight.

June 14. Got to Bacon Springs late. Did not waken anyone. Slept in the hay last night and left this morning for home.

June 15. Left Bacon Springs yesterday at 8 via [Jorden E.] McAllister's, took lunch at his ranch, and left for Zuni at 12:30. Got to Nutria at 2, but my stubborn mules kept me there until 3. Got home at 9 P.M.

June 16. Monday. The Indians are dancing every day and night to bring rain.

All during June the Indians danced day and night hoping in that way to get rain, for the soil was exceedingly dry on account of the lack of any rain for long time. One day they walked over 100 miles carrying an image to a lake [Lyman Lake]. They felt that surely that action would bring rain.

But the 18th Father was able to open school once more. Unfortunately the Indians were usually occupied with dancing and few came to school. They were also busy in the corn fields. Father was still holding his classes in town. Only seven pupils came one day.

Tenney came for the burlap bags of wool which had been bought and sacked by Father. He was provoked that the wool had to be stored in the miserable, dirty room where he taught. Sometimes he felt almost suffocated. He was relieved when Tenney took with him 11 burlap bags and 14 bales. It gave Father more chance to breathe. Tenney also took the mail, which Father and Mother had been busily preparing.

Any spare time Father had he worked in his garden. By June 22 his corn was beginning to sprout. That same evening he read the Bible to Pino. While Pino was there, he spoke to him about the Indians building a school house. Father felt that a school of their own would possibly make the Indians more interested in education.

On June 25 he wrote Dr. Jackson the following letter:

Zuni Pueblo, N. M.
June 25, 1879

Rev. Sheldon Jackson
Portland, Oregon

Dear Sir:

I was gone a month all but one day at Fort Stanton, Lincoln County.

While I was gone, Mrs. Ealy wrote to you about changing the date of our Presbyterian meeting from August 21st to October. As I have written to all the ministers fixing August 21st as the day of meeting and as our vacations come in August, I feel certain that it would suit all of the members in the Territory at that time – August 21st.

If you have business to bring before Presbytery have it there by letter, or an adjourned meeting can be called sometime in the fall which will probably be necessary anyway on account of the installing of a new man over the Church at Santa Fe.

As for me I may not be in Presbytery even in August, but all the men can leave their schools in that time. My Indians have just been off sixty miles to the sacred lake [Lyman Lake], carried an image all the way; they went to bring rain. Two Catholic priests were in town all night last Saturday. We are all well.

My fence around the premises cost me $350, but we could not live here without something to keep back Indians, burros, etc. etc. etc.

I want to try to build a school house in vacation.

Yours truly,
T. F. Ealy

The day after he wrote to Dr. Jackson, Father stated in his diary that that was the last day of school before vacation. The short vacation gave him an opportunity to do some work about the house. He bought from Dan Dubois 12 alamo (cottonwood) trees for which he paid $5. They were six feet high and had been brought 22 miles. They had to be planted. Such trees are found many places in New Mexico. Both his trees and garden had to be irrigated by bucket.

Meanwhile he kept up his Sunday School at 9:00 A.M. in town and his reading to Pedro Pino at dusk in his own home. The last day of June he began to build a room at the rear of the mission house.

The first time any mention is made in the diary of a second house is on this date. It is quite evident that the family house could not be used both as a dwelling and as a school house. At first Father speaks of building one room at the rear of the first house. Soon he changed his plans and built a second house, this time of adobe, which they planned to use as the schoolhouse. For some reason, possibly because it was more suitable for the climate, the adobe house became the family home.

In speaking of his work in Zuni Father said that besides teaching, preaching, and practicing medicine, he had built a mission stone building; also, for the Government he had put in another building as well as a school room and a store room. In the picture of the stone house, some Adobes for the second house can be seen in the foreground. At the sides of the stone house too, can be seen parts of the corral, which Father mentions many times in his diary.

It was not unusual to have people for meals. On July 1 McAllister came for supper. The next day two priests called: one returned the following day hoping to secure room and board but the folks were not yet ready to entertain people.

Meanwhile Father had bought two cows from Mr. Crane for $60.00. Some Navajos brought them over and received remuneration of $5.35 for the trouble. Father was busy sacking wool in costals [costales] or burlap bags; by the 5th he had a load ready for market. He and others were working also at making adobes for the new house.

Still holding Sunday School in the rented room the village, he was amazed on July 6 to find the house locked and the people gone to Nutria. He took the opportunity to read to Pedro Pino in Spanish. That same day McAllister brought the folks some mail from Wingate.

The dry weather continued, and Father had to buy grass for his two cows – the Zuni brought it every day On July 8 he and Romano Pino started for the Fort, but it was 3:00 P.M. when they arrived; therefore they had to remain all night. The errand Father went on was to post his bond for the Post Office. It wasn't until noon the next day that he reached home. To his great delight it rained all that evening and night. It was the first chance he had to see how the roof on the house worked. He was gratified that it turned the rain well. The rain also was good for his garden, which now began to grow rapidly. The Indians though were having trouble in their wheat because grasshoppers were exceedingly plentiful.

A number of different duties kept Father busy all through July; most of these were connected with the house. On July 10 he set a hen; on the 11th he sacked a costal of wool; on the same day an Indian worked nearly all day digging out space for another room; on the 12th he himself built a portion of a wall of adobe; on that day two men from Albuquerque (Mr. Clark and Mr. Bennett) came to town to buy wool and put their horses in his corral.

His Christian work was moving slowly. He tried to hold Sunday School each Sunday but he found appalling indifference among the children. Pedro Pino was always ready to have the Scriptures read and by this time Father was advanced enough in Spanish to read it well. On the 13th of July Pedro's son, the Governor, joined his father in listening reverently to the reading. Father thought that if he could gain them as servants to Christ, many of the Zunis would follow their example. The lack of a definite place to hold service worked against any active Christian work. Jennie Hammaker gathered the children outside to hear the teaching of the Sabbath School lesson. Father kept reading to Pedro Pino each Sabbath.

On July 14 the Albuquerque buyers bought some wool for which they paid 12 cents a pound for goat skins, 4 cents for sheep skins, and 5 cents for wool. They remained in the town until July 22. During that time they were busy buying wool. Father sold them 1900 pounds more of wool, 371 sheep, and 295 goats for Andrew Clark of Albuquerque.

On July 20 Father marked and shipped their wool. It weighed 900 pounds and covered half his room. Teams left at 3:00 P.M.

George, a Laguna Indian, worked at making adobes nearly every day. He was promised $15.00 a month and board. He began work on July 16 and on that day made 25 adobes. One day he attended the Indian dance, but was usually quite faithful to his work, not deterred even by a light rain. Father built an adobe wall around the whole compound. George not only worked at building adobes but he milked and watered the cows and calves.

Now rains came nearly every day, for the most part rather light, but an exceedingly heavy rain came on July 13. Although it stopped work for awhile on the building, this rain was gratefully accepted. Another heavy rain came on July 27 and on August 6. All people who live in a dry climate can understand how much the people of Zuni appreciated these rains and why they form important items in Father's diary.

At one time during the month of July Moquis [Hopis] called. They were having some difficulty with the Zuni Indians.

On the 17th of July Father wrote his annual report of the Zuni School for the year. Such a report can be found in the account of the next year. Most of those reports were published in the church paper. This report was sent to the Board by Mr. Hatchman on July 27, who came on his way to Albuquerque and remained all night.

The difficulty of buying lumber for the house was a pressing problem. Father could obtain it in Ft. Wingate for $80.00 per 1000 feet or from Albuquerque for $22.00 per 1000 feet. The great distance from the latter place would add greatly to the cost. He chose Ft. Wingate for most of his lumber.

Mr. McAllister had a coffee plantation half way between Fort Wingate and Zuni. As he was often in each town, he frequently brought the mail. In fact the mail was brought from the Fort by any person who happened to be traveling to Zuni. The Indians always told Father when they were going to the Fort so that they might take along any mail he had to send and bring his with them on their return. It was rather vexatious to live so far from the post office, 27 miles. While the folks lived in Lincoln Father had found the mail was frequently tampered with; not so in Zuni. There is not one word of complaint though many people handled the mail. He optimistically wrote that he expected mail in Zuni in six weeks.

It was not at all unusual for strangers to appear to eat a meal and to stay all night. A man by the name of Slackwood came on July 22. From him Father bought 600 pounds and 3 bales of wool. He sacked one burlap bag, besides taking in $8.00 in money for the sale of 2 yards of muslin, 2 of calico, and nearly 100 of sugar. By this time he had 4 costals [costales] of wool to sell; by the 29th he had 6.

Every chance he had Father worked at the house which he was building of adobe at the rear of the main house. The completion of the latter was held up because materials were slow in coming. On July 23 and the 25th Father mentioned in his diary that he built some of the adobe walls. The same day he taught and sacked wool. He incidentally said that he was very tired. Again two days later he mentioned he is not well.

One of the problems was the necessity of keeping plenty of supplies on hand which had to be brought the 27 miles from Fort Wingate. Once on July 24 Father found they were entirely out of flour though some corn meal and crackers were on hand. One time much later, when I was old enough to remember, Mother said she did not want any beans. I asked her in great wonderment why because beans were my favorite dish; her reply gives me an understanding of conditions under which the folks lived, "How would you like to have nothing but beans for three months?" Yes, they were frequently hungry.

It was not until July 26 that the materials were on hand to plaster the walls. That day George began to plaster the kitchen. On July 30 Father helped George at the plastering. The next day George worked at the hall. Father was not well enough to do much that day. While he and George were plastering, on August 2, they saw a snake on top of the wall in Jennie's room. Neither knew what kind it was, but they went on plastering. I am wondering how Jennie Hammaker felt about the snake, or was she told about it? Any how the snake disappeared and never appeared again.

When Sabbath came August 3 Father read from the Bible as usual to Pedro Pino. By this time he was rather proud that he was able to read well in Spanish. He on that occasion pressed Pedro Pino again for an answer about the Indians building a school house. He could not get a reply nor did he get one on the 5th when he called a meeting. The Indians were dancing and put him off.

The item from the diary for August 4 reads: "Got the mail by McAllister; two letters from the Indian agent, one about school desks; the other about keeping store." He and George plastered all that day and on the 6th and 7th.

By the 8th of August Father felt that the whole family needed a change. He secured a burro so that any one who became tired might ride and the family and Jennie started for the top of a high mesa back of the house, a trip of about three miles. It was a somewhat difficult climb and the grown people took turn about riding home. I judge we children rode most of the time. A hard rain at sunset completed the happy day.

A unique surgical operation was performed by Father on August 9. That day he was asked to cut the hoofs from a burro and so, as he said, for the first time he became a blacksmith.

The plastering continued every lay but Sabbath. George did a good bit, for Father had to fit the work into his schedule. They were now putting on the second coat and the house was beginning to look more like a home. It must have made Mother happy that she could now entertain the travelers who came for meals and for the night without being ashamed of conditions. Father says that Sam Tenney came for tea on August 11 and that they expected Bread's team with some of the material for the house the next day.

The matter that interested the folks greatly was the fact that the railroad was now in the territory and that the cars were running as far as Las Vegas. They knew that it would soon be extended, and of course they hoped it would come close to Zuni.

Today as we look out the window, we sometimes speak of the great amount of traffic. To the folks at the isolated Zuni mission the passage of one wagon caused comment. One can imagine then how they felt when 16 wagons passed one day, August 12.

The following day Father secured a horse from an Indian to go to Wingate. As he did not start until 11:00 A.M. he was not able to go the whole way and so stopped at the McAllister's coffee ranch for the night. The next day he started for the Fort, but by some mischance took the wrong trail and ended at Crane's at Bacon Springs. There he stayed for lunch and then rode to the Fort. While there he attended to the business for which he had gone, to settle up what he owed [Col.] Dudley, and was glad there was a balance of nine dollars. As soon as possible he left for home via Davelle and reached Zuni by bedtime.

The work of the first house was going on, and at the same time George was making adobes for the second house or room at the rear. One day he made 56. By August 17 Father said he hoped to have Sabbath School in that room by the following Sabbath. He also expected to teach in it for two or three months. He was not able to complete it until more than a month later.

Let us note an extract from the diary for August 16:

"Looks like rain – rained while I was at the Fort. Am buying corn fodder for winter and drying it; my cows are fat." Also one for August 22: "Am buying green corn fodder and drying it for winter. Have about 2 tons." He would have been glad to use a silo.

The following items are taken directly from the diary:

Aug. 19. Paid Ammon Tenney all we are owing him on the corral, $73. Gave him a check for $125 to take to Albuquerque.

Aug. 20. Built at the wall today. Yesterday plastered the parlor with George's help. Mr. [James D.] Houck took supper with us. Lives west of Peter's Station.

Aug. 22. Read. Bought feed. Did not work much. George plastered. Wrote home to Mother. Hasped the hall about half. Expect to finish it my noon tomorrow.

A letter to Dr. Jackson on August 22, 1879 explains something of what was going on at the mission.

Zuni Pueblo, N. M.
August 22, 1879

Rev. Sheldon Jackson

Dear Brother:

It is quite a good many days since I wrote to you as you were very much engaged, I thought I would not increase your labors. At the same time I have been quite busy.

Our house is only now ready to live in, although we have been living in it there 9 months. It was a great risk to health for us to live in it while plastering.

I have built one room and have another half built at the rear of the house joined to the main building. Dr. Thomas is under the impression that there was a school room attached to our house, similar to James. We want a school room removed at least thirty feet from the house we live in on account of filth, etc.

School opens the first Monday of September. We will teach in the two rooms three months as the number of scholars will be small until peaches and corn are gathered. The peach crop is fairly good. Everything is pretty fair but some of the wheat at Pescado ["fish," a Zuni pueblo] was eaten by he grasshoppers. I have three cottonwood trees growing in the yard.

As I was gone one month at Fort Stanton, did not think I could return to Las Vegas to Presbytery. Hope hereafter I can be present at all the sessions.

Miss Hammaker is very well and contented. I think she will be quite successful in the school room.

Pino is well. Tried to have the Indians make adobes for the school house; but when no pay was offered no work was done.

We are all well. Expect you out it in October. The R.R. is expected at Albuquerque in three months.

I was appointed Postmaster here but they have my bond in Wingate and I do not know but that it may be destroyed. They do not seem to want a post office here.

Yours truly,
T. F. Ealy

The following reports are taken directly from the diary:

Aug. 23. Plastered. Did not see the parlor finished. Put away corn fodder in the forenoon. Dubois brought the mail from Fort Wingate.

Aug. 24. Zunis nearly all out in the wheat fields harvesting and in their peach orchards. They have thousands of trees. Pedro Pino away at Pesco.

Aug. 26. Finished hall, also parlor with second coat. We are drying corn.

Aug. 26. Plastered half day. Will put 3rd coat on parlor. Geo. made adobes until noon and then went to the peach orchards. Was gone until dusk.

Father was fond of walking. On August 27 he, Jennie, and Pearl went for a walk on the mesa east of town. It was 2:00 P.M. before they reached the top. They were given some peaches before they returned by way of the west side, eating as they descended.

The next day George finished plastering the parlor; at the same time Father put two panes of glass in the windows and helped scrub out the parlor. He was proud of the result. On August 29 he continued to work at the parlor until noon; then helped Mother put up a muslin ceiling. Jennie was sick.

The garden was beginning to pay dividends. Watermelons, squash, and berries were just ripe and afforded a welcome change of diet to the people of the house. Meanwhile George was busy making adobes.

August 31 was the last day of vacation. Father planned to reopen the school the next morning, as he said D. V. This day he read to Pino in Spanish. The next morning Jennie had eleven pupils whom she had hunted up. Father had only one that day and two the next day. Most of them were in the corn fields or peach orchards. On September 1 Sam Tenney stayed all night and Bennett came from Albuquerque to sell some goods.

Sept. 3. Ammon Tenney offers me a windmill of Stover make for $110. (The fact that Father was trying to get a windmill proves that the water in the well was failing.) Three wagons came in today to sell goods of the firm of Bennett & Co., or Graham & Co., at 7:30 P. M. Pearl 4 yrs. old.

Sept. 4. Two wagons and a herd of cattle went through to Arizona, from Indian Territory. While they were resting I was called out quickly by an Indian to see my corral fence on fire. (From the' picture it is evident the fence was made of wood.) Think it caught from hot ashes.

Sept. 5. Left at noon for Ft. Wingate. Got to McAllister's at dark.

Sept. 6. Went to the Fort and returned at 11:30 P.M. Brought two kits for Pearl and Ruth.

Sept. 7. Read to Patricio, the Governor; his father not in town. Our S. S. room is not ready.

Sept. 8. Geo. made 62 adobes. I have the 2nd room ready for the roof. (It seems this means the adobe house.)

Sept. 9. Ordered a windmill of the Stover make 12 ft. in diameter with an attachment to grind corn. George and I built an outhouse of adobe.

Sept. 10. The windmill 10 ft. in diameter $110; 12 ft. in diameter $130.

Sept. 11. A surveying party of the A. T. & St. Fe. Road of 7 men. A Navajo delegation of 7 men from Ft. Defiance in my corral. Sen. Phillips of Kansas and Lieut. Mitchell of Wingate.

Sept. 12. Held a council before sun-up with Navajos in my house. Then went to Piscado; from there to Nutria and met the Navajos. Ordered them away in 9 days from the Zuni Reservation.

Sept. 13. Got home last night. The Indians all busy in the corn fields and peach orchard.

Sept. 14. We can do very little of a religious nature. The people need the day school first.

At first the children did not understand what was said to them. They spoke the Indian language and few spoke Spanish. It is true that Father began to study the Indian language almost at once. He was hampered by the fact that it was not a written language and therefore he had to point to an object and find the Indian word for it and then write it down. He spelled the words the way they sounded to him. I have a book in which he compiled many, many Indian words. Their words are formed for the most part by fastening one word to another. It is extremely complicated.

English was taught in the school and in time some of the Indians became proficient in it. I recall that one of the Zuni boys, who attended Carlisle Indian School, used to come to our home in Schellsburg for his vacations. "R" was a letter he could not pronounce, and so I was always to him, "Lucy." He spoke one day of a beautiful "led lose." Yet we children had no trouble understanding his English.

Sept. 15. Went with the Governor to the peach orchards west of Zuni. They are very nice. We walked on the mesa above the orchards – the sight was grand. The Indians gave me about a half bushel of peaches.

Sept. 16. Young Mr. Burgess here; came to meet his brother who is coming from Albuquerque. Two Mr. Burgesses and Mr. [Douglas D.] Graham called.

Sept. 17. Geo. did not work. The Navajos are leaving Nutria, I am so glad. Will not need to take them off the Reservation with soldiers.

Sept. 18. Geo. Sick. Gave him a dose of salts. Bennett gone to his ranch.

Frank Hamilton Cushing in Zuni dress. "Land of Sunshine," 1899.

Sept. 19. Graham gone to Wingate. 32 Government mules. Major Stevenson and lady, from Washington, Mrs. Ed. Buel, Lieut. Hagwald, Miss F. ____, Dr. Cochrane and lady from Wingate here. Mr. and Mrs. Baker – 3 meals and horse.

Matilda Coxe Stevenson later wrote a book on the Zuni Indians, their mythology, esoteric fraternities, and ceremonies. [She authored 8 books on the Zunis.]

Sept. 20. All the ladies and gentlemen visited Zuni. Francisco [Hamilton] Cushing from the Smithsonian Institution here; an artist.

Frank H. Cushing I have read had been sent by the Smithsonian Institution to secure information about the Pueblo Indians. He chose to concentrate on the Zuni Indians. In order to gather exact material he came to Zuni, lived among the Indians, and finally because they showed great hostility to him for sketching their dances, allowed himself to be adopted into their tribe. His coolness saved his life once as he was sitting on the rooftop sketching and making notes; suddenly a number of the dancers began to climb the ladder near him, at the same time shouting "Kill him! Kill him!" He drew his hunting knife and waved in the air so that the sun flashed on it. They desisted at once.

In old numbers of the "Century Magazine" (December 1882 and February and May 1883) Cushing gives an extremely vivid account of his first visit to the Zunis and of his impressions at that time. Such is an extract from his description of the town: "Imagine numberless long, box-shaped adobe ranches, connected with one another in rooms and squares, with others, more or less numerous stories piled on them lengthwise and crosswise, in two, three, even six stories."

"Everywhere this structure bristled with ladder-poles, chimneys, and rafters… wonderfully like the holes in an ant hill seemed the little windows and doorways which everywhere pierced the wall of this giant habitation."

Taken from the Smithsonian Institution Series, Inc.

Our own house, when Father finally had it completed, in spite of all the delays and frustrations connected with the building, was possibly one-quarter of a mile from the town.

Sept. 21. Sabbath. 16 mules left for Wingate. Pedro Pino came from Piscado this evening. He came over and later told us some things about their belief and government.

Sept. 22. Held a meeting with the officers and agent – not many other Indians. Mr. Stevenson presented the Indians with some flour, sugar, coffee, etc.

Sept. 23. Had more scholars today than usual. Mr. Mrs. Stevenson bought a great amount of pottery.

Sept. 24. Surveying party 30 miles off – coming. Mr. Heddington of Stover & Co., Albuquerque here. Sold his freight $132.50.

Father's great excitement and interest are reflected in the many references in his diary to the approach of the railroad. On September 24 he writes of it exultantly – "Coming!" The October 2 and 3 items both speak of the future railroad, inasmuch as the surveyors were now as far as Zuni. Then on October 4 he records that they passed within two feet of his fence. He was always interested in progress, but one can understand his special feeling for something that would link his out-of-the-way mission to the events of the rest of the United States. No doubt he envisioned a future when his Zuni people would throw off their habitual bowing to ancient customs and become truly a part of our civilization. Something like that was necessary before a soldier of the Cross could preach and teach effectively. He longed for their salvation.

Zuni Pueblo, N. M.
Sept. 24, 1879

Rev. Sheldon Jackson
Denver, Col.

Dear Brother;

Supposing your trip would so overburdened with correspondence and duties, I held back from writing many lines to you.

Had a note written by you, written on the train. Zuni is visited now by parties from Washington, D.C. Stevenson and lady from the Department of the Interior, Mr. Frank Cushing, connected with the Smithsonian Institution, the artist Mr. [John Karl] Hillers, and others.

Our yard is now ornamented with four white tents; a few days ago there were six tents, while a party of ladies and gentleman visited Zuni from Fort Wingate. A gentleman arrived from Albuquerque today and reported the surveying party of the A. T. & S. F. R. R. at Agua Trio, the top of the continental divide, about eighty miles from Zuni on the east.

All or many of the old pieces of pottery are being bought up, to be sent to Washington; every nook and corner of the Pueblo are being photographed. There will be a complete model of the town placed in the Smithsonian extension. It will perhaps measure 10 x 15 feet.

Our schools are not well attended this month, the children are out in the orchards and fields.

I have received a book called "Introduction to the Study of the Indian Language" [by John Wesley Powell]. This will help me get the language in a good shape.

Hope we will have a visit from you soon.

Yours with great esteem,
T. F. Ealy

On September 25 the lack of scholars vexed Father anew. He could not see why the Indians did not take advantage of the chance to learn when they were getting it free. Looking at it from our present standpoint, separated in time and place from Zuni, we can understand why the young Indians who had never been made to sit in a school room resented somewhat the restrictions on their liberty, especially when most of the parents had no desire for their children to have an education.

Mr. Cushing, the artist sent out by the Smithsonian Institution, was busy collecting sketches of the Indians. These were formerly published by that institution. Living as he did at the house of the Zuni governor, dressed as the Indians were, and sleeping on sheep skins with only two blankets over him, he had become almost an Indian and so was able to secure whatever sketches he wished. Instead of staying in Zuni three months as he had intended, he remained four years. He was part of Colonel Stevenson's collection party.

Dancing! Dancing! Dancing! September 28 and 29. This one was called the ripe corn dance and was carried out largely by the young people. A dance on October 3 was somewhat different from the usual dances. The day before the Indians had built a huge fire to burn out their sins; this day, as the danced, they had burdens on their back which the laid down at the Cacique's [Chief's] feet. Did it mean that thee burdens represented their sins?

Bennett had been absent from Zuni but returned on September 29. He had six mules which he put into the corral at the manse [minister house] while he fed them and ate his own supper. Then he left for Wingate to be gone four days. The next day Mr. Stevenson, who had gone to Old Ft. Wingate over the mountain from the other Ft. Wingate, had come back to fill all the canteens with water from the Springs. He put his two horses into the corral. It was the usual procedure when people came to town. Mr. Cushing kept his all the time in our corral. On October 6 there were seventeen mules and two horses in the enclosure. Mr. Stevenson and his party from Washington, except Mr. Cushing, left for the Moqui towns on October 10. They bought a great amount of wool and pottery. Father felt that they desecrated the Sabbath by doing such work on that day.

What excitement on October 31. A surveying party from the A. T. & Santa Fe R. R. surveyed up to Zuni and camped one-half mile below the town. Mr. Drake was the man in charge. The engineers surveyed within two feet of the manse fence.

It was no use to try to get the Indians into school on October 6. There was too much going on. Father's attempt ended in failure. Many people and such bustle and confusion were much more interesting than a day in school. Some of the items of interest, besides the Washington party buying wool and packing pottery, were the railroad surveying party, the great number of wagons passing through the town, eight in one day, and a photographer, who took pictures of the school and house. How could the Indian children be expected to do anything but watch these new developments? I wonder that Father was able to assemble enough children to have their picture taken. The photographer, Mr. Hillers, also took a picture of one of the Caciquis.

The Indians who were working for Father meanwhile were gathering corn fodder, finishing the plastering of the school room, making adobes, working at the stable wall, and doing various jobs around the house. Father took a hand now and then. He was extremely ill on October 13. That day he was not able to do anything. The day before, Sabbath, he spoke in his diary of being tired, although he had read the Bible to Pedro Pino and his son Jesus. Father was able on October 14 to pay the Navajos who had been helping on the wall. That same day there was a grand rain.

Cushing, who had remained in Zuni, was busy all day October 15 packing the pottery which had been bought by the Stevenson party. The next day the Government wagon filled with pottery left for Fort Wingate.

By October 16, Father had recuperated sufficiently to make a door for José Pallo and one for his chicken coop. The next day a boy from Virginia originally but now from Utah came to the house and helped Father make a chimney while he was waiting for a way to go further on his journey. At noon on the 18th he ran to overtake a wagon which had just passed.

George and Antonio took time off on October 20 to go to Wingate for the mail and had to stay all night. Antonio did not return until October 22 but George returned to his work the next day. Antonio came in time for tea.

A letter, written to Dr. Jackson on the same day, follows:

Zuni Pueblo, N. M.
Oct. 22, 1879

Rev. Sheldon Jackson
Denver, Col.

Dear Dr. Jackson:

I somehow think or for some reason imagine this will go to Denver and about the same time you will be in Zuni; I hope you will make one visit yet in advance of the R. R. Pedro Pino says he will accompany me in August next to Presbytery.

Hope you can meet us there if we are spared to go. I have baptized his grandson. I read to him from the Spanish on Saturday evening; my prayer is "Lord let him see Thee in Thy Word."

I was astonished – it was not the only astonishment in Zuni, however; three weeks ago a woman died and when her grave was prepared I heard they had dug up some skulls. I asked a medical friend who was visiting Zuni to walk around to the old churchyard and get a skull. Instantly he started in advance for the prize, and lo! when we arrived, sure enough there lay four skulls thrown up with the loose dirt, also many other loose bones from the human body.

He seized two, but I told him it looked like stealing, perhaps we had better ask the Governor if we might have them. We could not find the Governor, and when we got back to the grave, we were gone about twenty minutes, the corpse was interred.

A friend who saw the burial said that skulls were thrown in first then the body, which was carried to the grave in a blanket, was wrapped in another also and lowered.

When bodies are four or five deep it is time to look for a new cemetery, and this too, which is so full, is in the center of town. The Zunis are a little angry at the Navajos at trespassing upon their lands.

Two days ago they showed their hatred in a dance by killing a dog with clubs then tearing off his nose with their teeth, also tearing out his entrails and pulling them apart with their teeth, horrible to relate, but it is so, notwithstanding it's mirabile dictu [wonderful to relate].

We lie down and sleep at night because we trust in the Almighty.

Our little girls are doing splendid work in sewing; Miss Hammaker has finally won their esteem.

I have a good many boys on my roll, but they do not attend regularly. The Zunis have seven dances; all others are variations of these seven.

Your friend and humble servant,
T. F. Ealy

The matter which occupied much of the attention during the last of October was the new windmill, which arrived on October 24 but which was not put into running order until about a month later. Logs for the well had to be prepared. These were 22 feet long. Father cut two on October 28 and secured two more on November 3 and still two more on November 5. Meanwhile George and McClune, who had been helping since October 23, took the rocks or wall out of the well. Then Father put a rim under the wall and rebuilt the wall.

More and more people were traveling. The news about the coming railroad seemed to fill people with the desire to move. Father speaks of a Mexican family that had stopped in the yard on October 23; Bennett and Graham, who had been in Albuquerque, now returned; a man by the name of Miller stopped in the yard October 27. On November 3 Dr. Jackson came. He visited the dance which was going on that day and took notes. On the 5th he left for Fort Defiance. It was a great help to Father to be able to talk over his work with Dr. Jackson. On November 4 Major Stevenson and wife returned and took the parlor. The school at the house had to be abandoned for the present. Father still taught in town. Every time he could possibly secure the boys, Father taught them. Jennie was using the parlor for her school room.

After reading to Pino on November 2, Father had a talk with him about the danger to the health of the Indians of having the cemetery in the center of their congested town. He felt the great amount of sickness could accounted for partly by this fact. He begged Pino to speak to the Cacique about the matter and to try to get him to move the cemetery entirely away from the town.

It was early November now and the cold weather was really at hand. The wind blew very hard on November 7 and by the next day snow came. The weather was cold enough now so that it was possible to keep meat which came from the Fort – 75 pounds of beef. How the folks must have enjoyed the change of diet! The cold though had a disastrous effect upon me, then 2 years old. I had an extremely sore throat and fever.

My sister and I were made happy one day to receive some shoes in the mail. We were too little and young to bother much about our looks, but even at that early age every little present made us happy. I can still remember a tiny thimble that came in one of the mission boxes and I was overjoyed to have it assigned to me.

George, who was usually faithful to his work, could not resist occasionally going to the Zuni dance. One such time came November 1. George joined, in the dance although of a different tribe.

A man by the name of McClune had come to town on October 25. He helped Father build the stable wall. An incident on the last day of October was the setting of a hen by Father. That same day the Government team left for Wingate, and some more logs were hauled by Antonio for the well. The day Dr. Jackson came Father called a meeting of the men of the town at night. On the night of November 8 some Indian officers (New-Co-ya-ka-she) were inaugurated.

"Zuni Children with Teachers." The person standing on the left is Jennie Hammaker; the person standing in the center is We-Wa (We'wha); the person standing on the right is Taylor Ealy. Others unidentified. Photo by John Karl Hillers, 1879. Courtesy National Anthropological Archives, Smithsonian Institution.

The varied life of the missionaries can be seen by the following extracts from the diary:

Nov. 9. Mail came. Rained. Did not read to Pino. Taught sums. McClune left for Wingate.

Nov. 10. Rained. Stevenson took the parlor and drove out the school. We got the consent of the Cacique to give up the images.

Nov. 11. Carried over one of the images – the one containing the shield, a men king. A gov't. driver carried the other, a woman. Both about three feet high; weighed perhaps 30 lbs. Put pump in.

Nov. 12. Mrs. Ealy took sick at 11.P.M. We had just finished preparing our mail. Maj. Stevenson sent his team to Ft. Wingate.

Nov. 13. Born!!! After a tedious labor of 13 hours, our little boy [Albert "Bertie"] was born at 12 o'clock midnight in the first position the cord around his neck, short cord.

The intense delight of Father is shown by the three exclamation points with which he followed the announcement of the arrival of his first son. His sensitive mind must have locked into the future when this babe would be a grown man, active in the work of the Kingdom of God, for so Father naturally would look for him to be. The rest of the November 13 record is such as one would expect a physician to write. He was a very fine obstetrician and I am sure gave Mother the best of care, but how she must have longed for her own Mother during those thirteen hours of agony. Fortunately, she had a splendid constitution and soon was her own normal cheerful self; fortunately, too, she had Jennie to be with her.

In spite of the birth of a child and the attendant confusion two men from Prescott came the next day to remain all night. There were six in the party, but four stopped with Mr. Graham. On November 16 a wagon and six mules came from Ft. Wingate. Mr. Baker came from Albuquerque to join the party from Prescott. It was the time of the grand annual feast and dance in Zuni, an observance in which all the Indians of the reservation took part. This lasted for several days which were given over by the Indians to feasting and dancing.

At every chance new logs were prepared for the windmill until enough were hewed. These of course had to be hauled ready to be put into place. Father says two were made ready on November 17. He says incidentally the Belle, one of the two dogs he had bought to be with my sister and me all the time, had had pups the day before. These dogs kept the Indians away because for some reason we had a great fascination for them. When we left Zuni, Belle who was devoted to us, followed us a long way and would not return until Father said, "Go back!" We felt as if we were losing one of our best fiends, but of course it was impossible to take them east with us.

In his diary Father always calls Mother Mrs. Ealy or Mrs. E. I never heard him call her Mary. In later years, when he entered the house, if Mother were not present, his first words were, "Where's Mother?" He reported on November 15 that she had the baby were doing well.

November 13 was a busy day at our house. That day there were six horses in the yard and fifteen mules in the corral. Mother even had callers, Major and Mrs. Stevenson, at 8:00 P.M.

The windmill was on the ground; now it had to be put into running order. Mr. Williams, who had installed Ammon Tenney's mill came the evening of November 20 to install the one at the mission. The pump had been put in on November 11. The next day Williams began the work by working at the well. In the afternoon he went to see the Indians dance. The day following, November 22, both Father and Williams worked at the windmill, and again on November 24 Father helped with the work. On November 25 the windmill was finally put into position but it was not really in running order until November 29. A snow kept them from working on November 26 and 27. Even then the water was not sufficient and the corn grinder had not yet arrived. Father decided to clean out the well, hoping in this way to get sufficient water. So far as I can find that is the last reference in the diary to the windmill. It looks as if at last it were working properly. To erect it cost $25.00 Thanksgiving Day $10.00 came in the mail, and Mr. Stevenson gave Father $10.00 for the rent of the parlor. He now had almost enough for the windmill.

Father does say that he caught cold while working at the well and by Sabbath November 30 he was far from well. On this day Williams left for Albuquerque. Cushing went along to the mines.

The Indians meanwhile were occupied with the sun, moon, and stars dance and with the season dance. These were some of their important dances. Scholars did not come to school.

During this part of November the mission house had different callers and visitors. On the 23rd Perea came from Fort Wingate; on November 25 Mr. Graham and Mr. Bennett, who had returned November 20, were at the house for tea. Father also had, on November 23, a sick woman for patient, Yack's wife. The next day she was somewhat better. On November 25, Pedro Pino and his two sons went to Fort Wingate. When they returned, Thanksgiving, they brought the mail.

Father still taught in the town in a room he had rented from Pedro Pino: On December 1 he had eighteen boys, while Jennie Hammaker had only seven girls out at the mission house.

Some diary items are these:

Dec. 2. Three deaths in town, Yack's wife, a little baby, and Lucas Pino.

Dec. 3. Indians grinding and dancing. Each Cacique's house has two women in it grinding corn and dancing while the men sing and beat the drums.

These acts had an important place in their religious ceremony.

Dec. 4. Snowed last night about one inch. Wrote to Col. Garrick Mallery, Box 585, Washington, D. C. on the sign language.

This is the answer to the letter to which Father refers:

Smithsonian Institution
Bureau of Ethnology
J. W. Powell, in charge
P.O. Box 585

Rev. Taylor F. Ealy
Zuni, New Mexico – via Fort Wingate

Dear Sir:

I have received with very great pleasure your letter of the 6th inst. giving several signs, in response to request, and mailed to you yesterday some forms and outlines to facilitate further research and descriptions which I sincerely hope you will find time to use. The forms will be valuable to ensure accuracy of understanding; for instance – you give "liar" <u>run the index finger from each corner of the mouth</u>. Does this mean extend the index of the right hand successively forward or also downward from the two corners of the mouth? I take it so but without full understanding – it might mean that the forefingers of the <u>two</u> hands were at the same time extended from the two corners. You will see the Importance of a further elaborate description and if possible illustration in the manner, now, I hope, rendered comparatively easy by my forms.

I remain, in hopes of further kind assistance from you,

My Dear Sir,
Yours very respectfully,
Garrick Mallery

The Indian whom Father sent to Fort Wingate for the mail on December 5 was not able to return until the following day. The mail brought a letter with $16.00 in it, money returned by Dr. Palmer. On December 5 two Mexicans who lived in St. John's stopped at the house on their way home from Albuquerque; one had two sheep.

Though December 6 was Saturday Father taught all day. The next day he held Sabbath School at 11:00 A.M. and read from the Bible to Pedro Pino in the evening. Only 15 were present at school on December 8.

It was exceedingly windy that day and the next day was extremely cold, the coldest, day in the winter. In spite of the severe weather Graham and Cushing went to the mountain to pick up Cushing's saddle and bridle which he had left there. The cold continued the rest of the month until December 17. Then it became warmer for a few days, but the day before Christmas it was bitterly cold.

Father mentions on December 9 that the Indians were horse racing and on December 10, 11, and 12 they were dancing. They began dancing at sundown on December 10. He says there were 50 in the dance – 43 men, 7 women, also earth men.

Father was much interested in the earth men. This account he wrote in an old record book, not the diary.

GLIMPSE AT THE DANCE
by T. F. Ealy

"Scaling a ladder, I stood upon the top of a house, which facing the placita was two stories high."

"'In the placita were ten earth men, men whose skin is painted a grayish-red color like clay. These men wear a birch-cloth and a mask which looks repulsive at first sight. It is made of buckskin or goat skin with nodules sewed on like warts and the masks are all of different shapes. These ugly mugs, as we call them, or Coya Ma Sha, as the Zunis call them, seem to hold the spectators while the more elaborately dressed performers are gone."

"These earth men had a basket of corn; upon the corn a bunch of straw. One of them went to the crowd of spectators and picked a man and woman. They came forward and talked to one of these earth men. Then he gave each a double handful of corn. He then selected two others to whom he talked secretly a good while, when suddenly he appeared startled; told the rest to stop dancing. After that he took the bunch of sticks, laid them on four piles, then gave them to the woman. He also divided the basket of corn between the man and woman. About this time 50 of the dancers proper came into the placita from under a gangway which led into another part of the town. Of these, 50, 43 were men, 7 women. The earth men disappeared and the regular dancers took up the dance."

Meanwhile such activity as nine ox teams, going by on December 9 and wagons going west on December 11 are mentioned. Cushing and Graham went to Saballa [Cebolla] on December 10 but Graham returned the following day. He took us children over to the town that day; to us the visit to the Indian town was a treat.

Dec. 13. Taught in the forenoon and held a council in the afternoon with the principals concerning a trip to Santa Fe.

Dec. 14. Taught the boys and Jennie taught the girls. Read to Pino.

Dec. 15. Cushing returned and brought the mail. I sent Captain Pino or Kerr to Wingate with letters.

Dec. 16. Cushing and Graham called in the evening.

Dec. 17. Warm. Capitan (Indian) brought the mail. Taught school.

Dec. 18. Christmas for the Zunis. No boys came to school. All the people tying feathers upon a multitude of little sticks and tomorrow they go out to put them in the ground in the corn fields.

Knowing they thought that the gods clothe themselves with feathers, we can understand the necessity of planting prayer sticks with feathers attached to them. To Father this action appeared only a silly one, but to the Indians it was most important. With these prayer sticks in the corn fields the Indian gods knew, so the Indians thought, that they were asked to help the Zunis by bringing rain and in securing a good harvest. Prayer sticks are always planted before a sacred dance. Feathers are so important that dancers wear them as part of their costume. The eagle feather is the kind most desired.

Dec. 19. Mr. Graham went to Ft. Wingate. Indians planting feathers in the corn fields.

Dec. 20. Taught all day.

Dec. 21. Sabbath. Taught all the boys who came to the house. Read in Spanish to Pedro Pino. Mr. Graham brought the mail from Fort Wingate.

Dec. 22. Monday. A light snow fell last night.

Dec. 23. A man buried! Many of the Zunis went out to plant feathers in their corn fields. Snow falling. High wind. Rowan Pino [Pablo Pino's grandson] married.

Dec. 24. Very cold. Taught school. Visited a sick boy. Graham has a new clerk.

Dec. 25. Mr. Douglas D. Graham of Fishkill on the Hudson, N.Y. and Mr. Francisco Cushing of Washington, D.C. were here for dinner.

Dec. 26. Taught school. Cold – some snow. Moderated in the evening.

Dec. 27. Warmer – melting. The Indian we call the Lieutenant brought a girl 7 months old to be baptized. We called her Grace Kennedy at the request of Dr. N. A. Berber of Bergan Point, N.J.

Her father had accepted Christianity. Father speaks of this baptism in a letter to Dr. Jackson on January 9, 1880. The letter follows:

Zuni, New Mexico
January 9, 1880

Dr. Jackson

Dear Brother:

I am glad to say that another little Zuni child has been brought to our house to be baptized. December 27th I baptized her (1879). Her name is Grace Kennedy, after a little girl who died in N.J. Her uncle of Bergen Point, N.J. sent us $30 and pledges the same amount for her support each year.

Lord help us to lead her into the light of Thy Truth.

Your fellow servant,
T. F. Ealy.

Dec. 28. S. S. in the morning. Read to Pedro in the evening. Warm.

Dec. 29. Taught. Indians dancing – carried out five, who were overcome during the dance. Warmer.

Dec. 30. Taught school. Visited four patients. One was buried. School report: Boys 14; Girls 12.

Dec. 31. Taught school. Although it is vacation, I am eager to get the Indian boys in the habit of going to school. Pearl, Ruth, and Albert are well. We are all well.

Chapter 5 | The Silent Year – 1880

Six letters were written to Dr. Jackson during his year. Three of them came during January and March. The first and second ones have already been quoted. The third on March 1 deals with the matter of the post office in Zuni and with the school. Father was receiving from the government school books, medicine, and clothing for the school children. The fourth one also has something to do with the office. The matters treated are self explanatory.

Zuni, New Mexico
March 1, 1880

Dr. Sheldon Jackson

Dear Brother:

I ought to have written sooner about the P.O. but as I had gone to considerable trouble getting bondmen I felt some little perplexed to think my bond had never been forwarded to Washington. It must be in Wingate in charge of the P.M. [postmaster] if it is not in Washington. The bond was signed by Mr. Crane of Bacon Springs and Dr. Ealy of Dayton, Ohio. I do not care to get out a new one until I know why the first was rejected. Our boys' average for February is eighteen and girls' average is twenty-five. We are very much encouraged with the progress of our scholars. You have written nothing about the new school house; remember this is the one great thing needful. I am looking for the Indians back from Laguna with the good school books, medicine, clothing, etc. which the government is giving to the mission for distribution.

Regards from all,
T. F. Ealy

This letter too refers to the post office for Zuni. By this time Father had decided that the Government did not feel it necessary to have a post office in Zuni.

Zuni, New Mexico
March 7th, 1880

Dr. Sheldon Jackson

Dear Brother:

I drop you these lines to ask you a question – Will you be in Washington soon and if so would you have time to see as to the reason of the delay of Mr. Douglas Graham's bond? He is here in Zuni awaiting the decision of the commissioner of Indian affairs. He has written and telegraphed yet no answer, one way or the other, nothing but perfect silence. Young Mr. James Bennett has bought Navajo Springs west of us. Mr. B. is the son of an elder in the Presbyterian Church. His father lives in Wisconsin, I do not know where.

The boxes sent us from the East have not reached us yet. Today a wagon left here which will be back in about fifteen days and will then bring them to Zuni if they are in Albuquerque. It is reported that the old Padre is to be married. He passed through Zuni two days ago; baptized a child.

We are all well but all the time hungry. What is to be done about the school house or Chapel?

Your brother,
T. F. Ealy

It is important to note that the Indians now had gone far enough to wish for more education.

Zuni, New Mexico
June 15, 1880

Dr. S. Jackson

Dear Bro:

I send you a copy of a letter which I have just written to Dr. Thomas, Agt.

Dear Sir:

I am informed that if I know of any Zunis who wish to go to school at Carlisle, Pa, I am to report the fact to you.[1] There are now five offering themselves, one I suppose is beyond the required age, he is perhaps 21, but a very worthy boy, by name Pasqualito. I wish to inform you that they offer themselves, and to ask you if the way is clear for them to go, when and how shall they go, and how many years remain before returning?

Your Ob't servant,
T. F. Ealy, M.D.
U. S. I. Teacher

Father was delighted to report four had left from Zuni for the East to further their education.

Zuni, New Mexico
July 12, 1880

Dear Dr. Jackson:

With gratitude to God I have the honor to say that Agt. Thomas left Zuni this noon with two boys and two girls from Zuni.

We are sorry to miss seeing you but know just how full of work you must be. I very much wanted your counsel in starting on a house. Now I propose to build, of stone, a new dwelling house and to make a cellar under one room and make it a story and a half of stone.

Your brother,
T. F. Ealy

I have called this year silent because there seems to be no diary record for the year. For the following year I have diaries written by both Father and Mother, but so far no diary for his year has turned up. I do know that my brother Albert, or Bertie, as he was called, died on June 4, 1880 and was buried in a grave close by the side of the house. Both parents in their diaries for June 4, 1881 mention that Bertie had died a year before on that day. The last item in 1879 is to the effect that all the children are well and we were mentioned by name.

Just what was the cause of Bertie's death we were never specifically told, but I judge it was a house far too cold for an infant and the fact that Mother was too busy with her school teaching, baking, entertaining strangers, who came to stay all night, washing, cleaning, and numerous jobs she was compelled to do to give as much attention as she would have liked to her darling boy. To both parents his loss was a terrific blow.

In July of this year Father wrote a poem about Bertie's death which reflects something of the agony that his death caused. As he was a doctor, I know he felt that he should have saved him and yet as a Christian he knew that he should not grieve. Both moods are shown in the poem.

"Oh my little Bertie Darling!"
"I know thou art in the skies;"
"No more I hear thee warring"
"With pains and groans and cries."

"Oh my little Bertie Darling!"
"When my summons calls me home,"
"When I hear the Savior calling,"
"Then I will gladly come."

"Oh my little Bertie Darling!"
"I am longing to meet thee;"
"I long to hear thee warbling"
"Songs, not groans of misery."
    – July, 1880

It is, so far as I know, the only attempt at poetry Father ever wrote. The depth of the sentiment excuses the lack of real poetry.

One story about Bertie's grave has come down through the years. My sister and I spent our time, after the grave was dug, until the burial, in sitting by the side of it with our feet in the grave. Evidently it caused us much concern that Bertie was to go to Heaven and yet was to be put into the ground. We must have talked the matter over – a two and a four-year-old – for we went to our parents and begged them to put a ladder into the grave so that the angels could take Bertie out of the dark place.

Aunt Mary Ealy in her diary, which I had a chance to read just this summer, in telling of Albert's death says that his funeral was attended by 13 Americans and 100 Indians. It must have been an extremely sad occasion.

It was in this year that Mother took the two of us with her and went for a visit to Father's brother, Dr. Albert [E.] Ealy of Albuquerque. Something of the journey thither has been told to me. It seems we went in a prairie schooner, and while crossing the Rio Grande, since there were two wagons drawn by the same team, the load became bogged in the sand. The driver then unhitched the second wagon, in which we were, and left us while he took the first one over the stream. Then he came back for us. By this time the wagon was somewhat settled in the sand and it took a long time for the oxen to pull us over. Mother had not been well when she started and this additional strain and worry made her ill. The driver too became ill and died. Mother was ill for several weeks at Uncle Albert's. Her disease was typhoid fever. He, however, gave her the best of attention and Aunt Effie proved a splendid nurse. In short, good medical attention, fine nursing, and her naturally good constitution combined to restore her to health.

Naturally, she felt that she must return as soon as possible to Zuni. The work there was still going on and Father, she knew, needed her help badly. By the time of her 1881 diary, though, one can see that she needed a much longer rest. She speaks frequently of being exceedingly tired. She spoke too with joy of the fact that they planned a trip to the East. The desire for companionship with the people she knew, on an equal plane, amounted almost to nostalgia now. Yet she went on faithfully with her daily work. Now, many of the Indian women were learning to sew and she was enjoying their interest in this type of work.

Among the people Father treated for various types of illness in 1880 Father mentions, in his medical record, the fact that in March he treated the whole family for influenza. He mentions Mrs. Ealy, Pearl, Ruth, and himself. It was possibly the same trouble that carried off Bertie in June. Father speaks of treating Bertie on May 31. It must have grieved him sorely that he could not save his first son.

Zuni, New Mexico
July 17, 1880

Dr. Sheldon Jackson

Dear Sir:

I have given up seeing you on this trip. Thought I had better let you know what my plan is as soon as possible. Now the ice is fairly broken in Zuni. We have borne the burden and heat of the day, and, if it is the Lord's will, we would like to be honorably discharged or relieved from future duty after Sept. 30th, 1880.

Could you have a man, if possible with a knowledge of medicine and in every way qualified to carry on the good work without any break, and, in order to do this, I now ask that a man be sent to Zuni six months before I leave in order that I may help him in the study of the language and ways of the people. Then it will be as if no break had been made. I can teach a man in six months what it has taken me nearly two years to learn. I speak of this matter in time so that you may be able to select a suitable person.

The going away of the children [to Carlisle] have bound the people closer to us and we love them more for what they have done. One little girl who wanted to go was hidden away by some relatives the morning we wanted her. One boy about 21 years, who claimed to be the brother of one José who went, almost begged to go. He is a very pious young man. I told him that perhaps some good people after a little would send for him. His name is "Pasqualito."

Your brother,
T. F. Ealy

This one is especially important since it concerns Father's desire to be relieved of his Zuni post. His Father had been writing for him to come to his assistance as a country doctor and his own health was becoming more and more precarious. He chose, with great sorrow to surrender, at least for the present, his station in Zuni.

In August, the following annual report was sent to Presbytery. This report gives an idea of conditions in Zuni. It was published in the mission paper called "Presbyterian Home Missions." I shall conclude the year with this report.

ZUNI – ANNUAL REPORT, 1880
By Rev. T. F. Ealy

"The condition of the Pueblo this year is better than last, from the fact that the rains have been more abundant. These rains cause all vegetation to grow very rapidly. Hence, good crops, fat animals, greater increase of flocks, and a general encouragement to all to push forward. The habits of the Zunis are almost as regular as summer and winter, spring and autumn, day and night; for their habits are regulated by the sun, moon, and the changes of the seasons. They have a house where the Cacique of the Sun sits, and through a hole in the wall tells, by the sun's rays shining in, what time of the season it is. Especially does he watch carefully when the sun travels his last day north, and, with joy and dancing, they welcome his backward march."

"The disposition of the Zunis is that of perfect quiet. They wish to take part in no wars. Their decision, when asked, or when it was rumored that there was to be a general Indian outbreak, and that the Zunis were expected to join, was, that if all the Pueblos and all other Indians banded together to whip the Government and drive Americans from the country, Zuni would not join them."

"They are disposed to, and always have supported themselves. Their economy goes so far that they waste almost nothing. In the spring of the year, when vegetables are unseen in Zuni, they eat the grass from the sheep's stomach; they drink his blood; they clean and eat all his entrails; they use his coat to save the burro's back as he staggers along under his heavy load, and at night their sheep pelts are spread down upon the ground or floors of their houses for the inmates to sleep upon. After these pelts become too filthy for the house, they usually sell them to traders, and thus get rid of he old and supply their place with new."

"They are a people in themselves who make very little progress, and if left to themselves would rather recede. But progress has been made. They have sent some of their children to school. They have in use one steel plow. Alas, with an immense crop of wheat they have not a single fanning mill. One Indian has a team of horses. I am trying to persuade them to build a reservoir which will hold water enough to supply a population five times as great. This can easily be done. It is simply the building of a solid masonry wall against the water in the shape of a rainbow, or, perhaps triangle shape. The cost of the wall would, perhaps, be from five to seven hundred dollars. It is where the Piscado Creek enters the Zuni Valley through a narrow opening in the 'black rock.' If the Government would help them in this they would need no more territory."

"One sad event of the year was the trial, and, I have no doubt the death, of an old Indian, who by the others was supposed to be a witch. The charges laid against him were: 1. As is their custom, they all plant plumes, but this old man was charged of having planted owl feathers, and such feathers are used only by witches. Another charge was, that he had bewitched two young girls of the village, who afterward died of rheumatism; 2. By his owl feathers he caused an unusually high wind. This wind raised the sand and killed their corn by its blowing over the fields."

Four students from Zuni to Carlisle Indian School, Carlisle, PA. Taken before they went to Carlisle. Standing: Tsai au-tit-sa (Mary Ealy) and Jan-i-uh-tit sa (Jennie Hammaker). Sitting: Teai-e-se-u-lu-ti-wa (Frank Cushing) and Tra-we-ea-tsa-lun-kia (Taylor Ealy). English names in parentheses. Image from book.

The four students after they returned to Zuni from Carlisle School. [Students attending the school were forced to adopt English names, dress in Western clothing, and cut their hair.] Standing: Frank Cushing and Taylor Ealy. Sitting: Mary Ealy and Jennie Hammaker. Image from book.

"At 2 o'clock in the night, an alarm was raised in the town. At sun-up the next morning the witch was caught and tied with his hands behind his back to a pole above his head. While in this position, his life was threatened, and there and then they made him confess the charges laid against him. I told them that if they killed him I would report the whole matter to the Agent, who was expected in Zuni in a few days. Everything was quiet until the Agent came and went. On morning the old witch was reported dead and buried."

"This year four children from the Pueblo have gone to Carlisle, Pa. to school. Never before have any of this Pueblo been much east of the Rio Grande. They say 'Zuni is the center of the whole world.'"

"We are now erecting a new building to be used in connection with our school work. The completion of this building will put the school work upon a fair footing."

"No epidemics have broken in upon the people during the year."

Chapter 6 | The End of Life in Zuni

Since both Father and Mother kept diaries this year, I shall supplement Father's report by those of Mother. Unfortunately letters sent to their homes were not saved, and so I shall have to depend almost wholly upon these diaries for information.

From the first item in Father's diary on January 1, I judge all of the folks at the mission were busily at work. It was bitterly cold weather, but not too cold for the Indians to dance. Snow covered the ground. Mother had a nice Indian girl by the name of We-Wa [modern spelling We'wha][1] to help her with her work. That fact gave her more time to devote to her school teaching, an occupation natural to her, since she was a teacher when Father married her.

An Indian school had opened in Albuquerque the last of the previous year. It was co-educational, a boarding school of the Pueblo Indians. The citizens of Albuquerque had donated a tract of land for the establishment of such a school, but the school began in a rented building. On January 4 Mr. Conklin came to Zuni to recruit scholars for both the Carlisle and Albuquerque schools. The man back of the whole project was Mr. Thomas, the Indian Agent.

A boy in an article published in the December "Rocky Mountain Presbyterian" speaks of seeing an Indian girl, Nellie, who was attending the school at Carlisle. She was in the company of four from Zuni, three from San Felipe, and three from Laguna. The day Mr. Conklin left, Mr. [Richard Henry] Pratt, head of the Carlisle Indian School was in Zuni. Father showed him around in the morning and taught in the afternoon.

The weather still continued cold. The school rooms were not properly heated. The Indian children were accustomed to improperly heated rooms, but the mission people suffered severely. Mr. Frank Cushing, who had been visiting the caves in Arizona, returned to Zuni.

By January 9, the new house was sufficiently advanced for Sabbath School to be held there. During the next few days Father secured some of the girls who came to school to help with the plastering. He speaks of seven of them helping to plaster the kitchen on January 11, 12, and 13, and by January 14 he was able to teach in the new house, even though the plastering was not entirely dry. He was eager to get to work at home. He had secured school desks, which he found most helpful in his class room work. Heretofore, the children had no place to rest the papers on which they were writing.

Jan. 15. Started on a mule to Ft. Wingate. Got as far as Nutria and camped all night in an old Indian house. Found corn shucks in the house, which made a good bed. Ate two slices of bread for my supper. A good deal of snow at Nutria although at Zuni it was all gone.

Jan. 16. When I got up and went to saddle my mule, he did not care to be saddled and so ran off, after kicking at me with all his might, with a log dragging over the snow. I had the pleasure of walking home. Never was I more hungry and tired. This was a Sabbath spent in torture.

We'wha (we-wa). Photo by John Karl Hillers, circa 1886. Courtesy National Anthropological Archives, Smithsonian Institution.

THE OLD WHITE MULE

(This is a paper which Father wrote on June 26, 1889, relating the above incident.)

"In 1881 I hired a horse to go from Zuni New Mexico to Old Ft. Wingate, 45 miles. It was a lonely and unsafe ride over the mountains. When the mount came, lo! It was a white mule."

"I mounted and set off early in the morning, but by late afternoon, by kicking and whipping the mule I had reached only Nutria, a village of deserted houses, where the Indians formerly planted wheat. It was a cold evening, night was coming on, snow was on the ground, and the mule planted himself as if say, 'thus far and no farther.' I took off his saddle and bridle, tied him to a large log with a lariat, hunted up some husks which the Indians had left, and gave them to him to eat. I myself backed up into the corner of the ugly old adobe house to sit the night through without a fire. I had a small lunch which I divide between supper and breakfast."

"At long last the morning dawned. I fed the mule the little handful of husks I could hunt up in several houses. These the Indians had stuck up in folded packs for making cigarettes. The ground was covered with about five inches of snow. I started to saddle the mule to complete my journey, but to my consternation the old 'white' said No! He came at me with his mouth open and both forelegs extended. I knew that meant extermination. It is said that the bite of a mule produces death. He had a most convincing argument. There was no safety at either end of that nag. Soon I renewed my effort to bridle him; he repeated his ugliness. Then he started to drag away his moorings. When I ran after him, he would run; when I stopped, he stopped."

"I determined to make an effort to walk and carry saddle, bridle, and an old blanket home. I had not trudged long through the melting snow when my right leg began to hurt. I slowed up my gait and walked on. Oh, how I longed for the sight of a human being. Some time in the day a Navajo Indian hove in sight on horseback. When he came up, I tried to hire him to take me back, but he soon bolted past and left me pleading in vain."

"Later in the evening I found it would be impossible to carry my saddle any farther; so I threw it to one side and by a desperate effort reached some little springs where bulrushes grew. These rushes I pulled up by the roots; they nourished me. By that time I was five miles from home. That five miles was the hardest struggle I ever had to get home. Hungry, sleepy, and worn out, I did not dare to rest long for fear of falling asleep and to have slept out on the ground would have meant my death. It then became a struggle, not for home but for life. When I reached my door, I sank down from exhaustion before I could enter it. Finally I got enough strength to open the door of the house where I fell safe upon the floor."

It was March before he was able to go for his saddle but by that time he could find no trace of it.

Jan. 17. Teaching. The Indians have no Governor to push them on. Patricio [Pino] is nominally the Governor but he is not a man of any influence.

Jan. 18. Our school was very good today. Two women plastering.

Patricio Pino, Zuni Governor after Pablo Pino. "My Adventures Zuni" by Frank Hamilton Cushing, 1882.

Jan. 19. Mail. Two women plastering. We have very little wood. A stranger came in after dark. Fed him and sheltered him – he had no money.

By January 21 Father was able to secure two burro loads of wood. Heating the whole house by wood with one stove was difficult. That same day he and Mother made an issue to the scholars. The issues were various types of clothing supplied by the Government. The next day the 13 girls who were present the day before received dresses. Each boy was given a pair of stockings. The same day Father rubbed each head with blue ointment. I suspect the presence of lice explains the ointment.

The diary item for January 23 is interesting.

Opened Sabbath School at 8 because the scholars came in early. It was not ended until 11. About 50 scholars present. Sang "Come to Jesus." Read Matt., II Chpt. Gave little papers to all the scholars.

Mr. Blanchard who had come through Zuni on January 23 and taken dinner at the house passed with his teams on January 24 for Albuquerque. Through the rest of January the three of them were busily teaching, Mother Jennie, and Father. The Indians had begun another dance and so were not much interested in school. Sometimes the dance was in the evening and that fact helped the attendance at the school.

During the time he was in Zuni Father translated the second chapter of the Gospel of St. Matthew, the Lord's Prayer, and the Commandments into the Indian language. He had begun the study of the Indian languages as early as October 1878. He made a record of the words and expressions he had collected in 1879-1880.

Mother's notation in her diary on January 29 shows that her life was very full:

Today baked six loaves of bread, taught school – busy all day. Wrote to Miss Gates [now Mrs. Perea] and home. We made in all this week five garments; a shirt and two basques [jacket with long tails] for We-Wa, a dress for Grace, a dress and skirt for her sister, besides one for which they found the calico. (We-Wa was the Indian girl who helped around the house; helped with the washing, ironing and the general housework. Grace is the Indian girl whom Father baptized under the name of Grace Kennedy.)

Jan. 20. Held S. S. in the new building. We had a nice school – 3 teachers. Began the shorter catechism. Indians dancing.

Jan. 31. Taught. (Mother says for the same day) Jennie, We-Wa and I washed. I taught awhile. Scrubbed front room in the new house. Taught. Made out the school report. Girls average 20; boys average 11 – total 31. Warm and pleasant. Indians dancing – many of our pupils in the dance. Ruth reading in the first reader.

When February came Father succumbed to a severe spell of bronchitis and a bad cold in his head and left ear. February 2 he had to give up teaching and stay in bed all day. At the same time Jennie became ill. Mother took over our house, the teaching and the nursing. On Sunday she took charge of the Sunday School and gave out papers. Father tried to get up on February 3, but had to return to bed. His cough was most distressing. We children too were sick with bed colds; Pearl coughed most of the night. On the 7th Father went to school but still felt extremely bad; stayed only for the morning session. One evening Mr. Cushing, who had just returned from hunting his horse called.

Meanwhile we children, who practically lived in the school room, were advancing rapidly in our school work. I was advanced to a high reading chart which I received from Albuquerque, while Pearl was given a copy book and promoted.

Father did many imprudent things, which he as a doctor would have condemned in others, and of course he had to pay the penalty. This spell of bronchitis seems to have come as the result of his teaching in the new house of adobe, before it was sufficiently dry. One can understand his great eagerness to leave the small room in the Indian village in which he had been teaching and his desire to use the new desks which would help him to be an efficient teacher, but he should have waited. Now he was able to be in school only part of the day. His cough was so bad that it interfered with his teaching in the day and at night kept him from sleeping; in fact, he spent most of the day in bed.

Added to other inconveniences was the fact that it was cold weather and there was very little wood. One day Mother took her pupils to the kitchen for their classes, the only really warm room in the house. The ground was covered with snow. By February 11 the whole family was sick with bronchitis and it was impossible to hold school. On February 12 Father reported he felt better though his cough was still bad.

It was too much for mother to do everything and Mrs. Burgess from the town was secured on February 12 to help. Mother became ill too and was unable to carry on. All coughed day and night. Father developed symptoms of rheumatism to add to his distress. He explained the sickness by saying that the unusually heavy rains on the Pacific had caused a wave of cold air to sweep over New Mexico and penetrate their region. I feel the real cause could be found closer home. Their school work now became uphill business.

In the mail on February 16, Father received a cheering letter from Mr. Thomas, the Indian Agent at Santa Fe, who said that he was raising Father's salary as of last July. This was indeed good news.

On the 19th, since the Indians were in the midst of another dance, the folks moved their school room to the new house. Father, though still far from well, washed the floor, blackened the stove, and did all he could to make the place presentable, for he wished to hold the Sunday School the next day in that room.

The railroad by this time had advanced as far as Old Fort Wingate, about forty-five miles from Zuni. On February 20 Captain Hentig and his wife and Mrs. Henderson came from Apache on their way to Washington with the intention of taking the railroad at the Old Ft. Wingate. How fortunate they were to be able now to leave the territory by train.

The Dance of the Great Knife, Zuni. "My Adventures Zuni" by Frank Hamilton Cushing, 1882.

It is interesting to note how far the railroad had advanced by February, 1881. By March 10 it had advanced to Bacon Springs.

About the railroad situation in 1881 a note in an old magazine says that "the year 1881 brings a second transcontinental railway route, as the Atchison, Topeka, and Santa Fe Railroad has made a connection in New Mexico with the Southern Pacific R. R. in Arizona so that travelers can now go in good cars from Kansas City to San Francisco through New Mexico and Arizona.

Feb. 21. Taught in our old house. Indians dancing – not many came. Jennie, Mrs. E., and Josanna scrubbed the two rooms in the new house. The sun came up on the north end of Tah Yallaryne, the mesa back of the house, and shone in the kitchen window of the old house.

Feb. 22. Indians dancing. One beautiful boy fell through the roof of a house and broke his neck. I slept in the new house while the others slept in the old one. Mail came.

Feb. 23. Moved to new house. Indians dancing.

Feb. 26. Taught school. We employ our spare moments out of school fixing the two houses but we are all still very unwell with bronchitis. I have planted 3 trees N. and S. between the two houses.

On February 27 Sabbath School was held in the old stone house. The next day during the school session a captain of the army, Captain Hentig, happened to come in. Almost at once an old woman came running into the room and called out the children. It seems the Indians have been told that soldiers would come to send their children to the East to school. She wanted to keep that horror away from the children.

On March 1 a young man (who said he was the son of a Reformed Minister) came from Ft. Wingate. He stayed all night and went with Father during the evening to see the Indians dancing. The next day he started on his mule for Ft. Wingate. Evidently he did not impress Father very much because he speaks of him as a dead-beat.

Father on March 1 had a letter from Schellsburg which caused him much concern. His Mother, who was then 66, had been ill. At such times he realized keenly how far away he was from his own people. Grandmother was always an exceedingly frail person, but in spite of that fact she had a family of seven children and lived to the age of 74.

On March 4, Friday, the pupils came only in the morning. Even that short time was better than usual, for a dance was going on in the village. The next day was Saturday, therefore they should have stayed at home, but they came to school earlier than usual. Father felt the mission folks should have rest on that one day. Of course on Sabbath they always held Sabbath School in the morning with Bible School in the evening. That Sabbath, March 6, 30 were present. Mother and Jennie had gone to town and hunted them up.

The new house still had many things to be done around it. For instance, on March 4 Father had secured some Indian men to put dirt all over the roof. For this job each received a pair of trousers and a shirt.

On Wednesday March 7 the scholars arrived early, 7:00 A.M. even though 9:00 is the hour for school. A man, middle-aged, came to look through the windows, as he had done for about two months. Father felt he had been sent to find out the number and names of those attending and to report them. On March 12 at 8:30 he was again at the window. Father went out and told him to leave immediately. The man left with any further trouble. That day the school numbered 30. By March 11 the school had grown to 50. Every day Miss Hammaker went to town to hunt up pupils. Issues of clothing were made to those who have not yet received them.

The weather was extremely cold, so snowy and cold that on March 10 no mail came, although the following day it came at 1:00 P.M. Father speaks of the fact that the nights were bitterly cold. I have an idea that the folks had scarcely enough bed clothes to keep them warm. All during the rest of March there were many days that were very cold. On March 15 it was not only cold but the snow drifted and there was much snow on the ground.

Mr. Graham, who had a [trader's] store in the village, often went to Albuquerque for goods. On March 10 he returned from such a mission. Father mentions that on March 15 he settled his whole bill with Graham. Father now bought his household supplies from him.

As a preliminary to the dance on March 15 for eight days the Indians had exercises, and on that day babies were whipped and pottery was thrown from the houses and broken Another of their strange customs.

Let's take a few items directly from the diary and a letter to Dr. Jackson.

March 16. 50 scholars. A Navajo brought the mail late in the evening. A short note from Dr. Jackson offering me [a position at] some Mexican Church and school. Very cold last night.

March 17. 61 scholars. Very cold – snow on the ground. Mother Ealy is 66 today; Aunt Mat 81.

March 19. I have been writing up the issue papers. I was busy at the papers most of the day.

March 20. S. S. in morning. Bible Class in evening. Gave Sunday School papers to the scholars. The children are beginning to take some interest in the school.

Zuni, New Mex.
March 20, 1881

Doctor Jackson

Dear Brother,

I meant to write to you yesterday in regard to the field of labor you spoke of in your last, but the whole day was taken up in making out issue papers to Governor. As we only have one mail a week and to delay answering for a week more might cause you much delay in getting the field manned, I will drop you a line and say that I would not wish to take a new field in New Mexico or Colorado.

Yours fraternally,
T. F. Ealy

March 21. Indians dancing. 40 scholars came to school. Mr. Graham and Mr. Clark, an engineer on the A & P Road, called: Billy Hathaway called in the evening.

March 22. Indians dancing – over 50 in the dance. 32 scholars present.

March 23. Teaching. School large.

All of March shows a gratifying attendance at school. In spite of the dance many scholars preferred to attend school and evidently were allowed to do so. By this time many of them had learned enough English to understand the instruction and they were eager to take part in the singing. The illustrated papers too were full of interest to them. The three teachers were happy in their work; they felt at last the school was a going concern.

One of the out-of-town trips to see a patient Father made on March 24. He was asked to ride 15 miles below Navajo Springs to see Mr. William Jennings, a man at a railroad camp there who was ill of pneumonia. Not able to secure a horse that day, Father was forced to wait until the following morning when he set out at sunrise to ride the 58 miles. When he reached there at sundown the man had been dead eleven hours He received $40.00 for the trip. Realizing that he could not rely on hiring horses, Father returned at eight o'clock the following day with a pony which he had bought for $25.00. Now he had a mount of his own and no longer had to depend on the Indians.

The Sabbath School the next morning and the Bible School in the evening were very nice, but strange to say, Father recorded that he felt very tired. Even a young person such as he was then could not stand the punishment to which he was subjecting his body by his unceasing work added to his duties as a physician. A vacation of a week, which the folks took at this time, helped them to regain a little strength. They both were feeling the strain of the life in Zuni. On March 29 Mother says in her diary that they had not yet heard when they would be relieved of the Zuni post. This was a "consummation devoutly to be wished." They both realized now that the work there was too hard for them; it was a constant strain without any change, any relief.

Father worked on March 30 at putting up some benches for the school room and for the house in general. We girls I have heard had a bench to sit on at the table. The reason I know that fact is that a story is told about Pearl emitting a loud scream while we were sitting together on the bench one day. At once my parents said, "Ruthie, what are you doing?" It seems that I was cutting my teeth on Pearl's arm. My answer to the question was merely, "Yones please." I meant pinones [piñónes], a nut [from the pinyon pine tree] of which I was inordinately fond.

John Sullivan and two men from San Juan County came that evening; also a Miss McKee from Hollidaysburg, Pennsylvania. They were all at the parsonage for tea. The next day John Sullivan left for St. John's [Arizona] where he expected to work at the building of a court house. In his diary Father mentioned that Jennie rode the pony astride. Since that method for ladies was then taboo, Father felt it was worth a passing notice. I believe he was a little scandalized.

Dust storms bothered the folks often. Even the dishes in the cupboards were filled with dust at times and it was difficult to keep sand particles out of the food. Fortunately the latter part of March was beautiful without much wind and no dust.

In his diary for April 1 Father speaks of Pearl's reading ability and the accident with the pony. Let us note his record:

April 1. Pearl today finished the Second Reader. She is writing in copy book No. 2. Both Jennie and Mrs. E. fell off the pony today. The pony is not badly disposed but he is not used to seeing American women. Wrote to Mary Ealy.

April 2. Rained in evening.

April 3. 26 in S. S. The Indians have been going out for several days to plant wheat. A Mr. [Milo Lucius] Pierce came from Ft. Wingate last night and stayed all night. I had met him at Lincoln, N. Mex.

April 4. My school is gradually getting smaller on account of the Indians going out to plant wheat. About 13 present. Sent in school report and sanitary report but no medical property return. Sent in a general property return.

April 5. Teaching but the school is small. Mail came; got a letter from Mrs. Shaw, Rochester, N.Y., asking for a statement about the religion of the Pueblo Indians.

April 6. Bought 50 lbs. of flour of D. D. Graham. Paid $4 for the flour – the R. R. is only 40 miles off. I think this very dear. I wrote to Mrs. Shaw about the Pueblo Religions.

The account which Father wrote about the religions of the Pueblo Indians I have not found. This was written by Rev. John Menaul:

"The Pueblo Indians are of all people the most religious. Religion enters into everything they do, i.e., everything is done according to ancient custom – in fact, the whole inner and outer life of he Indian is one of perfect devotion to religious custom."

"It is this complete and perfect devotion to custom which has kept the Indians a separate and distinct people until this day."

"The Pueblo Indians are exceedingly slow from the fact that for centuries they haven set their faces like flint against anything foreign; especially Mexican."

The work of the various schools met the approval of Presbytery.

After the reports by various schools, the following resolution was passed:

"Resolved, that having reviewed the condition of all the schools under the care of Presbytery, we as a Presbytery do express our satisfaction with the status of this branch of the Church's work in this territory; and we heartily commend our teachers, and we will continue to labor to extend the influence of these schools and multiply their number."

April 7 turned out to be an extremely cold and windy day. Father was not at all well in the evening of April 8. He had taught though all day and written to Miss Lauderdale about the windmill in the evening. That same day Cushing went to Fort Wingate and Billy Davis and George Bruner came to Zuni from Navajo Springs. These movements of the white people were a source of great interest to the folks at the mission house. It was about their only contact with the outside world.

In addition to his other duties Father milked morning and evening. He wanted us children to have plenty of milk to drink. As he said, we practically lived on it. He saw too that the pony was well fed; the grass which it ate was cut with a sickle by the Indians and carried to the house in blankets.

Since nearly all the Indians were out of town, there was no Sabbath School on April 10. In the evening Father preached on 2nd Timothy 1:12. Besides our family there were present John Sullivan, Billy Davis, Billy Free, and George Bruner. You may note that Mr. Frank Cushing never attended any of these meetings. The following day Sullivan went to Fort Wingate, and Davis and Bruner back to Navajo Springs.

The mail, always a great boon to people separated from their own folks, was especially watched during these days. The mission folks, at least our family, were planning to go east as soon as possible, and were hoping to receive their salary from the Indian Agent. It had not been paid for a quarter and the promised increase in Father's salary had not been sent since July. He needed the money very much and so the next day when no money came, Father wrote to Dr. Thomas asking him to remit.

On April 14 the Indian Alcalde or magistrate was buried. Mr. Graham, who kept a store in the town itself, usually bought his goods in both Albuquerque and Wingate. He had difficulty in keeping his little girl from running away to play with the Indians. One of the few things I remember about our being in New Mexico is that I saw this little girl tied to the bedpost by a rope; my Father explained that the girl had to be tied up to keep her from running off. That scene made a great impression upon me. Mr. Graham was kind to us children. One day he took us for a short ride on horseback and entertained us also by making his dog go up and down a ladder placed against the house. He gave Father some bugs which he got in an Indian house. These bugs, roasted in fat, were eaten by the Indians. They looked like a young grub.

School kept up each day but now and then no pupils came for school. On April 18 Mother and Jennie went to town and compelled the children to attend school and thus had a few pupils. On the 17th so few people were in town that it was impossible to have Sabbath School. Father was able to have a Bible Class in the evening. He was pleased to see Billy Free present. It was probably his first day of attendance in a Sabbath School. It looked as if he enjoyed the class for he came to Bible Class the next Sabbath. That day Father had sufficient pupils to have Sabbath School in the morning.

Father had retired at 11:00 P.M. on April 24 when shortly he heard someone at the door. Graham had come for him to attend Mrs. Burgess. It was the next evening at 7:00 P.M. before she was delivered of a girl. Mother says in her diary that she went every day for awhile to bathe Mrs. Burgess' baby. At the time Mother felt she was in rough surroundings, among rough people.

It is interesting how many different people brought the mail in April. On April 15 Enos Cushing [Frank's brother] brought it from Fort Wingate, in it a letter from Mother's Father; on the 19th the mail came by buckboard with a new driver; on April 25th John Sullivan came from Wingate with the mail.

On April 19 Dubois, wife, and sister came from Deer Springs to spend the night. Jennie went with Mrs. Dubois the next day for a short visit. Deer Springs is 22 miles from Zuni in Arizona.

By April 20 Father reports that I began reading the First Reader for the second time though I was only three and a half years old. Pearl about the same time finished the Second Reader and began the Third Reader. She also was busy with arithmetic questions – had worked 89 by May 4.

The school had been small for some time but by April 29 the Indians were returning to town from planting wheat. Also, the time spent out of school had a disastrous effect upon the boys; most of them spent the time now in catching black birds instead of coming to school. Father was disgusted that the Governor, Patricio Pino, did not take a hand and make the boys attend school. On May 2 the school was full again.

A good rain and showers on April 16 made the country look much better than it had the previous April. The weather began to be very warm.

Frank Cushing came over from Fort Wingate on April 21 to secure Indians to make adobes. He stayed at the manse for super. The next day Mr. Graham returned from Fort Wingate.

Meanwhile Jennie was making several visits. From Deer Springs she went to Ojo Vennado [Venado]. While she was away Mother had much more to do. She reports that on April 22 she both washed and baked. In those days one could not run out to the nearest grocery to get a loaf of bread. All bread had to be baked on the premises. The washing too had to be done by hand with hard rubbing.

The Zuni Indians were usually peaceable, not easily aroused to anger; therefore Father as amazed one day to see an Indian strike a woman with the round of a ladder.

One of the things in the Zuni village that worried Father was the lack of water and the poor sanitation. For some time he had been trying to persuade the Indians to dam a place in the Black Rocks and make there a large reservoir. He was sure this result would be possible if a V-shaped dam could be built. He tried hard to get the Government to help in this project. On April 28 he persuaded Mr. Graham to go with him to Pescado to view the site he had in mind.

On the last day of April Father sprained his leg when he jumped from his pony while it was running. That same day both Mother and Father made out the property return and the abstracts, A, B, C, D sanitary reports of the school.

The next day, Sabbath, was spent in teaching Sabbath School at 9:10 and Bible Class in the evening. Mr. Freeman Hathaway was present.

A story came with the mail man on May 3 to the effect that Mrs. Thackeray had been found dead in her bed with her head split open. It was thought that her husband had killed her in a drunken row. They lived 30 miles north of Zuni.

Father made a kite for Pearl on May 5. The next day, when he flew the kite, the Indian children came flocking and of course were persuaded to go into the schoolroom. Then Father planned to make a larger one and use the same scheme the next day. That day there were about 25 pupils.

With the warm weather, aided by that number of showers the country now looked green and beautiful. Father planted his lot in corn.

Mother wrote in her diary that on May 5 Jennie, Pearl, and I dressed in our Indian clothes and went over to the town. We still had these dresses after our return to Schellsburg and were very proud of them. When settled in Schellsburg, the family had a number of extremely pretty Indian blankets and several pieces of potter which are still in the family.

Cushing came from Wingate on May 7 with two mules and a driver intending to go exploring. The next day, Sabbath, after the Sabbath School of twenty-five was over, Father walked over to the town to talk with Mr. Graham, and while he was there Mr. Frank Cushing entered and asked to buy something from Mr. Graham's store. To Father's disgust Mr. Graham accompanied him to the store. He said, "Such a way to keep the Sabbath!" It was a day of great activity for Zuni for seven wagons and almost 31 horses passed. Some statements from the diary:

May 9. Teaching. Mail came by Mr. Freeman Hawthorne. Not much wind and no drifting up at this time.

May 10. Windy and drifting – the scholars did not come in the afternoon except 2. Mail came by buckboard.

May 11. Not so much wind. Cushing left for the caves in Arizona. He came into the schoolroom and three girls ran off – evidently afraid.

May 12 & 13. The Indians are busy at the corn fields planting. Ruth finished the first reader today. She is 3 ½ years old. I was in the schoolhouse about 8 hours.

By May 14 everything was moving along quietly. Father taught those who came and in the afternoon read Still's "Materia Medica [Medical Material]" on the therapeutical action of Calomel [a mercury chloride mineral, used to relieve constipation]. The following day Mr. Armstrong, Mr. Gregory, and a German came from the railroad to visit Zuni. They liked what they saw. It was Sabbath and therefore Sabbath School was held in the morning and in the evening singing exercises for all who wished to come. Though it was May, a hard shower with hail came up in the evening. Two men who were often at the exercises left for Navajo – Free and Bennett.

On May 19 Lieutenant John G. Bourke came from Wingate and Lieutenant Carl F. Palfrey, 1st Lieutenant of Engineer Corps of Arizona on General [George R.] Crook's staff. Both Lieutenants remained over night and put their ten mules in the coral. Though they called on the folks, neither one visited the mission school. They left on May 21, one for Wingate, the other for Navajo Springs. They felt they were roughing it but Father thought not. By this time the scholars were beginning to return to school. On may 19 the General Assembly of the Presbyterian Church met at Buffalo, N. Y.

The mail now was reaching Zuni from two directions, from St. John's by buckboard and from Fort Wingate, often by the hands of friends. On May 16 it failed to arrive, Father thought it was due to the fact the stock was attached.

Father performed a wedding ceremony on May 25. Mr. William Davis married Mrs. Carrie Burgess. There were Americans who lived for the most part in the Indian town at this wedding, thirteen in all, an unusual occurrence in Zuni. Cushing had gone away on May 11 but he returned in time for the wedding. With him were two men from Arizona; Graham, who had gone to the Fort on the 23rd was on hand also. Mother says she baked the wedding cake.

As the school at this time was not large, Mother took the two of us and started at noon on May 26 with Mr. and Mrs. Dubois to pay a short visit to them on their ranch twenty-two miles west of Zuni. Meanwhile Father was able to do all the teaching. Mother wrote of her starting with Mr. and Mrs. Dubois, but as she relates when they were nearly there, she and we children met John Sullivan, who persuaded us to go with him to Mr. Stevens' home. There Mother met a number of Mexican ladies.

What does Father say about our absence?

May 28. It seems lonely with the children away. About 10 P.M. Jennie and I were startled while at worship by a knock, Albert and Effie and Nora and Mr. and Mrs. Kuhns had come from Albuquerque; Mr. Wiswell and Mr. Billings from the R. R. They had all started to visit us but failed to reach Zuni before night.

Father had been greatly delighted when his brother Albert had moved to Albuquerque. It brought his home folks nearer. You can imagine his joy now when the whole family came to Zuni to visit them. This trip was made possible by the new railroad which linked Albuquerque with this part of the country.

May 29. It was a scene of confusion. But we were delighted to see them. Mrs. Ealy got home at 11 A.M. After they had seen some of the people and houses of the Indians, we had dinner. Wiswell and Billings started for the R. R. tie camp on the mountain, and in another hour the ambulance started with the other folks. In the evening singing, Sullivan, Free, Underwood, and Graham.

It must have been difficult to settle down the next few days to the routine work of teaching and making out necessary reports, which were constantly required by the Indian Agent. Father sent in his reports on June 1.

June 2. Lieut. Emmet, a reporter, and an artist, [Willard Leroy] Metcalf, for Harper's Weekly, came to Zuni. Cushing came with them from the Ft.

June 3. Small school. John Sullivan brought the mail from Ft. Wingate.

June 4. Threatened rain all day. Messrs. Emmet, Bagster, Metcalf expect to remain several days. One year ago today we laid our little darling Bertie in the grave.

Early in June Father had a call to come to Bacon Springs to see Mrs. Bishop, seventy-nine years old, who had broken her upper femur. She had had a similar accident on the other leg eight years before. In order to reach Bacon Springs he took the buckboard in the evening for Fort Wingate but stopped off at Nutria, twenty-two miles from Zuni. He had held Sabbath School in the morning before he left. The following morning June 6 he left Nutria at sunup and got to Wingate at nine o'clock. The days were now very warm. He ate his dinner with Mr. Fisher at the A. & P. Railroad station and his supper with Mr. Crane at Bacon Springs. After helping to make Mrs. Bishop comfortable he left Crane's early the next morning and walked to the depot for breakfast. Then at 9:00 A.M. he took the train for Wingate and at 10:00 took the buckboard for Zuni, were he arrived at 10:00 P.M. Father's delight in the railroad may be sensed from this part of his diary. He ate at the station at Wingate, went by rail to Crane's at Bacon Springs, and the next morning walked to the station at Bacon Springs for breakfast.

On June 8 he had a different type of patient. Mrs. Davis was very much distressed with a bad case of quinay [tonsillitis]. A gargle which Father gave her caused the swollen gland to burst in a short time and almost at once she became much more comfortable.

By June 8 the folks had heard that they were to be relieved at the mission by Rev. Mr. S. A. Bentley. It was not until ten days later that Mr. and Mrs. Bentley appeared unexpectedly at sundown to take their position as U.S. Indian Teachers. Since they had not written, the folks felt that the house was not left as it would have been had they known just when the Bentleys would come.

The days were warm; the nights extremely cool. The school remained quite small.

On June 10 Mr. Davis started with his family for his ranch in Arizona and when eight miles out, little Willie tumbled out of the wagon. They were fearful lest the wheel had run over him and so returned to have him near a doctor should any bad symptoms arise. Finding Willie was not hurt they started again the following day. The air was hot and dry with much wind in the afternoon.

A doctor from Fort Wingate came to the village on June 13; his purpose seemed to be to vaccinate the Indians. Evidently he had very little practice at the Fort. On the same day the Adjutant and his wife from Fort Wingate and Miss B. arrived in town. Two days later the stage contained a Sioux Indian, Tito-Com-at Se, who lived then in Indian Territory.

In a talk with the chiefs of the town on June 15 Father found that the children who came to school were those who disobeyed their elders, for they had been forbidden to attend the mission school. In spite of this fact the attendance during May had been fairly good because the children had learned to like school, interested as they were in the cards issued to them and in the singing. Father told the war cacique he was a bad man valueless to the community. The children enjoyed the singing and always entered heartily into it. Sometimes the whole Sabbath evening service was a song service. The few Americans in the town did not attend the meetings. What a great help they would have been had they done so!

Some horse thieves were prowling around taking horses whenever possible. On June 17 the men who had been after them to try to get back the horses were able to overtake the thieves and recover seven of them. The robbers lived in Colorado on the San Juan River.

As I have mentioned, the Rev. Mr. and Mrs. Bentley had come to Zuni on June 18. The folks were glad to see them, but somewhat surprised that they had not been notified the time of their arrival, nor were they given any chance to explain the work of the mission. The new minister and his wife appeared late at Sabbath School the following day. The Indian pupils, as their custom was when any strangers appeared, began to leave one by one. It was not a very propitious beginning for their work.

Thus the departure of Father, Mother, and us children came more suddenly than any one anticipated. Everyone was up early Monday morning getting the final packing done and the transfer papers made out before the government ambulance left at 9:00 A.M. for Fort Wingate and the railroad three miles below the Post. Too weary to care, the night was spent in sleep even though a bed on the floor of the box car was the only place to rest. The next morning, Father who had ridden his pony and driven the two cows and three calves went first to the Post and then to Crane's at Bacon Springs, where he left his pony and cattle. Mother and we children went by the railroad to the same place and by six o'clock that evening all were ready to take the train for Albuquerque. The trip was made in a caboose.

Father notes that his official connection with Zuni ended on June 21, 1881, and that he was succeeded by S. A. Bentley.

When we reached Albuquerque, we were met at the station by uncle Albert, whom we had promised to visit later. First though we went to Bernardillo [Bernalillo] by train to pay a promised visit to Susan Gates Perea. At this town where Mr. Perea's brother lived, we were met by Don Jesus Perea, who sent us in his carriage to Carrola where Susan, her husband, and their little boy now lived. All of us were delighted to see Susan once again. Alas! By this Pearl and I somewhere had contracted measles, and so the folks thought it better to take us at once back to Albuquerque.

The family stayed there until June 29. Mother and Father did not want to wait any longer, for they were eager to get settled in a home. Father in the few days he was in Albuquerque went with his brother, who also was a doctor, to dress a fracture of a leg and to visit his patients.

The trip home was an exceedingly great improvement over the trip four years before. Now we could go by train almost to our destination with no traveling by buckboard or wagons drawn by mules or oxen, no sleeping in the open with wolves howling all night and no lack of food. Instead comfortable trains took us along at what then seemed a rapid rate to our home. The very luxury of it all entranced us, we children were especially pleased. The baggage had to be checked to Philadelphia, Pennsylvania. We left Albuquerque on June 29.

By July 1 we were in Kansas City. The next day word came while we were on the train that President Garfield had been shot, a rumor later confirmed when we reached Columbus. Early on July 3 we came into Altoona, which appeared to be a large place to eyes long accustomed to a small Indian village. There we found everybody greatly excited over the attempted assassination of the President [he died of his wounds September 19, 1881]. We went to Huntingdon from Altoona in order to take the Monday morning train for Mann's Choice, the nearest railroad point to Schellsburg, four miles away. It was three in the afternoon when the train reached Mann's Choice, and somewhat later we were in Schellsburg. Aunt Mary said in her diary that our family arrived unexpectedly and that Father and Mother were much broken in health. Father found all his folks well. He offered sincere thanks to God for our safe journey of 3,000 miles. It was the Fourth of July.

Father at once took his place in the life of Schellsburg. On Wednesday night he was at prayer meeting, which he speaks of as a blessed privilege. He also began to go with his Father to see patients. On July 8 he mentions one as very bad and on July 10, just as he was starting for Sunday School, a boy came into the office breathless to report a run-off and to say his Father and a woman were badly hurt. Both doctors went to see the inured. The woman had her leg broken and man had a gash torn in his left arm.

On July 10 at 8:00 P.M. Father spoke in the Presbyterian Church on the work in New Mexico.

Grandfather Ealy had some farms near Schellsburg. Father says that on July 11 he went to the Grove farm for cherries. I can remember that as children my sister and I frequently went to this same farm for cherries. Unfortunately I was a poor climber and so Pearl, who was like a squirrel, was able to pick all around me.

On July 13 Mother and we girls left Mann's Choice for her home at East Waterford, where Father was to join her later.

Aunt Effie Ealy, Uncle Albert's wife, came for a visit to her home in Schellsburg on July 15. On that same day Father received a letter from Jennie, who had decided to stay behind at Zuni when the folks left. He also had a letter from Dr. Agnew, Philadelphia, Pennsylvania.

In October of that year Mother wrote the following letter about the recent sudden death of Jennie Hammaker:

Schellsburg, Bedford Co., Pa.
October 3, 1881

Dear Dr. Jackson:

You have been informed ere this of the death of Jennie Hammaker. It seems so hard to understand and yet we know that it is the "hand of God" that hath done this. It came like a thunder bolt to her parents. Will you be at Albuquerque soon; if so please let me know. There are so many things we should like to know and her parents are so anxious to have all her books, etc. Please inform us if you expect to be there soon. I was anxious to have our baby's body brought East, but if Jennie could be buried on the Zuni Mission ground I think it would be best to leave it there. The Hammakers are not able to bear any heavy expenses or would have had the body brought home right away but all was so sudden and the telegrams to be answered immediately, it was difficult to tell what to do.

Kind regards to Mrs. Jackson.
Very respectfully,
Mrs. T. F. Ealy
Schellsburg, Bedford Co., Pa.

Father meanwhile was doing all he could to relieve his Father of the heavier part of his practice, which extended for many miles all around the town and even far up into the mountain. One case was that of Mrs. Hinton, whom he took to Philadelphia for an operation. Mrs. Hinton was a great sufferer and both doctors hoped something could be done for her in a city hospital. They took the train at Napier and reached Philadelphia by 6:50 that evening. The patient by that time was frightened and almost exhausted. They stopped at the European Hotel for the night but changed to the boarding house of Mrs. G. H. A. Camp, 3305 Walnut Street the next noon where the price was much less, only $4.50 a week. Father, realizing his shabby clothes, took some time to buy (at Wanamaker's) a suit for $7.00 and a hat for 75 cents.

Let us close with Father's July 17 entry in his diary:

Was at Sabbath School at 9 A.M. and at church at 10:30 and also in the evening at 8 P.M.

Chapter 7 | Conclusion

The first part of Father's life was spent in preparing for what he intended to be his life's work. It had been his great desire to be a missionary, if not to the foreign field, at least to the people of the West. He gladly went to the fields selected for him by the Board. The climate at Fort Arbuckle proved such that he felt he could stay no longer; then came the chance to go to New Mexico. Now, he surely had found the right place. Alas! The fighting which raged during much of the time he was in Lincoln, New Mexico, was a deterrent to any sort of Christian work. When it came to be almost constant, he decided that the only course to follow was to leave for the present. He hoped later that it would be possible for him to return, for he realized the great need for just such spiritual leadership as he hoped to furnish.

The Board decided to send him to a struggling Mission Station in the town of Zuni, New Mexico, a pueblo town occupied by about fifteen hundred Indians. These people were the least approachable of all the tribes, not because they ware unfriendly, but because they were perfectly satisfied with the type of religion which they had and were utterly indifferent to any attempt to educate or to Christianize them. This situation was complicated by the fact that Father did not know their language and his knowledge of Spanish was inadequate, by the fact that he was supposed to build a mission house with little idea of the way to go about such a task, by the lack of such comforts he had always considered necessary, and by his somewhat isolated situation. Fortunately he had the help of a devoted wife and a good assistant.

He at once set about the task of supplying the things which he lacked. He studied both Spanish and Indian. He gathered the materials for the house, with as much speed as possible and at once set about building it. He rejoiced in the approach of the railroad as a means of securing more comforts and of gaining more contact with the outside world. He welcomed visitors from the East who came to learn about the Zuni Indians. Finally he took every opportunity to broaden himself.

By the time he left in 1881 be had a mission station of two houses, with cottonwood trees between, a stable, and a corral, all surrounded by a wall. He had gained the respect of many of the Indians who more and more were beginning to realize the value of an education. The religious dances still interfered with the school attendance, it is true, but the children seemed to be enjoying their school work. He had learned to like his Indian friends.

When he had to leave because of his health he was sorry. He hoped some time to return to his work in New Mexico. Meanwhile, he went to Schellsburg, Pennsylvania to help his Father with his wide country practice. He remained in this town the rest of his life and there his family grew up. The practice of medicine was natural for him and I know he enjoyed it, but I believe that he always, after his missionary experience, longed for that type of work and hoped some day to return to the mission field in New Mexico.

Some changes through the years have occurred in Zuni. First of all the houses are built of red sandstone rather than adobe; the cause of education has been advanced, for now the town has four schools, a public school, a government school, a Protestant Mission

School and a Catholic Mission School, and a Governor who really has a great interest in the educational advancement of his people; he also is trying to improve the sanitary conditions in the town by securing a better water supply and a sewerage system, but the Zuni still need many improvements. The pueblo style of architecture is not adaptable to modern life, the Indians need to have some definite means of earning a living, for some still come to school poorly clad and poorly fed, and they need to learn to look forward rather than back. They need to become really a part of the great Christian World.

Father's work may appear to many as unimportant. He seemed to change very little the lives of the Indians among whom he worked; his life in Schellsburg was only that of a country doctor. When he was a boy he longed to be a soldier, but he never fought in the United States Army. He was always, though, a fighter for the cause of righteousness. Wherever he went, in the West, on the mission field, in his home in Schellsburg, he worked faithfully to advance the cause of the great Master, under whom he enlisted. He could truly say at the end of his life, "I have fought a good fight." His was an influence which only a true Christian possesses. Who can say how far that influence has reached?

Appendix A | Taylor F. Ealy's Testimony at Dudley Court of Inquiry

The Dudley Court of Inquiry was held from May 2, 1879 to July 6, 1879, at Fort Stanton. The purpose of the Inquiry was to determine whether Colonel Dudley should be court-martialed for his actions – or lack of actions – in Lincoln during the 5-day shootout which ended with the burning of Alexander A. McSween's house on July 19, 1878. McSween, Harvey Morris, Vincente Romero, and Francisco Zamora were killed attempting to flee the burning building. Deputy Robert Beckwith – a Dolan man – was killed in the "promiscuous" shooting that accompanied the attempted escape.

The judges in the Inquiry were Colonel Galusha Pennypacker, presiding, Major N. W. Osborne, and Captain H. R. Brinkerhoff. The prosecutor, representing the Army, was Captain Henry H. Humphreys. Assisting Captain Humphreys was attorney Ira Leonard, who was Susan McSween's personal attorney. Defending Colonel Dudley was Santa Fe lawyer Henry L. Waldo. Dudley was exonerated by the Court for his actions in Lincoln and not ordered to stand trial in a court marshal.

Ealy's testimony in the Inquiry, which he writes about on page 115, follows. Although he writes that he only testified for one day, on June 2, 1879, he actually asked the Court for permission to amend his testimony and testified briefly the next day. The "Recorder" (prosecutor) in the trial transcript is Captain Humphreys. For much of the trial, as shown by the transcript, Dudley represented himself.

Testimony

Mr. TAYLOR F. EALY, a witness being duly sworn testified as follows.

Q. by Recorder [prosecutor]. *State you name and occupation and place of residence?*

Answer. *T. F. Ealy, teacher to the Zuni Indians, live at Zuni, N.M.*

Q. by Recorder. *Were you in Lincoln, N.M. on the 19th day July last and did you see Col. Dudley there that day, if so state when and where you first saw him, and what time of day?*

Answer. *I was in Lincoln on the 19th, saw Gen'l Dudley about dusk in the evening. I first saw him about 10 or 12 paces from my door. I lived in the easterly end of the Tunstall building.*

Q. by Recorder. *How far was he from the residence of McSween when you saw him?*

Answer. *I think less than 200 feet.*

Q. by Recorder. *State, if you know, whether at the time you saw Col. Dudley, when you state, the McSween house was burning.*

Answer. *The McSween house was then burning.*

Q. by Recorder. *In which direction did Col. Dudley go, or was he going when you saw him, towards or from the McSween house?*

Answer. *Towards the McSween house.*

Q. by Recorder. *Did you have any conversation with Col. Dudley that day, if so, state what it was, if it had any reference to the events that were then transpiring there, if so, state fully all that occurred between you and him?*

Answer. *About 30 minutes after I passed him, I spoke to him in camp asking him to save some property I had in front of my building. He said he could not send his men up there to be shot, that he himself had been shot at. I replied that I did believe that he was shot at, he said that is all he wanted to talk to me and that I had to leave the camp.*

Q. by Recorder. *State what further, if anything, occurred about your mission that day, and what [was] done, if anything?*

Answer. *I told Dr. Appel that I would write a note to Gen'l Dudley. He said no, he will not receive it from you. I told the parties standing by to note what he said. Dr. Appel said he would receive a note from Mrs. Ealy. She wrote him a note asking him to save the property in front of the house, the property was safely returned.*

Q. by Recorder. *What kind of property was it?*

Answer. *An organ, my books and a few other things. Just what I could grab and throw into a box in haste, a clock, and so forth. We understood they were going to set fire to the building. That is why we hurried out.*

Q. by Recorder. *Is that all that transpired between you and Col. Dudley that day?*

Answer. *Yes Sir.*

Recorder stated he had finished with the witness.

Cross Examine:

Q. by Col. Dudley. *Do you swear that you first saw Col. Dudley about dusk in the evening of the 19th of July last?*

Answer. *Yes Sir.*

Q. by Col. Dudley. *Do you swear that you first saw Col. Dudley about 10 or 12 feet from your door on that day?*

Answer. *Yes Sir.*

Q. by Col. Dudley. *Was not Dr. Appel and some other officers with a detachment of troops coming down the road to your house with a wagon to get some things of yours and was not Col. Dudley on the opposite side of the street coming along at the same time when you say you saw him about 10 or 12 feet first from your front door?*

Answer. *Yes Sir. That was the time I saw him first.*

Q. by Col. Dudley. *You say you passed him. Where was he at the time you passed him, and in what direction was he going?*

Answer. *I have already answered that, the same answer that I gave you, 10 or 12 steps from my house, Gen'l Dudley towards the burning building, I towards the camp, Patron's house. With my little babe in my arms.*

Q. by Col. Dudley. *On which side of your house was he at the time, on the side towards Col. Dudley's camp, if not, state on which side it was?*

Answer. *On the eastern side towards the camp going in the opposite direction from the camp.*

Q. by Col. Dudley. *Were not the things that were taken away at the time the wagon came down with Dr. Appel and the other officers, and when, as you say, you saw Col. Dudley the first time that day, the last things that were taken away from your house?*

Answer. *No Sir. They were not. My library was left back. He refused. That is what I wanted brought back when I talked to him in camp.*

Q. by Col. Dudley. *How many times were things taken away from your house that day?*

Answer. *Once before when I talked with him in the camp, which I had forgotten. There was nothing left but my library which they afterwards brought. Twice.*

Q. by Col. Dudley. *Now Doctor, to please to refresh your memory to ascertain if you had not been to Col. Dudley's camp and had an interview with him before you saw him down near your house?*

Answer. *No Sir. I was not out of my building that day that I know of previous to the time I saw him in front of my house.*

Q. by Col. Dudley. *Was it not in regards to getting those things which were come for, at the time you saw Col. Dudley the first time that day, that your wife wrote the note to Col. Dudley?*

Answer. *She wrote a note from the house asking for an escort to take us out.*

Q. by Col. Dudley. *What things were come for at the time you saw Col. Dudley the first time that day?*

Answer. *I remember now more distinctly that there were two trunks and the organ, taken in the first load, three trunks, perhaps Miss Gates had one.*

Q. by Col. Dudley. *Had anything been taken from your house to the camp before Mrs. Ealy wrote the note to Col. Dudley?*

Answer. *No sir, they were not taken to the camp at any time, nor was any guard placed around us. Nothing had been touched, we were in a house, four ladies and seven children, doors locked, windows covered. Part of the sheriff's posse in front of the door firing. We were there from about 1:00 o'clock until dusk, shut up.*

Col. Dudley, by his Counsel, then submitted a note from Mrs. Ealy as evidence. See Exhibit No. 37. Read to Court after showing same to witness.

Witness resuming. *Nothing had been taken before the first note was written. This is the second note.*

Q. by Col. Dudley. *Were the things taken from your house moved by the soldiers? If so, to what place were they taken?*

Answer. *They were removed by the soldiers to the Patron house.*

Q. by Col. Dudley. *Was not Patron's house near the camp?*
Answer. *Yes Sir.*

Q. by Col. Dudley. *Now Sir, what time was that note, the note of your wife you have just read, written with reference to the taking of the things from your house by the soldiers. Was it the first load, or the second load that was taken?*
Answer. *It was after the first load.*

Q. by Col. Dudley. *Did you not just a second ago say it was the second load?*
Answer. *That did not go down on paper. I said I did not. I can say to that, that I do not remember saying that.*

Q. by Col. Dudley. *Now please to state in reference to what things your wife wrote this note, was it the library of yours?*
Answer. *Mrs. Ealy wrote the note because Col. Dudley refused. Yes Sir, this is note No. 1, the first note written.* (Lieut. Col. Dudley handing same to witness.)

Note submitted in evidence. See Exhibit No. 39. Read to Court.

Q. by Col. Dudley. *Is the note just shown to you the one in which your wife asked for an escort from the Tunstall building?*
Answer. *It is, Sir.*

Q. by Col. Dudley. *What time of day was it when your wife first wrote the note to Col. Dudley asking for an escort?*
Answer. *After we had been in the house for about 5 hours, about dusk.*

Q. by Col. Dudley. *Was an escort, or guard, furnished in response to this note? If so, how long after it was sent?*
Answer. *Yes Sir. A few minutes.*

Q. by Col. Dudley. *Now, did your wife and children, Mrs. Shields [Shield] and children, Mrs. Ealy and Miss Gates go to the camp or to some house near the camp at some time between 12 and 2 o'clock on that day?*
Answer. *About dusk they went to the Patron house.*

Lt. Col. Dudley then submitted to the witness a paper dated Fort Stanton, NM 7-26-78 which witness identified as his hand writing. Lt. Col. Dudley then submitted to witness a paper endorsed July 20, 1878 which he acknowledged to be his hand writing.

Answer. *These are to the best of my knowledge.*

Q. by Col. Dudley. *Now Sir. Did you not on that day go to Col. Dudley's camp and ask for soldiers to go to Tunstall's building and when told by Col. Dudley he would not order his soldiers under the fire of the contending parties prevailing at and near the Tunstall store, and did you not in an angry, violent, impervious and arbitrary manner, demand of him, what United States troops were for if not to protect you and your property?*
Answer. *I do not remember of using that language. I don't know if I told him that the U.S. soldiers were there to protect my family. I asked for soldiers in the camp to save my library and was refused.*

Q. by Col. Dudley. *Did he not assign as a reason that he would not order his soldiers to expose themselves to such a fire as prevailing at that time near the Tunstall building?*
Answer. *He said he did not wish to send his soldiers up there [to] be shot.*

Q. by Col. Dudley. *Did you not at the time fall into a passion at his refusal?*
Answer. *I was excited.*

Q. by Col. Dudley. *Did you not use some very violent language to Col Dudley?*
Answer. *I don't think so. Sir.*

Q. by Col. Dudley. *What was it then to which your wife referred to in her note and what was it in your conduct she apologized for?*
Answer. *For saying I did not believe he was shot at.*

Q. by Col. Dudley. *Was it not on account of that refusal of Col. .Dudley to send his soldiers under fire, and expose them to be shot, that your wife wrote the note in question asking him for soldiers to get the remainder of the things?*
Answer. *The note embraced two things, that my asking that my books be brought and offering him an apology for my saying I did I did believe he had been shot at. My reason was a double reason, what I have stated was her reason, I don't know of any other reason for writing it.*

Q. by Col. Dudley. *Did you go down yourself with the wagon and volunteers and two officers the last time they went down after your library and other things?*
Answer. *No Sir.*

Q. by Col. Dudley. *Where was the library and other things at the time, the last time I mean, the soldiers went down, in the building or outside it?*
Answer. *I don't know what time you refer to, I don't know, I think they were partly inside and the box outside.*

Q. by Col. Dudley. *You are a Minister, or profess to be a Minister of the Gospel, do you not?*
Answer. *Yes Sir.*

Lieut Col. Dudley, by his Counsel, stated he was finished with the witness.

Re Direct:

Q. by Recorder. *You stated that you desired to explain about how the things were taken away from your house. What explanation did you desire to make?*
Answer. *I want to explain about the note. Mrs. Ealy wrote it because Col. Dudley refused me, the getting of the box also, because he, through Dr. Appel, refused to receive any communication from me.*

Witness was warned of the ruling of the Court. [Rule regarding hearsay.]

Q. by Recorder. *Explain why you was excited on Col. Dudley's refusal to send soldiers down to your residence for the things you wanted taken away from there?*
Answer. *I was not accustomed to seeing such inhumanity exhibited.*

Q. by Recorder. *Explain what the guard or escort did when you went with them and how long they continued to guard you and family, and what protection, if any, they gave you?*

Answer. *The escort, when I left, I do not remember seeing a gun, when the escort arrived I do remember of seeing a gun. I took my babe and went in advance, I did not go with them. They come with the ladies to the Patron house. They escorted them to the house without guns, and left them there soon after.*

Recorder stated he had finished with the witness.

Lieut. Col. Dudley, by his Counsel, then requested the Recorder to read a letter previously submitted to witness this day. See Exhibit No. 40.

Q. by Col. Dudley. *Were you and the persons mentioned in the note just read to you taken to the fort, and if so, by whom were you taken and by whose order?*

Answer. *About 4:00 o'clock, July 20th, we were furnished with transportation to the post. The troops were under command of Gen'l Dudley. It was government transportation. We were either in advance or behind them.*

Q. by Col. Dudley. *How long did you remain at the fort?*
Answer. *Nine days I think.*

Lieut. Col. Dudley, by his Counsel, offered in evidence a letter previously submitted to the witness this day. Read to Court. See Exhibit No. 41.

Q. by Col. Dudley. *Was transportation furnished in pursuance of the request?*
Answer. *I think not Sir.*

Q. by Col. Dudley. *Who was in command of the post at that time?*
Answer. *Col. Dudley was called commander.*

Q. by Col. Dudley. *Did you not go along at the same time?*
Answer. *Yes Sir.*

Q. by Col. Dudley. *Did not a guard of soldiers accompany the transportation?*
Answer. *I think the transportation and driver of the ambulance were all.*

Lieut. Col. Dudley, by his Counsel, then submitted a letter dated August 1878, which he admitted to be in his hand writing. Submitted into evidence, read to Court. See Exhibit No. 42

Q. by Recorder. *Explain how you came to the fort and your treatment while here by Col. Dudley?*
Answer. *Came by government transportation. I felt that I was a prisoner at the post.*

Q. by Recorder. *State if while you were here at the post you received any communication from Col. Dudley inviting you to leave the post, or otherwise?*
Answer. *Yes Sir, I have one in my pocket. This is the original.* Witness handed to the Recorder a letter dated July 23, 1879. Recorder submitted same in evidence. Read to Court. See exhibit No. 43.

Witness resuming. *I have another in my possession but not here.*

Q. by Recorder. *Explain how you happened to receive this letter and what induced it?*

Answer. *By request of the ladies I wrote a note requesting an axe. I did not know if I was allowed to touch the wood or not. I did not know where to get an axe. I was abundantly willing and able to cut my own wood. Mrs. Ealy was doing cooking for as small a family....*

Recorder stated he had finished with the witness.

Witness then withdrew.

[Lieut. Samuel S. Pague, 15th Infantry, was called as a witness and after being duly sworn, questioned by both sides. The Court adjourned at 4:10 P.M to meet the next day, June 3, 1879, at 10 A.M.]

[When the Court opened the next day, Mr. Ealy asked to make a statement.]

Witness Dr. Ealy wished to make the following correction in his testimony. Witness desired to add to question, "Please refresh your memory," as follows. "I was not out of my house after the troops come in until I left the house to go to Patron's house."

Lieut. Col. Dudley, by his Counsel, then submitted to witness a note dated July 23, 1878, 5 PM, which he acknowledged to be his hand writing. Read to Court. See Exhibit No. 40.

Q. by Col. Dudley. *Is that your hand writing here?*
Answer. *Yes Sir.*

Q. by Col. Dudley. *Is that the note to which the letter from Col. Dudley produced by you yesterday and read to court was a reply?*
Answer. *It was.*

Q. by Col. Dudley. *Did soldiers go to your house after the remainder of the things in response to Mrs. Ealy's request contained in her second note to Col. Dudley? If so, did they bring them down to the Patron house?*
Answer. *Yes Sir.*

Witness then retired.

Exhibit No. 37

To the President
Court of Inquiry
Fort Stanton, N.M.

Sir:

I have the honor to request that the following name persons be subpoenaed to appear without delay as witnesses for Col. Dudley.

The Recorder having attempted to establish, by two or three of their witnesses, that soldiers belonging to the infantry detachment forming party of the command at Lincoln on the 19th of July last, fired at and took an active part on his attempt to leave the McSween house on the night of July 19, 1878.

There was not a single soldier present at the time the alleged firing took place.

Very respectfully,
N. A. M. Dudley
Lt. Col. 9th Cav.

Exhibit No. 38

Lieut. Col. Dudley

Please accept the thanks from Mrs. Ealy for protection here. Also please accept an apology from me on behalf of my husband. I am very sorry he lost his temper.

With many thanks,
Mr. T. F. Ealy

Exhibit No. 39

July 19, 1878

Lieut. Col. Dudley

Please give us a guard of soldiers for this building. We have no place to go. We ask for your protection.

Very respectfully,
Mrs. T. F. Ealy

Exhibit No. 40

Lieut. Col. Dudley

We respectfully ask you to take Mrs. Shields [Shield] and her five children with Miss Gates, Mrs. Ealy, my two children and myself to the fort for protection.

Very respectfully,
T. F. Ealy

Source: Dudley Court of Inquiry Records, report to Act. Asst. Adjutant General, July 20, 1878, Letters Received by the Office of the Adjutant General, 1871-1880, RG 153, NARA.

Appendix B | Rynerson Letter to "Friends Riley and Dolan"

The letter addressed to "Friends Riley and Dolan" and signed by W. L. Rynerson dated February 14, 1878, in which Rynerson, U.S. Attorney for the Territory of New Mexico, calls for physical violence against Alexander A. McSween and his allies, is given below:

Law Offices of William L. Rynerson
District Attorney 3d Judicial N.M.
Las Cruces, N.M. Feby 14, 1878

Friends Riley and Dolan:

I have just received letter from you mailed 10th inst. Glad to know you (Dolan) got home O.K. and that business was going on O.K. If Mr. Widenmann interfered with or resisted the sheriff in discharge of his duties, Brady did right in arresting [him]. Any one who does so must receive the same attention.

Brady goes into the store in McSween's place and takes his interest. Tunstall will have same right there he had before, but he must not neither obstruct the sheriff or resist him in the discharge of his duties. If he tries to make trouble the sheriff must meet the occasion firmly and legally. I believe Tunstall is in with the swindlers with the rogue McSween.

They have the money belonging to the Fritz estate and they know it. It must be made hot for them all the hotter the better, especially is this necessary now that it has been discovered that there is no hell.

It may be that the villain "Green Bautista" Wilson will play into their hands as Alcalde [magistrate]. If so he should be moved around a little. Shake that McSween outfit up till it shells out and squares up and then shake it out of Lincoln.

I will aid to punish the scoundrels all I can. Get the people with [you]. Control Juan Patron if possible. You know how to do it. Have good men about to aid Brady, and be assured I shall help you all I can, for I believe there never was found a more scoundrely set than that outfit.

Yours &c
W. L. Rynerson (signed)

Source: Thomas, *The Frank W. Angel Report on the Death of John H. Tunstall*, p 134.

Appendix C | Timeline

Here are the dates of the most important events related to *"Water in a Thirsty Land."*

- 1788 – Pedro Pino (Lai-iu-ahtsai-lu) born in Zuni
- August 24, 1821 – Mexican Independence from Spain
- May 18, 1834 – Sheldon Clinton Jackson born in Minaville, NY
- April 23, 1837 – José Ynes Perea born near Bernalillo, NM
- September 12, 1848 – Taylor Filmore Ealy born in Schellsburg, PA
- September 6, 1850 – Susan Gates (Perea) born born in Schellsburg, PA
- December 23, 1850 – Mary Elizabeth Ramsey born in East Waterford, PA
- 1856 – Jennie M. Hammaker born in Schellsburg, PA
- July 22, 1857 – Frank Hamilton Cushing born in North East Township, PA
- 1872 – Taylor graduates from Western Theological Seminary, Allegheny, PA
- 1874 – Taylor receives a medical degree from the University of Pennsylvania
- October 1, 1874 – Taylor marries Mary Elizabeth Ramsey
- October 6, 1874 – Taylor ordained as an evangelist by the Presbytery of Pittsburgh
- November, 1874 – Taylor begins teaching school at Fort Arbuckle, Indian Territory
- September 3, 1875 – Daughter Anna "Pearl" Margarette born at Ft. Arbuckle, OK
- June 5, 1876 – Ealy family returns to Schellsburg for a visit
- October 15, 1877 –Ruth Rea Ealy born in East Waterford, PA
- January 29, 1878 – Ealy family and Susan Gates leave Schellsburg for New Mexico
- February 3, 1878 – Ealys and Gates arrive in Denver, Colorado
- February 6, 1878 – Ealys and Gates arrive in El Moro, Colorado
- February 13, 1878 – Ealy and Gates arrive in Anton Chico, New Mexico
- February 18, 1878 – John Henry Tunstall murdered
- February 18, 1878 – Ealys and Gates arrive at Fort Stanton
- February 19, 1878 – Ealys and Gates arrive in Lincoln at about 11 a.m.
- February 21, 1878 – John Henry Tunstall's funeral in McSween's house
- February 28, 1878 – Ealys and Gates move from Shield's wing of house into McSween's wing
- March 9, 1878 – Governor Axtell arrives in Lincoln and issues proclamation illegally "removing" John B. Wilson as JP and "nullifying" his arrest warrants
- March 30, 1878 – McSween meets with supporters at Chisum's ranch
- March 31, 1878 – Billy and others sneak into Lincoln and camp in Tunstall's corral
- April 1, 1878 – Sheriff William Brady and Deputy George Hindman killed
- April 5, 1878 – Richard Brewer and "Buckshot" Roberts killed at Blazer's Mill

- April 15, 1878 – Frank Warner Angel appointed Special Agent to investigate Tunstall's murder
- April 26, 1878 – Ealys and Gates move into Tunstall residence/store
- May 4, 1878 – Angel arrives in Santa Fe
- May 30, 1878 – George Peppin appointed Lincoln sheriff
- June 1, 1878 – Angel arrives in Lincoln
- June 6, 1878 – McSween gives sworn statement to Angel for his Report
- June 6, 1878 – Juan Patron gives sworn statement to Angel for his Report
- June 6, 1878 – Widenmann gives sworn statement to Angel for his Report
- June 8, 1878 – Billy the Kid gives sworn statement to Angel for his Report
- July 15, 1878 – First day of 5-day shootout in Lincoln
- July 19, 1878 – Last day of 5-day shootout – McSween and four others killed
- July 20, 1878 – Ealys, Gates, and Shields escorted under guard to Fort Stanton.
- July 29, 1878 – Ealys and Gates leave Fort Stanton for Las Vegas
- August 2, 1878 – Ealys and Gates arrive in Anton Chico
- August 3, 1878 – Ealys and Gates arrive in Las Vegas
- August 14, 1878 – Ealys and Gates rent house in Anton Chico
- August 14, 1878 – Angel leaves New Mexico for New York
- August 16, 1878 – Taylor offered position at Zuni Pueblo
- September 4, 1878 – Axtell fired as governor and replaced by Lew Wallace
- September 23, 1878 – Ealys and Gates Leave for Zuni
- October 12, 1878 – Ealys and Gates arrive at Zuni
- October 14, 1878 – Taylor begins digging water well and planning a residence
- November 17, 1878 – Ealys and Gates move into partially completed house at Zuni
- December 25, 1878 – Susan Gates marries José Ynes Perea
- February 3, 1879 – José and Susan Perea move to St. James, AZ
- April 25, 1879 – Attempt by unknown parties to assassinate Ira Leonard by firing at night into his bedroom
- May 7, 1879 – Dudley Court of Inquiry begins at Fort Stanton
- May 12, 1879 – Taylor and Mary receive summons to appear at the Court of Inquiry
- May 13, 1879 – Taylor leaves Zuni for Fort Stanton
- May 14, 1879 – Mary and two children left at Bacon Springs
- May 20, 1879 – Taylor arrives at Santa Fe
- May 21, 1879 – Taylor meets Governor Lew Wallace at Santa Fe
- May 26, 1879 – Taylor arrives at Fort Stanton
- June 2-3, 1879 – Taylor testifies at the Dudley Court of Inquiry
- June 3, 1879 – Taylor leaves Fort Stanton for Zuni by way of Roswell
- June 7, 1879 – Taylor arrives in Las Vegas
- June 7, 1879 – Taylor meets Jennie Hammaker at Las Vegas
- June 8, 1879 – Taylor and Jennie arrive in Santa Fe
- June 11, 1879 – Taylor and Jennie arrive at Zuni
- June 25, 1879 – Taylor begins building second house at Zuni

- July 6, 1879 – Dudley Court of Inquiry ends with Dudley's acquittal on all charges
- September 19, 1879 – Cushing arrives in Zuni as part of the Stevenson anthropological expedition
- November 13, 1879 – Albert "Bertie" Ealy born in Zuni after 13 hours of labor, delivered by Taylor
- November 29, 1879 – Windmill installed and working at Zuni
- June 4, 1880 – Albert "Bertie" Ealy dies in Zuni
- July 17, 1880 – Taylor requests that he be permitted to resign and leave Zuni
- June 21, 1881 – Last day in Zuni and end of official service
- June 29, 1881 – Ealys leave Albuquerque
- July 4, 1881 – Ealys arrive in Schellsburg
- September, 1881 – Jennie Hammaker dies of typhoid fever at Zuni
- 1883 – Pedro Pino dies at Zuni, date unknown
- July 6, 1887 – Taylor's father John Cyris Ealy dies in Schellsburg
- March 6, 1888 – David P. Shield dies in Las Vegas
- 1891 – Taylor's mother Anna Maria Clark dies in Schellsburg
- April 10, 1900 – Frank Hamilton Cushing dies in Washington, DC
- December 29, 1908 – Anna Margarette (Ealy) Appleman dies
- July 17, 1910 – José Ynes Perea dies in Albuquerque, NM
- February 19, 1915 – Taylor Filmore Ealy dies in Schellsburg
- December 13, 1916 – Elizabeth (Hummer) Shield dies of pneumonia in CA
- November 26, 1924, Susan Gates Perea dies in Falmouth, KY
- September 6, 1930 – Sheldon Jackson dies in Nassau, NY
- January 3, 1931 Susan Ellen (Hummer) McSween dies at White Oaks
- May 31, 1935 – Mary Ealy dies in Schellsburg
- 1955 – *"Water in a Thirsty Land"* issued
- October 9, 1959 – Ruth Rea Ealy dies in St. Petersburg, FL.

Notes

Introduction by Editor

1. The Ealys and Gates moved from Shield's wing to the McSween (Eastern) wing of the building Feb. 28, 1878.
2. Albert Howe deposition, Frank Warner Angel Report, Interior Department Papers 1850-1907, RG 60, NARA; David G. Thomas, *The Frank W. Angel Report on the Death of John H. Tunstall*, (Doc45 Publishing, 2021), pp 86-87.
3. Thomas, *The Frank W. Angel Report on the Death of John H. Tunstall*, p 112.
4. Maurice G. Fulton, interview with Juan Peppin, 1930, Fulton Papers, Special Collections, UA.
5. David G. Thomas, *The Trial of Billy the Kid*, (Doc45 Publishing, 2020), pp 77-94.
6. N. A. M. Dudley, report to Act. Asst. Adjutant General, July 20, 1878, Letters Received by the Office of the Adjutant General, 1871-1880.
7. Dudley, report to Act. Asst. Adjutant General, July 20, 1878, Letters Received by the Office of the Adjutant General, 1871-1880.
8. Dudley, report to Act. Asst. Adjutant General, July 20, 1878, Letters Received by the Office of the Adjutant General, 1871-1880.
9. Here is Deputy John Long's sworn testimony at the Dudley Court of Inquiry regarding his attempt to to start a fire at the wing of the house occupied by Elizabeth Shield and her five children:

> "*QUESTION*: Do you know anything about setting fire to the McSween house that day?"
>
> "*LONG*: Yes sir, I know about setting the house afire. I poured coal oil on the floor and gave a man some matches out of my pocket to start the coal oil fire."
>
> "*QUESTION*: About what time did you pour the coal oil on the floor of the McSween house?"
>
> "*LONG*: About half past one in the afternoon."
>
> "*QUESTION*: In what part of the house was the coal oil poured?"
> "*LONG*: In the northeast kitchen, they did have two kitchens."
>
> "*QUESTION*: State whether or not this attempt to set the house on fire was successful."
> "*LONG*: It was not."
>
> "*QUESTION*: After you poured the coal oil on the floor of the kitchen, where did you go?"
> "*LONG*: I was shot at and I ran outside the fence and got into a privy sink, it was dug into the bank, privy sink was open facing the river. Buck Powell was with me." [Thomas Benton "Buck" Powell was one of Peppin's deputies.]

> *"QUESTION: How long did you remain there?"*
>
> *"LONG: I was there until after dark. Ascequa [sic] was running within 15 feet but I could not get to it, neither me or Buck."*

Dudley Court of Inquiry Records, RG 153, NARA.

10. Here is Deputy Andrew Boyle's sworn testimony at the Dudley Court of Inquiry regarding his starting a fire at the McSween wing of the house:

> *"QUESTION: Do you know when the McSween house was set on fire at the place where the fire was successfully started?"*
>
> *"BOYLE: It was about one o'clock in the afternoon."*
>
> *"QUESTION: Where you present at the time?"*
>
> *"BOYLE: I was."*
>
> *"QUESTION: On which side of what part of the house was this?"*
>
> *"BOYLE: It was at the back door of the kitchen on the northwest corner of the house."*
>
> *"QUESTION: Describe, if you know, the way the fire took effect and its course of progress upon the house."*
>
> *"BOYLE: I set it on fire with a sack of shavings and chips and used what timber there was on top of the stable to make it burn. It burned very slowly all the afternoon from one room to another turning a circle around the house."*

Asked under oath, Boyle confirmed the firing was ordered by Sheriff Peppin:

> *"QUESTION: When did Sheriff Peppin order you if you could not get the McSween party out without burning it, to burn it?"*
>
> *"BOYLE: In the morning when I started to go down there."*

Dudley Court of Inquiry Records, RG 153, NARA.

11. Thomas, *The Trial of Billy the Kid*, p 91.

12. Yginio Salazar, fleeing with McSween's group, was shot in two places and knocked unconscious. He was assumed to be dead by the victors, so was further ignored. Yginio was 15 years old. Yginio crawled 1,000 yards to his sister-in-law's house, leaving a trail of blood and reaching the house about midnight. Dr. Appel was called and he treated Yginio's wounds. Thomas, *The Trial of Billy the Kid*, pp 91-93.

13. Dudley, report to Act. Asst. Adjutant General, July 23, 1878, Letters Received by the Office of the Adjutant General, 1871-1880.

14. Thomas, *The Trial of Billy the Kid*, pp 111-117.

15. Thomas, *The Trial of Billy the Kid*, p 117.

16. Frank Hamilton Cushing, "My Adventures Zuni," *Century Illustrated*, 1882, p 192.

17. Thomas, *The Frank W. Angel Report on the Death of John H. Tunstall*.

18. Thomas, *The Trial of Billy the Kid*, p 207.

19. Donald R. Lavash, *Sheriff William Brady, Tragic Hero of the Lincoln County War* (Sunstone Press, 1986).

20. *Albuquerque Journal*, Feb. 7, 1883.

21. Ralph Emerson Twitchell, *The Leading Facts of New Mexico History*, Vol 3 (The Torch Press, 1917), p 375.
22. Frank Hamilton Cushing, *Zuni Breadstuff*, Indian Notes and Monographs, Vol VIII (New York Museum of the American Indian Heye Foundation, 1920), pp 9-14; Cushing, "The White Indian," *The Land of Sunshine, The Magazine of California and the West*, Vol. XI, (Land of Sunshine Publishing Co., 1899), pp 8-17.
23. *Tennessean* (Nashville), Nov. 10, 1882.
24. Cushing, *Zuni Breadstuff*, pp 55-58.
25. *Evening Star* (Washington, DC), April 10, 1900.
26. *Santa Fe Weekly New Mexican*, July 26, 1879; *Santa Fe Daily New Mexican*, March 2, 1898; "Flying H Ranch," National Register of Historic Places, 85003633, NARA.
27. E. Donald Kaye, *Nathan Augustus Monroe Dudley, Rogue, Hero, or Both?* (Outskirts Press, 2007).
28. *Santa Fe New Mexican*, July 28, 1882; *Albuquerque Journal*, Nov. 14, 1882.
29. *Pittsburgh Press* (Pittsburgh PA), Oct. 7, 1959.
30. *Evening Star* (Washington DC), Nov. 16, 1925.
31. Robert Laird Stewart, *Sheldon Jackson, Pathfinder and Prospector of the Missionary Vanguard in the Rocky Mountains and Alaska* (Fleming H. Revell Co. 1908).
32. Burton,They Fought for "The House." Jeff Burton, ed., Philip J. Rasch, They Fought for "The House," English Westerners' Society (The English Westerners' Society, 1971);
33. Don Cline, *Antrim and Billy* (Creative Publishing Co., 1990), pp 47-59; Some sources argue Catherine McCarty and her sons arrived in Kansas from Indianapolis, but offer no documentary evidence.
34. Don Cline, *Antrim and Billy* (Creative Publishing Co., 1990), pp 47-59; *Mining Life*, September 19, 1874: *Arizona Republic* (Phoenix), Dec. 30, 1951; Thomas, *The Trial of Billy the Kid*, pp 172-178.
35. Susan E. Barber, letter to J. Evetts Haley, Aug. 16, 1927, Panhandle Plains Historical Museum Research Center (PPHMRC); Robert N. Mullin, ed., *Maurice G. Fulton's History of the Lincoln County War* (University of Arizona Press, 1968).
36. Kathleen P. Chamberlain, *In the Shadow of Billy the Kid* (University of New Mexico Press, 2013); Frederick Nolan, *The Lincoln County War, A Documentary History*, (Sunstone Press, 2009).
37. *Las Vegas Gazette*, March 16, 1878; *Mesilla Valley Independent*, March 16, 1878.
38. George W. Peppin statement, Exhibit 8, Dudley Court of Inquiry Records, NARA; *Lincoln County Leader* (White Oaks, NM), March 29, 1884; *White Oaks Eagle* (White Oaks, NM), Jan. 20, 1898.
39. David Whiteley, "José Ynes Perea," unpublished manuscript, July 4, 2021; *Santa Fe Weekly New Mexican*, Sept. 13, 1880.
40. The Zunis who accompanied Cushing to Washington D.C. were: Naintche, First High Priest of the tribe, First Warrior of the Order of Fire, and First Cacique of War; Ki-a-si, Second High Priest of the Priesthood, Warrior of the Order of Hunters, and Second Cacique of War; Lai-in-atsae-bin-kai, Second Priest of the Temple or House of Medicine, Cacique of the Order of Fire and of the Parrot Gews; Pa-lo-wat-te-wa, Head Chief Warrior of ht Order of Fire, and Priest of the Order of Law; Lai-ai-a-tsae-lu (Pedro Pino), previous Governor of the Zunis and father of the present Governor; Wa-na-he, a Moqui (Hopi) by birth, married and adopted into the tribe of Zuni, Chief of the Sacred

dance for the year. E. Richard Hart, *Pedro Pino, Governor of Zuni Pueblo 1830-1878* (Utah State University Press, 2003); *Daily Commonwealth* (Topeka KS), Feb. 28, 1882.
41. Philip J. Rasch, *The Men at Fort Stanton, English Westerners' Society* (The English Westerners' Society, 1961); Thrapp, *Encyclopedia of Frontier Biography: P-Z*, Vol 3, p 1179.
42. Gary L. Roberts, *Death Comes for the Chief Justice* (University Press of Colorado, 1990); Darlis A. Miller, "William Logan Rynerson in New Mexico, 1862-1893," *New Mexico Historical Review*, Vol. 48, No. 2, April, 1973, p 101-130; *Rio Grande Republican*, Sept. 26, 1893.
43. *Las Vegas Gazette*, August 24, 1878; *Lincoln County Leader* (White Oaks), March 24, 1888; Nolan, *The Lincoln County War*, p 486.
44. *Santa Fe New Mexican*, Dec. 12, 1916.
45. *Courier News* (Bridgewater NJ), Aug. 7, 1888.
46. Nolan, *The Lincoln County War*, pp 76-102.
47. Nolan, *The Lincoln County War*, pp 428-433.

Chapter 3 - Zuni

1. A brief history of European and Zuni contacts: The first known contact between Zunis and Europeans was in May, 1539, when Franciscan priest Fray Marcos de Niza viewed the Zuni village of Hawikuh from a distance. He was ordered to the area by Antonio de Mendoza y Pacheco, Viceroy of New Spain, to determine the truth of tales collected by Álvar Núñez Cabeza de Vaca of seven fabulously rich cities in the region. Fray Marcos took "possession" of the land in the name of the King of Spain.

The next European "visitor" was Francisco Vázquez de Coronado y Luján, who – guided by Fray Marcos – attacked and captured Hawikuh on July 7, 1540, after a fierce battle. The Zunis reportedly fielded over 200 warriors. Coronado named the area Cibola and renamed Hawikuh Granada. He wrote a celebratory letter to the Viceroy "from the province of Cevola, and this city of Granada." Cibola (or Cevola) was a Spanish translation of the Zuni word for pueblos (villages).

Following other explorations, Coronado returned to Hawikuh in the spring of 1542. He left some Native Mexicans at the pueblo, who were accepted into the community by the Zunis.

In the summer of 1581, Francisco Sánchez Chamuscado visited Cibola. He found the Zunis living in six pueblos, one pueblo having been abandoned after Coronado's visit.

Two years later, Antonio de Espejo and Fray Bernardino Beltran with fourteen soldiers visited Hawikuh. They were surprised to discover still alive three of the Mexican Natives that Coronado had left behind forty-one years earlier.

In November, 1598, Juan de Oñate y Salazar, the colonizer of New Mexico, visited Cibola and forced the Zunis to swear obedience to the King of Spain. In his report, Oñate said there were six Zuni villages: He found at Hawikuh crosses and children of the Mexican Natives left by Coronado. On a later visit, in 1605, Oñate reported that Hawikuh was the largest of the Zuni villages, containing about 110 houses.

In late July, 1629, the Governor of New Mexico, Don Francisco Manuel de Silva Nieto, with several Franciscan priests, visited Hawikuh. Nieto left behind three priests and three soldiers to convert the Zunis to Christianity. A native house purchased in the pueblo was consecrated as the first mission church.

The three priests left by Nieto disappeared within a few years, fate unknown. On February 22, 1632, the Zunis killed Fray Francisco Letrado who had been sent to replace the missing priests. A few days later Fray Marin de Arvide and his escort, who were travelling to Hawikuh, were murdered. Following these killings, the Zunis moved to the nearby flat mesa known as Dowa Yalanne ("Corn Mountain"), an often-used refuge site.

On March 23, 1632, Tomas de Albizu confronted the entrenched Zunis at Dowa Yalanne. The Spaniards were eventually admitted to the summit of the mesa and Albizu negotiated a peace agreement with the Zunis.

About 10 years later, missionaries were again sent to Hawikuh. They rebuilt the church, naming it La Concepción de Hawikuh.

On October 7, 1670, Navajos raided Hawikuh. Surprised, the Zunis abandoned the village for their mesa refuge. The priest at the village was Fray Pedro de Avila y Ayala. Avila was so zealous about evangelizing the Zunis that – when he was assigned the mission two years earlier – he walked alone the entire 1,500 mile distance from Mexico City to Hawikuh. Avila locked himself in the church in response to the raid. The church was breached and Avila brutally beaten and finally killed by blows to his head. A fire, started in the center of the church, badly scorched the structure, causing it to be abandoned, never to be used again. The cemetery of this church are alluded to by Taylor on page 160.

In August, 1680, there was a general revolt against the Spanish by the Native Americans in New Mexico. The Zunis murdered their missionary, Fray Juan de Bal, who resided at Halona Pueblo. At that time there remained only four Zuni pueblos, Hawikuh, Halona, Kiakima, and Matsaki. Two pueblos, Canabi and Aquinsa, had been abandoned. The Zunis, who numbered about 2,500, retreated to their mesa stronghold and remained there for twelve years.

When the Zunis chose to return to pueblo life, they built a new pueblo, Zuni, on the ruins of Halona. This village was visited in July, 1699, by New Mexico Governor Pedro Rodríguez Cubero. The next year, Padre Juan Garaicoechea was assigned to Zuni as their priest. Another conflict with the Spanish and the killing of three Spaniards drove Garaicoechea away and forced the Zunis to seek refuge again on Dowa Yalanne. Two years later, Garaicoechea convinced the Zunis to leave the mesa and return to Zuni.

For the next 100 years, contacts between Zunis and Spaniards are too frequent to list. This period was a time of repeated wars between the Zunis and their Native American neighbors, the Navajos and Hopis.

In 1820, the Spaniards abandoned efforts to evangelize the Zunis, leaving no priest with the people. The abandonment was caused by continued resistance by the Zunis and by political and military disruptions in Mexico during the Mexican War of Independence. Spain recognized Mexico's Independence August 24, 1821.

Richard B. Woodbury, *Zuni Prehistory and History to 1850*, (Smithsonian Institution, 1917); Tilly E. Stevenson, *Zuni and the Zunians* (Smithsonian Institution); David Grant Noble and Richard Woodbury, ed., *Zuni and El Morro*, Past & Present (Ancient City

Press, 1983); *Twenty-Third Annual Report of the Bureau of American Ethnology 1901-1902* (Government Printing Office, 1904).

2. The *Albuquerque Journal* wrote of Field's action:

> "What Field did, with a wide knowledge of Indians, their rites and their costumes, was to fashion and wear an authentic version of a Kachina costume as his Fiesta garb over the Labor Day weekend."

> "Field wore the costume and mask downtown (Santa Fe) and at a private party. A picture showing him at the party with a group of young women and captioned 'Ever See a Kachina Charleston?' was published by the 'Santa Fe New Mexican.' The newspaper today apologized editorially for having thus aggravated the affront to the Indians."

> "When two Indians approached the costumed youth on the plaza, it was learned, they told him he was 'doing a very bad thing and he should go home right away and take it off.' Field did so."

> "A few days later he apologized to governors of three pueblos at the home of writer Oliver La-Farage, president of the Amererican Assn. on Indian Affairs."

Albuquerque Journal, Sept. 24, 1952.

Chapter 4 - Second Year

1. Earle was a member of the U.S. Board of Indian Commissioners. He was asked to visit the Indian Agencies and villages of New Mexico and Arizona and produce a condition report. In his official report to the Commission in 1879, he wrote:

> "The Pueblo Indians are so called because they live in towns, as they have lived for generations past. Their dwellings are made of adobe, in compact groups, portions of which are three and four stories high. There are nineteen of these pueblos, with an aggregate population of about 9,000, scattered over an area of about 150 miles from north to south and 200 miles from east to west. They are under the supervision of Agent B. M. Thomas, located at Santa Fe...."

> "In all these nineteen pueblos there are only four schools established, viz: at Jesnis, Laguna, Isleta, and Zuni. This is owing mainly to the inadequate compensation allowed by the government, a sum for which no competent teacher would enter the field. At three of these places the amount is increased by one of the missionary societies sufficiently to afford a bare living, and at these places there are faithful, devoted, self-denying teachers, acting also in the capacity of physicians, who are making encouraging progress in educating the children...."

Eleventh Annual Report of the Board of Indian Commissioners for the Year 1879 (Government Printing Office, 1880), pp 55-61.

2. Edwin Corle, *Billy the Kid* (Duell, Sloan & Pearce, 1953).

3. The Washington shooting happened May 31, 1879. The *New Mexico Herald* reported:

> *[Washington], while attempting to shoot a dog, accidentally shot his wife and child, killing them both. The woman had the child, an infant, in her arms and the bullet passed through the child and entered the mother's breast.*

Washington was indicted for first degree murder for the killings on November 10, 1880, but the case was dismissed five days later.

Las Vegas New Mexico Herald, July 2, 1879.

4. Not staying in the same room with Leonard was a wise move. Less than a month earlier two never identified men attempted to assassinate Leonard by firing into his bedroom at night. He was uninjured. Letter G. Taylor to Lew Wallace, April 25, 1879, Lew Wallace Collection, Indiana Historical Society.

Chapter 5 - The Silent Year – 1880

1. The Carlisle Indian Industrial School opened in Carlisle, PA., on November 1, 1879. It was the first U.S. government-run school for Native Americans. The founder and first superintendent was Lt. Col. Richard Henry Pratt. *"Students were forced to cut their hair, change their names, stop speaking Native languages, convert to Christianity, and endure harsh discipline including corporal punishment and solitary confinemnt."* https://carlisleindianschoolproject.com/past/ accessed May 1, 2022.

Chapter 6 - The End of Life in Zuni

1. We'wha (we-wa) was a lhamana, a Zuni word for a two spirit person. A lhamana was an individual who took on both male and female tasks in Zuni culture.

> *"In traditional Zuni culture, the lhamana are male-bodied people who take on the social and ceremonial roles usually performed by women in their culture, at least some of the time. They wear a mixture of women's and men's clothing and much of their work is in the areas usually occupied by Zuni women."* – https://en.wikipedia.org/wiki/Lhamana, accessed April 25, 2022.

We'wha was born in 1849 in Zuni. In 1853, We'wha was orphaned when her parents died of small pox. We'wha was adopted and raised by her aunt on her father's side. In late 1885, We'wha, identified in the newspapers as a "Princess of the Zuni tribe," travelled to Washington DC with Matilda Coxe Stevenson and stayed nearly a year as Stevenson's house guest. By the time of We'wha's visit to DC, We'wha was an accomplished weaver and pottery maker. On June 12, We'wha gave a public demonstration of Zuni carpet weaving at the National Museum.

On June 23, We'wha met with President Grover Cleveland in the White House. We'wha died in 1896.

Daily Eagle (Wichita KS), April 22, 1886; *Evening Star* (Washington DC), June 12, 1886; *Boston Globe*, Nov. 19, 1886.

Index

A

Agnew, Dr. 163
Alexander, Beatrice 31
Alexander, Colbert 31
Alexander, Lawrence 31
Allen 56
Angel, Frank Warner 13, 56, 178
Annin, John A., Rev 39-40, 74, 76, 79
Annin, Miss 82
Annin, Mrs. 40
Annin, Rebecca 75, 80
Antonio 130
Antrim, William H. 16
Appel, Daniel M., Dr. 13, 47-48, 56, 117, 168-169
Appleman, C. W. 31
Arbuckle, Matthew, Gen. 1
Armstrong 159
Arthur, Chester A., President 18
Axtell, Samuel Beach, Governor 13, 17, 48-49, 66, 70, 114, 177-178

B

Bagster 160
Baker, Frank 49, 133
Baker, Mrs. 127
Ball 72
Bancroft, Dr. 37
Banning 95
Barber, George L. 17, 79
Bates, Sebrian 9, 60, 64, 68-69
Beckwith, Robert W. 9, 68, 71, 167
Bell, Charley 95
Belle, (dog) 133
Bennett, James 98, 105, 120, 124-125, 129, 131, 134, 139, 159
Bentley, Mrs. 161
Bentley, S. A. 160-162
Berber, N. A. 136
Billings, Mr. 160
Bishop, Mrs. 160
Blanchard 150
Boggs, Thomas O. 40
Bourke, John G. 159
Bowers, George 9
Boyle, Andrew 9, 182
Brady, William 5, 7, 10, 13, 16-17, 19, 49, 51-52, 60-61, 175, 177
Brewer, Richard "Dick" 17, 19, 52, 56, 62, 66, 177
Brinkerhoff, H. R., Captain 167
Bristol, Warren Henry, Judge 53, 63
Brown, Henry 5
Bruner, George 156-157

Buel, Mrs. 127
Bunzel, Ruth L. 85
Burgess 95, 105, 111, 125, 151
Burgess, Mrs. 157, 159
Burns, Walter Noble 69

C

Calhoun, A. J. 76
Camp, Mrs. 163
Campbell, Billy 72
Capitan 136
Carson 115
Carter 63
Catron, Thomas Benton 71
Chapman, Huston Ingraham 72
Chaves, Florencio 9
Chavez y Chavez, José 6, 9
Chisum, James 79
Chisum, John S. 5, 16, 49, 52-53, 56, 66, 71, 81, 177
Clark, Andrew 120, 155
Clark, Anna Maria 179
Clark, Rush 56, 62, 103
Cochrane, Dr. 127
Coe, George W. 52, 54-55, 62
Colbert, Adelaide 31
Colbert, Lena 31
Compton, Col. 111-112
Conklin 147
Conway, Thomas 53
Copeland, John N. 52, 58, 63
Corbet, Samuel, "Sam" 5, 45, 51, 61, 69
Corle, Edwin 114
Coronado y Luján, Francisco Vázquez de 85
Crane, William W. 13, 92-93, 98, 101, 107-108, 110-111, 113, 117-118, 120, 122, 139, 160-161
Crawford, Charlie "Lallacooler" 71, 73
Crook, George R., Gen. 159
Cullins, Thomas 9
Cushing, Enos 157
Cushing, Frank Hamilton 11, 14-15, 18, 85, 127-129, 133, 135-136, 147, 151, 156-160, 177, 179, 109, 116, 126, 152

D

Darby 79
Davis, Mrs. 160
Davis, William "Billy" 156-157, 159, 161
Dawson, Raher 114
Delphia, Aunt 32
Dolan, James J. 7, 9-10, 14, 17, 48, 59, 61-63, 65, 71-72, 167, 175

190 ~ Index

Donaldson, Dr. 81
Donley, Mary 39
Dowlin, Paul 41, 43, 47-48, 65, 71, 114-115
Drake 129
Dubois, Dan 119, 124, 157
Dubois, Mrs. 157, 159
Ducero, Juan Don 90
Dudley, Nathan Augustus Monroe 7-12, 14, 55, 58-59, 63, 66, 68-74, 77, 112, 115, 117, 122, 167-174, 178

E

Ealy, Albert "Bertie" 12, 179, 132, 140-142, 160
Ealy, Albert Elijah, 14, 27, 45, 105, 109, 137, 141, 160, 162
Ealy, Anna Margarette "Pearl" 1, 31, 35-37, 41, 45, 47-49, 51, 60, 68, 80, 106, 111, 124-125, 137, 142, 151, 155-158, 162, 177, 179
Ealy, Anna Maria Clark 153
Ealy, Charles, 21
Ealy, Corrie, 35, 47, 56
Ealy, Effie, 109, 142, 160, 163
Ealy, John Cyris 179
Ealy, Mary Elizabeth (Ramsey) 1, 3, 7-9, 15, 25, 28-30, 34-37, 39, 43, 45, 49, 51-52, 59, 65, 70, 73-74, 76-78, 79-80, 82, 89, 94-98, 100-101, 105-108, 111-113, 115, 117-119, 121-122, 124, 132-133, 140-142, 147, 150-151, 153-161-163, 168-170, 173-174, 177-179
Ealy, Nora, 160
Ealy, Ruth Rea 1, 15, 19, 37, 41, 49, 53, 108, 111, 125, 137, 142, 159, 177, 179
Ealy, Taylor Filmore 1, 3, 5, 7-9, 12, 15, 18, 21, 23-25, 27-30, 34-37, 40-41, 46-47, 49, 51-52, 55-57, 59, 64-67, 69, 70, 72-73, 75-78-79, 80-83, 85, 87, 90, 92, 94-99, 101, 103, 105-111, 113-115, 117, 119-125, 127-129, 131-135, 137, 139-140-143, 147, 150-151, 154-162, 165-167, 173-174, 177-179
Earle, Abraham L. 103, 105, 114
Eaton, David 81
Ellis, Isaac 48, 55-56, 59, 62-63, 67-69, 115
Ellis, Robert. 31
Elrood 106
Emmet, Lieut. 160

F

Field, William 86
Finnigan, Father 21
Fisher, 160
Fitzpatrick, George 21
Forbes, Rebecca 33-34
Franklin, Alfred 31
Free, Billy 157, 159-160
Freeman, Dinah A. 31
Freeman, Galatan 32
Freeman, Minerva 31
French, Jim 60, 5-6, 9-10

Fritz, Emil Adolf 175, 50, 66
Fulton, Maurice 49, 58, 65, 114, 117

G

Gallegos, Raphael 75-76, 80
Galpin, A. G. 35
Garfield, James Abram, President 162
Garrett, Patrick Floyd "Pat" 16, 70-71
Gates, Susan, See Perea, Susan
George 109-110, 122-123, 125, 130-131
Godfroy, Frederick 53
Gonzales, Ignacio 9
Goodwin, Millard F. 64
Grace 150
Graham, Douglas D. 15, 108, 125, 127, 131, 133-136, 139, 154-155, 156-159
Grant, Calvin, 32
Grant, Thos. 32
Gregory 159
Griffith, Mrs. 79

H

Hagwald, Lieut. 127
Hamilton, R. J. 74, 76, 103
Hammaker, Jennie M. 12, 15, 108, 114, 117-118, 120, 122, 124, 130-132 135, 150-151, 153-155, 157-158, 160, 163, 177-179
Happy 32-33
Harras, E. S. 105
Harris, Chas. 31
Harrison, Lizzie 31
Harwood 77
Hatch, Edward, Gen. 113
Hatchman, 121
Hathaway, Billy 155
Hathaway, Freeman 158
Hawthorne, Freeman 159
Hayes, Rutherford B., President 49, 13, 70
Heddington, 127
Henderson, Mrs. 151
Hentig, Captain 151, 153
Hepburn 27
Hill, Tom 3, 17, 19
Hillers, John Karl 15, 100, 104, 128-129, 132, 148
Hindman, George 5, 15, 17, 52, 60, 177
Hinton, Mrs. 163
Hoerade, Jiconas J. 73
Hollman 82
Homer 17
Hopkins, Jr., L. N. 90, 92
Hoppy, Louisa 31
Houck, James Dennis 123
Howard 38
Howe, Albert 3
Huff, Daniel 57, 59, 67
Huff, Mrs. 67
Humphreys, Henry H. 167, 10

I

Ingalls, G. M. 29

J

Jackson, Sheldon Clinton, Dr. 12, 16, 49, 52, 53, 57-58, 64, 74, 76, 78-83, 87, 91, 93, 95, 97-99, 103, 105, 107-108, 113, 118-119, 123, 128, 130-131, 136, 139-140, 142, 154, 163, 177, 179
Jackson, Sheldon Jackson, Mrs. 37, 97
Jacobs, Willie 31, 161
Jan-i-uh-tit sa (Jennie Hammaker), 144
Jenkins 112
Jennings, William 155
Jesus 129
Jewett, Lieut. Major 113
Johnson, William Harrison 58, 79
Jones, John A. 70
Josanna 153
Juanita 55

K

Kendall, Henry 74, 77-78
Kennedy, Grace 136, 150
Koko 86
Kosboski 79
Kroeber 85
Kuhns, Mrs. 160

L

la Farge, Oliver 86
Lauderdale, Miss 156
Launderdale, J. V. 103
Lea, Joseph C. 53
Leach, Miss 117
Leonard, B. M. 109
Leonard, Ira 10, 114, 167
Leverson, Montague Richard 49-50
Loftus, George 30
Long, Jack 5, 9, 16, 48, 50, 62, 68

M

MacNab, Francis "Frank" 5, 55, 62
Mallery, Garrick 134
Marston, Sylvester W. 48
Mary, Sister 81
Mathews, Jacob Basel 5, 58, 61, 72
Maxwell, Pete 16
McAllister [Jorden E.] 118, 120-122, 125
McCarty, Catherine 16
McCarty, Joseph (Billy's brother) 16
McCarty, William Henry "Billy the Kid" 5-7, 9, 16, 19, 61, 66, 70-71, 114, 177-178
McClelland, 28, 33-35
McCloskey, William 49
McClune 131-132
McKee, Miss 155

McLaughlin, Mary 31
McSween, Alexander Anderson 3-7, 9-10, 17, 19, 37, 39, 45-50, 52, 55, 58-72, 74, 77, 117, 167, 173, 175, 177-178
McSween, Susan Ellen (Hummer) 3-4, 9-10, 17, 19, 46, 51-52, 58, 65-67, 167, 179
Menaul, John, Rev 89, 92, 156
Menaul, Mrs. 98
Metcalf, Willard Leroy 160
Middleton, John 5, 19, 52, 61
Miller 131
Mills, Mrs. 60
Mitchell, Lieut. 125
Moffat, James D. 27
Montaño, José F. 67, 69
Montgomery, Dave 114
Moor, Laurie 31
Morris, Harvey 6, 9, 68-69, 71, 167
Morton, William "Buck" 3, 17, 19, 49
Moss, Felix 76
Mullin, Robert N. 21
Murphy, Lawrence 10, 14, 17, 61, 65, 68-69, 71

N

Neadems, Mary 31
Nellie 147
Nelson, Andres 38-39, 42, 78
Newman, "Stanley Stewart, Dr. 87

O

O'Folliard, Thomas 6, 9
Oñate, Juan de 85
Osborne, N. W., Major 167

P

Pague, Samuel S. 114, 173
Palfrey, Carl F. 159
Pallo, José 129
Palmer, Henry 86, 135
Partridge, Mrs. 98
Pasqualito 140, 142
Patron, Juan Batista 45, 66, 68-69, 169-170, 173, 175, 178
Pennypacker, Galusha, Col. 167
Peppin, George W. 5, 7, 9, 17, 49, 58, 70-71, 178
Peppin, Juan 5, 60
Perea, Jesus 162
Perea, José Ynes 12, 15, 17-18, 39, 75, 82, 85, 87, 89, 91-93, 95-100-101, 105-106, 111, 134, 177-179
Perea, Susan (Gates) 3, 9, 11-12, 15, 18, 37, 43, 45-46, 51, 59, 64-65, 68-69, 74-78, 80, 82, 91-92, 95, 97-98, 100, 105, 107, 115, 117, 150, 162, 169-170, 174, 177-179
Peters, Brown 32
Phillips, Sen. 125
Phoust, E. W. 29
Pierce, Milo Lucius 156

Pingry, Dr. 100
Pino, Captain 136
Pino, Lucas 134
Pino, Patricio 18, 100, 112, 125, 149-150, 158
Pino, Pedro 12, 18, 179, 89, 95, 97, 99-101, 105-106, 108-109, 112, 118-120, 122, 124, 127, 129-131, 134-137
Pino, Pedro Bautista 18
Pino, Romano 120
Pino, Rowan 136
Pottinz 95
Powell, John Wesley 128, 15
Prague, Lt. 115
Pratt, Richard Henry 147
Purington, George A. 18, 48-49, 52, 61, 115

R

Ramsey, Charley 81
Read, Rev. 37
Reed, Walter, Dr. 110, 112, 114
Richards, Daniell 31
Richter, Conrad 21
Riley, John 10, 61, 62, 65, 71, 175
Roberts, Andrew L. "Buckshot" 2, 52, 62, 115, 177
Robinson, George S. 52-53, 61, 64
Romero, Vincente 6, 9, 68, 71, 76, 167
Rynerson, William Logan 18, 52-53, 61, 63, 71, 175

S

Salazar, Yginio 9
Samson, Calvin 52
Sargeant 56
Saunders, James Albert 55, 62, 73
Schafer, George 16
Schell, Iona J. 31
Scott, Lizzie D. 34
Serge 82
Sharon, Mrs. 113
Shaw, Mrs. 156
Shield, David Pugh 3-4, 6, 19, 39, 46, 48, 50, 52, 60-62, 66-67, 73, 177-179
Shield, Dr. 80, 113-114
Shield, Elizabeth (Hummer) 3-4, 9-10, 19, 45, 170, 174, 179
Shield, Mrs David Pugh 46, 51, 59, 64, 66, 68-69, 74, 77
Shield, Mrs. Dr. 98
Slackwood 121
Smith 52, 61, 113
Smith, Alice M. 111
Spiegelburg 81
Springer, Frank 74
Stafford, Lt. 111
Stevens 160
Stevenson, Albert 31
Stevenson, James 14-15, 19, 127, 129, 131-133, 179
Stevenson, Mary 31

Stevenson, Matilda Coxe 85, 127
Stevenson, Robert. 31
Stockton, Ike 60
Sullivan, John 155, 157, 160
Swaine, Peter T., Col. 108, 114

T

Taylor, Henry 31
Teai-e-se-u-lu-ti-wa (Frank Cushing), 144
Tenney, Samuel B. 101, 106, 109-112, 118, 122-124, 133
Thackeray, Mrs. 158
Thomas, Ben M. 103, 123, 140, 147, 151, 157
Tra-we-ea-tsa-lun-kia (Taylor Ealy), 144
Tsai au-tit-sa (Mary Ealy), 144
Tunstall, John Henry 2-3, 6, 9, 13-14, 16-17, 19, 39, 41, 45-46, 50, 52-53, 56-57, 60-63, 65-66, 69-70, 117, 167, 170-171, 177
Turner, Marion 58
Twitchell, Ralph E. 13

U

Underwood 160

V

Vargas 99

W

Waite, Fred 5, 66
Waldo, Henry L. 10, 114-115, 167
Wallace, Lewis "Lew" 178, 42, 70, 16, 113, 178
Walsh 37
Wanamaker, John 98, 163
Washington, George 9, 52-53, 61, 69, 115, 125
We-Wa, 132, 147-148, 150
Widenmann, Robert Adolph 4-5, 19, 46, 48, 51-52, 56, 60-61, 63, 69, 175, 178
Williams 133
Williams, Aubrey H. 21
Williams, Betsy 31
Williams, Geo. 31
Williams, Linda 31
Williams, Rachel 31
Wilson, John B. 17, 58, 67, 175
Wiswell 160

Y

Yack, Mrs. 134
Young, James 31

Z

Zamora, Francisco 6, 9, 68, 71, 167
Zschokke, Johann Heinrich Daniel 50

Doc45 Publications

Killing Pat Garrett, The Wild West's Most Famous Lawman - Murder or Self-Defense?

Pat Garrett, the Wild West's most famous lawman – the man who killed Billy the Kid – was himself killed on leap day, February 29, 1908, on a barren stretch of road between his Home Ranch and Las Cruces, New Mexico.

- Who killed him?
- Was it murder?
- Was it self-defense?

No biographer of Garrett has been able to answer these questions. All have expressed opinions. None have presented evidence that would stand up in a court of law. Here, for the first time, drawing on newly discovered information, is the definitive answer to the Wild West's most famous unsolved killing.

Supplementing the text are 102 images, including six of Garrett and his family which have never been published before. It has been 50 years since a new photo of Garrett was published, and no photos of his children have ever been published.

Garrett's life has been extensively researched. Yet, the author was able to uncover an enormous amount of new information. He had access to over 80 letters that Garrett wrote to his wife. He discovered a multitude of new documents and details concerning Garrett's killing, the events surrounding it, and the personal life of the man who was placed on trial for killing Garrett.

- The true actions of "Deacon Jim" Miller, a professional killer, who was in Las Cruces the day Garrett was killed.
- The place on the now abandoned old road to Las Cruces where Garrett was killed.
- The coroner's jury report on Garrett's death, lost for over 100 years.
- Garrett's original burial location.
- The sworn courtroom testimony of the only witness to Garrett's killing.
- The policeman who provided the decisive evidence in the trial of the man accused of murdering Garrett.
- The location of Garrett's Rock House and Home Ranches.
- New family details: Garrett had a four-month-old daughter the day he killed Billy the Kid. She died tragically at 15. Another daughter was blinded by a well-intended eye treatment; a son was paralyzed by childhood polio; and Pat Garrett, Jr., named after his father, lost his right leg to amputation at age 12.

Garrett's life was a remarkable adventure. He met two United States presidents: President William McKinley, Jr. and President Theodore Roosevelt. President Roosevelt he met five times, three times in the White House. He brought the law to hardened gunmen. He oversaw hangings. His national fame was so extensive the day he died that newspapers from the East to the West Coast only had to write "Pat Garrett" for readers to know to whom they were referring.

    2020 Will Rogers Medallion Award Finalist for Excellence in Western Media
    2020 Independent Press Award Distinguished Favorite, Historical Biography
    2019 Best Book Awards Finalist, United States History
    2019 Best Indie Book Notable 100 Award Winner.

Doc45 Publications

La Posta – From the Founding of Mesilla, to Corn Exchange Hotel, to Billy the Kid Museum, to Famous Landmark, David G. Thomas, paperback, 118 pages, 59 photos, e-book available.

"For someone who grew up in the area of Mesilla, it's nice to have a well-researched book about the area – and the giant photographs don't hurt either.... And the thing I was most excited to see is a photo of the hotel registry where the name of "William Bonney" is scrawled on the page.... There is some debate as to whether or not Billy the Kid really signed the book, which the author goes into, but what would Billy the Kid history be without a little controversy?" –Billy the Kid Outlaw Gang Newsletter, Winter, 2013.

Giovanni Maria de Agostini, Wonder of The Century – The Astonishing World Traveler Who Was A Hermit, David G. Thomas, paperback, 208 pages, 59 photos, 19 maps, e-book available.

"David G. Thomas has finally pulled back the veil of obscurity that long shrouded one of the most enduring mysteries in New Mexico's long history to reveal the true story of the Hermit, Giovanni Maria de Agostini. ...Thomas has once again proven himself a master history detective. Of particular interest is the information about the Hermit's life in Brazil, which closely parallels his remarkable experience in New Mexico, and required extensive research in Portuguese sources. Thomas's efforts make it possible to understand this deeply religious man." – Rick Hendricks, New Mexico State Historian

Screen With A Voice - A History of Moving Pictures in Las Cruces, New Mexico, David G. Thomas, paperback, 194 pages, 102 photos, e-book available.

The first projected moving pictures were shown in Las Cruces 110 years ago. Who exhibited those movies? What movies were shown? Since projected moving pictures were invented in 1896, why did it take ten years for the first movie exhibition to reach Las Cruces? Who opened the first theater in town? Where was it located? These questions began the history of moving pictures in Las Cruces, and they are answered in this book. But so are the events and stories that follow.

There have been 21 movie theaters in Las Cruces – all but three or four are forgotten. They are unremembered no longer. And one, especially, the Airdome Theater which opened in 1914, deserves to be known by all movie historians – it was an automobile drive-in theater, the invention of the concept, two decades before movie history declares the drive-in was invented.

Billy the Kid's Grave – A History of the Wild West's Most Famous Death Marker, David G. Thomas, paperback, 154 pages, 65 photos.

"Quien es?"

The answer to this incautious question – "Who is it?" – was a bullet to the heart.

That bullet – fired by Lincoln County Sheriff Patrick F. Garrett from a .40-44 caliber single action Colt pistol – ended the life of Billy the Kid, real name William Henry McCarty.

But death – ordinarily so final – only fueled the public's fascination with Billy the Kid. What events led to Billy's killing? Was it inevitable? Was a woman involved? If so, who was she? Why has Billy's gravestone become the most famous – and most visited – Western death marker? Is Billy really buried in his grave? Is the grave in the right location?

These questions – and many others – are answered in this book.

Doc45 Publications

The Stolen Pinkerton Reports of the Colonel Albert J. Fountain Murder Investigation, David G. Thomas, editor, paperback, 194 pages, 28 photos.

The abduction and apparent murder of Colonel Albert J. and Henry Fountain on February 1, 1896, shocked and outraged the citizens of New Mexico. It was not the killing of Colonel Fountain, a Union Civil War veteran and a prominent New Mexico attorney, which roused the physical disgust of the citizenry - after all, it was not unknown for distinguished men to be killed. It was the cold-blooded murder of his eight-year-old son which provoked the public outcry and revulsion.

The evidence indicated that although Colonel Albert J. Fountain was killed during the ambush, his son was taken alive, and only killed the next day.

The public was left without answers to the questions:

- Who ambushed and killed Colonel Fountain?
- Who was willing to kill his young son in cold-blood after holding him captive for 24 hours?

The case was never solved. Two men were eventually tried for and acquitted of the crime.

The case file for the crime contains almost no information. There are no trial transcripts or witness testimonies. The only reports that exist today of the investigation of the case are these Pinkerton Reports, which were commissioned by the Territorial Governor, and then stolen from his office four months after the murders. These Reports, now recovered, are published here.

These Reports are important historical documents, not only for what they reveal about the Fountain murders, but also as a fascinating window into how the most famous professional detective agency in the United States in the 1890s - the Pinkerton Detective Agency - went about investigating a murder, at a time when scientific forensic evidence was virtually non-existent.

Torpedo Squadron Four – A Cockpit View of World War II, Gerald W. Thomas, paperback, 280 pages, 209 photos, e-book available.

"This book contains more first-person accounts than I have seen in several years. ...we can feel the emotion... tempered by the daily losses that characterized this final stage of the war in the Pacific. All in all, one of the best books on the Pacific War I have seen lately." – Naval Aviation News, Fall 2011.

Doc45 Publications

The Trial of Billy the Kid

This book is about Billy the Kid's trial for murder, and the events leading to that trial. The result of Billy's trial sealed his fate. And yet Billy's trial is the least written about, and until this book, the least known event of Billy's adult life.

Prior biographies have provided extensive — and fascinating — details on Billy's life, but they supply only a few paragraphs on Billy's trial. Just the bare facts: time, place, names, result.

Billy's trial the most important event in Billy's life. You may respond that his death is more important — it is in anyone's life! That is true, in an existential sense, but the events that lead to one's death at a particular place and time, the cause of one's death, override the importance of one's actual death. Those events are determinative. Without those events, one does not die then and there. If Billy had escaped death on July 14, 1881, and went on to live out more of his life, that escape and not his trial would probably be the most important event of Billy's life.

The information presented here has been unknown until now. This book makes it possible to answer these previously unanswerable questions:

- What were the governing Territorial laws?
- What were the charges against Billy?
- Was there a trial transcript and what happened to it?
- What kind of defense did Billy present?
- Did Billy testify in his own defense?
- Did Billy have witnesses standing for him?
- Who testified against him for the prosecution?
- What was the jury like?
- What action by the trial judge virtually guaranteed his conviction?
- What legal grounds did he have to appeal his verdict?
- Was the trial fair?

Supplementing the text are 132 photos, including many photos never published before.

Available in both paperback and hardcover.

Paperback, 254 Pages, ISBN 978-1-952580024
Hardcover, 254 Pages, ISBN 978-1-952580048

Doc45 Publications

The Frank W. Angel Report on the Death of John H. Tunstall

"In the matter of the cause and circumstances of the death of John H. Tunstall...."

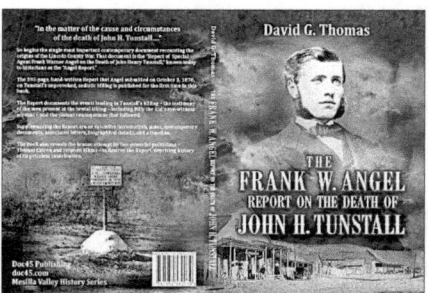

So begins the single most important contemporary document recounting the origins of the Lincoln County War. That document is the "Report of Special Agent Frank Warner Angel on the Death of John Henry Tunstall," known today to historians as the "Angel Report."

The 395-page, hand-written Report that Angel submitted on October 3, 1878, on Tunstall's unprovoked, sadistic murder is published for the first time in this book.

The Report documents the events leading to Tunstall's murder – the testimony of the men present at the brutal killing – including Billy the Kid's eye-witness account – and the violent consequences that followed.

It includes sworn accounts by William "Frank" Baker, Robert W. Beckwith, Henry N. Brown, James J. Dolan, William Dowlin, Pantaleón Gallegos, Godfrey Gauss, Florencio Gonzales, John Hurley, Jacob B. Mathews, Alexander A. McSween, John Middleton, Lawrence G. Murphy, John Wallace Olinger, Juan B. Patron, George W. Peppin, David P. Shield, Robert A. Widenmann, and 18 others.

Supplementing the Report are an extensive introduction, notes, contemporary documents, associated letters, biographical details, and a timeline.

The book also reveals the brazen attempt by two powerful politicians – Thomas Catron and Stephen Elkins – to destroy the Report, depriving history of its priceless contribution.

Forty three images, many never published before.

Available in both paperback and hardcover.

Paperback, 254 Pages, ISBN 978-1-952580079
Hardcover, 254 pages, ISBN 978-1-952580055